MILITANT NATIONALISM

Social Movements, Protest, and Contention

Series Editor: Bert Klandermans, Free University, Amsterdam

Associate Editors: Sidney Tarrow, Cornell University
Verta A. Taylor, The Ohio State University
Ron Aminzade, University of Minnesota

MILITANT NATIONALISM

Between Movement and Party in Ireland and the Basque Country

Cynthia L. Irvin

Social Movements, Protest, and Contention
Volume 9

University of Minnesota Press
Minneapolis • London

Published by the University of Minnesota Press
111 Third Avenue South, Suite 290
Minneapolis, MN 55401-2520
http://www.upress.umn.edu

Library of Congress Cataloging-in-Publication Data

Irvin, Cynthia L.
    Militant nationalism : between movement and party in Ireland and
the Basque country / Cynthia L. Irvin.
        p.   cm. — (Social movements, protest, and contention ; v. 9)
    Includes bibliographical references (p.   ) and index.
    ISBN 0-8166-3114-X (H : acid-free paper). — ISBN 0-8166-3115-8
(PB)
    1. Ireland—Politics and government—20th century. 2. Political
violence—Ireland—History—20th century. 3. Political violence—
Spain—País Vasco—History. 4. País Vasco (Spain)—Politics and
government. 5. Nationalism—Ireland—History—20th century.
6. Nationalism—Spain—País Vasco—History. I. Title. II. Series.
DA959.I75   1999
320.54'09415'09045—dc21   99-13672

Printed in the United States of America on acid-free paper

The University of Minnesota is an equal-opportunity
educator and employer.

10 09 08 07 06 05 04 03 02 01 00 99   10 9 8 7 6 5 4 3 2 1

For my family

Contents

Preface

In August 1983, while working and traveling in Ireland, I knocked on the door of the central Sinn Fein office in Dublin. I did so because, while many people I had met spoke about or against Sinn Fein, I had never encountered anyone who had actually spoken (or, at least, would admit to me to having spoken) with anyone in Sinn Fein. Given the role that Sinn Fein and the IRA had played and continue to play in Irish politics, I was, at the time, puzzled by the official and informal censorship and repressive measures applied to Sinn Fein activists. The omnipresence of members of the *Garda Síochána* (Irish Police) in Parnell Square, admittedly, further encouraged my interest, because previous experiences in Paris with political exiles from around the world had led me to believe that the more a government must rely on intimidation to suppress a political voice, the more likely it is that the voices being silenced need, at least, to be heard.

By stepping through that door, I began a journey that would later lead me to graduate school and to the study of issues of ethnic identity, historical memory, nationalism, and conflict. A fortuitous encounter with an Herri Batasuna delegate to the 1986 Sinn Fein *ard fheis* (party conference) and a visit to Donostia (San Sebastián) later that year would expand the horizons of my research and enrich its findings.

As a native of the American South, where many of these same issues lie dormant but not resolved, despite the passage of time since the Civil War, the terrain I would cover in the next ten years would at times appear startlingly familiar and at others, exceedingly strange. At each step of the way, however, I was accompanied by those who both believed in themselves and in me and who were glad to guide but never dictated what path to choose. No traveler could have had better companions.

In July 1993, at journey's end when I finished the doctoral thesis from which this book has evolved, I concluded:

1. Herri Batasuna is likely to continue to pursue a strategy designed to mobilize a popular movement in support of the demand for Basque independence and to participate only on a limited base in either Basque or Spanish political institutions.

2. Sinn Fein will continue to endorse a mixed strategy of armed struggle and electoral mobilization and is likely to increase its participation in the parliamentary process if provided with strong incentives by the British and Dublin governments.

3. The very nature of the IRA's and ETA's struggle renders disarmament improbable, if not impossible, before securing their inclusion in the negotiation process via Sinn Fein and Herri Batasuna.

These conclusions were based on insights gleaned from a collection of formal and informal interviews and extended conversations with Sinn Fein and Herri Batasuna activists. Their insights form the foundation of this book.

Since July 1993, events in Northern Ireland and the Basque Country have largely confirmed the accuracy of those earlier predictions. In Northern Ireland, Sinn Fein, having finally secured both Dublin's and Westminster's acceptance of its status as a legitimate political party and its incorporation in the all-party negotiations which on 10 April 1998 led to an agreed settlement (Good Friday Agreement) of the Northern Ireland conflict, is now working to secure the decommissioning of IRA weapons. In the Basque Country, Herri Batasuna continues to struggle to define its own role within the parliamentary process and has yet to secure its full acceptance by either the Basque or Spanish government representatives as a legitimate political actor. The declaration of a unilateral cease-fire by ETA on 18 September 1998, however, suggests that talks between Herri Batasuna representatives and those of other Basque nationalist parties have led, at a minimum, to a grudging acceptance by those parties of its critical role in the nonviolent resolution of the Basque conflict and any future Basque political institutions. As this study illustrates, the ties between Herri Batasuna and Sinn Fein are both deep and strong and certainly the Irish Peace Process has led to much discussion within ETA and Herri Batasuna, as well as among other Basque and Spanish political actors, regarding the successful as well as the failed strategies adopted in that process. While the question of whether the lessons learned from the Irish Peace Process can help create a similar process in the Basque cannot yet be answered, what I believe is already evident is that violence has never been the preferred choice of struggle by the majority of Basque *abertzales* or Irish republicans. Rather, as this study argues, the IRA and ETA have "spoken" most loudly when their political grievances were ignored, their political voices repressed, and their political goals dismissed. As I was once told by an Irish republican with a long history in both the IRA and Sinn Fein, "If you want the IRA to go away, it's not really the IRA you have to convince, it's the people who support us. Convince them that politics offers them a real possibility to secure their goals and we [the IRA] will no longer be needed, and if we aren't needed, we can and will go away." Whether the Spanish government and, indeed, the other Basque parties, will choose to listen to Herri Batasuna and those it represents and seek to find a way to guarantee not outcomes, but opportunities for political change will, perhaps, one day reveal the significance of particular strategies adopted by the various players in the Irish Peace Process and provide support for the findings of this study.

However, as any scholar who attempts to analyze ongoing events knows, history has both subtle and dramatic ways of revealing the inadequacies of our analyses. Therefore, while I believe that this book makes an important contribution to our understanding of the dynamics of militant nationalism in Ireland and the Basque Country, I also understand that the very factors that I identify as shaping the dynamics of these struggles, that is, ethnic identity, government responsiveness, organizational resources, and political competitiveness, are themselves dynamic in nature. As the relationships between these factors are better understood, we will no doubt come to yet more complete understandings of the politicization process by which insurgent social movement actors opt, at a minimum, to engage the ballot as well as the bullet in their political struggle and, ultimately, to fight for political goals, without recourse to the gun, within, and not without, the political institutions of the state. To address the issues of why and how those who have adopted armed struggle, through choice or necessity, to secure national self-determination reenter the explicitly political arena of elections and negotiations and opt to rely on nonviolent rather than violent forms of direct action to mobilize support for national independence, this study focuses on two sets of questions.

First, why and under what circumstances do some revolutionary movements decide to abandon long-established policies of opposition to electoral politics and opt to participate in the existing political institutions of their respective regimes, while others single-mindedly pursue the path of political violence? For example, in the case of Sinn Fein and Herri Batasuna, electoral campaigns have run simultaneously with the armed struggle of their military wings, the IRA and ETA. In Colombia, the M-19 insurgents agreed to turn in their weapons in exchange for seats in parliament. In Sri Lanka, the Tamil Tigers alternate between electoral participation and abstention, while in Peru, Sendero Luminoso (Shining Path) continues to reject electoral politics and is committed to destroying the electoral process.

Second, what are the strategic and organizational consequences for revolutionary movements that make the decision to participate in electoral politics and in the existing institutions of the state? Are there inherent contradictions in the organizational and operative demands, structures, and strategies of armed and civil political struggle that prohibit an effective coordination of military and political action and render organizational splits over choices of strategy inevitable? Will the armed organization's need to maintain sufficient popular support to ensure its survival require the subordination of the resources and political initiatives of the political organization to its needs? Will increasing success at the polls lead to increasing autonomy for the political organization, or will that organization need to reaffirm its identification with the armed organization to maintain its electoral support, hence limiting its ability to broaden its electoral base?

In addressing these questions, this study proposes to meet the following specific objectives, which broadly parallel the organization of the book. First, it examines in detail two specific West European militant nationalist movements and thus contributes to increasing the existing knowledge and data related to these movements. Second, it attempts to identify characteristics common to such movements and their activists. Third, it develops a set of testable hypotheses that account for variations in structures and strategy within militant nationalist movements over time and between movements across space, and thus proposes a framework for a broader cross-national analysis of insurgent nationalism. Finally, by examining the journey from political violence to political participation that some of the organizations in this study have completed and that others are still traveling, this study attempts to illumine those paths that lead most successfully to political resolutions of violent nationalist conflicts.

At the heart of this book are the Sinn Fein and Herri Batasuna activists who shared their views, their homes, and their friendship with an outsider and it is to them I owe the first acknowledgment.

I especially wish to thank Anne-Marie, Brian, Eileen, and their families in Portadown; Helen and Seán in Sligo; Teresa and Patsy in Derry; Bríd, Joelle, Geraldine and Frank, Marguerite and Jim, and all my Iris Court neighbors in Belfast; and Jim and his late mother in Armagh, who all provided me with a home away from home. Tish, Mary and family, Ruth, Máirtín, Bobby, Mick, Richard, Chrissie, and Brendan offered invaluable support in many ways. Tom, in particular, I wish to thank for sharing his knowledge and understanding of people, politics, and places Irish, as well as his gift of music.

Eddie Moxon-Browne and Adrian Guelke generously gave of their time to assist me while at Queen's University. Robert Bell and Yvonne Murphy not only explained the intricacies and eccentricities of the political collection at the Linen Hall library but also provided good company on many a dreary day. I must also thank Pat Rice and Robert Clark, who cleared my way to the Basque Country.

In the Basque Country, Jasone, "Gorri," Josune, "Txiki," Iñaki, Itziar, Jon, Sylvie, Myriam, Bego, Joseba, and my Galdakao and Lemoa companions shared countless insights, much laughter, many magnificent mountain peaks, and innumerable amazing meals. Lupe, Marga, Marie-Jésus and her family often provided a much-needed balance in my life. Alfonso Perez-Agote shared a wealth of knowledge and provided me with a quiet place to work at the University of the Basque Country.

At Duke, where theory began to inform my experiences, my advisor, Donald Horowitz, continually fostered a deep appreciation for the richness, complexity, and dignity of peoples everywhere and, thankfully, often rescued me from my dogmatic impulses. I could not have asked for a more rigorous, demanding, or supportive intellectual mentor. I can only hope to emulate his scholarship. I also wish to thank Peter Lange and Herbert Kitschelt for a myriad of intellectual exchanges. Their influence runs through this book, and its best points reflect their skills.

At the Harvard Center for International Affairs, where the thesis was actually completed, Doug Bond and Bill Vogele were a constant source of personal encouragement and excellent critiques of my work.

In Kentucky, Karen Mingst and Vince Davis have facilitated my work in many ways. I have also benefited from innumerable discussions, personal and professional, with Stuart and Nita Kaufman. Stephanie, Robin, and Beverly, who looked after the details I often overlooked, also provided invaluable assistance. I must also thank the Graduate School for the financial support that enabled me to conduct a final round of interviews.

I also wish to thank the United States Institute of Peace, which provided much-needed support in the form of a Jennings-Randolph Peace Scholar

Fellowship. In particular, I wish to thank Joe Klaits for his continuing interest in my work. I am also grateful to the Council for European Studies, the Tinker Foundation, and the Center for Basque Studies at the University of Nevada in Reno, which provided support for various stages of my research.

Finally, a few very special thanks are in order. To my friends who have encouraged and supported me throughout the various places and stages of my research, especially Marti, Vanessa, Anne-Marie, Celia, Dan, Beth, Terry, Janet, and Axel, I would not have wished to do it without you. To my family, especially my mother, Lorraine Irvin, I can only say I could not have done it without you.

List of Abbreviations and Organizations

Eire

FF	Fianna Fail
FG	Fine Gael

Basque Country

ANV	Acción Nacional Vasca (Basque National Action)
ASK	Abertzale Sozialista Koordinadora (Patriotic Socialist Committees)
EA	Basque Solidarity
EAS	Euskal Alderdi Sozialista (Basque Socialist Party)
EE	Euskadiko Ezkerra (Basque Left)
EHAS	Eusko Herriko Alderdi Sozialista (Basque Popular Socialist Party)
EIA	Euskal Iraultzale Alderdia (Basque Revolutionary Party)
ELA-MSE	Solidarity of Basque Workers (Basque Socialist Movement)
ESB	Euskal Sozialista Bilzarrea (Basque Socialist Assembly)
ESEI	Organization for the Basque Socialist Unification
ETA	Euskadi 'ta Askatasuna (Basque Homeland and Freedom)
ETA(M)	ETA faction committed to armed struggle and separate organizational structures for the political and military wings
ETA(PM)	ETA faction committed to political and military strategy and joint organizational structures
FOESSA	Fundación Fomento de Estudios Sociales y de Sociología Aplicada
GAL	Antiterrorist Groups of Liberation
HAS	Herriko Alderdi Sozialista (Popular Socialist Party)

HASI   Herriko Alderdi Sozialista Iraultzalea (Popular Revolutionary Socialist Party)

HB   Herri Batasuna (Popular Unity)

IRAULTZA   Revolution

IZQUIERDA ABERTZALE   Patriotic Left

JARRAI   Revolutionary Patriotic Youth

KAS   Koordinadora Abertzale Sozialista (Patriotic Socialist Coordinating Council)

LAB   Langille Abertzalean Batzordeak (Patriotic Workers' Council)

LAIA   Langille Abertzale Iraultzalean Alderdia (Patriotic Revolutionary Workers Party)

LAK   Langille Abertzale Komiteak (Patriotic Workers Committee)

MCE   Movimiento Comunista de España (Spanish Communist Movement)

MLVN   Movimiento Liberación Vasco Nacional (Basque Movement for National Liberation)

ORT   Organización Revolucionaria de Trabajadores (Revolutionary Organization of Workers)

PCE/EPK Partido Comunista Español (Communist Party)

PNV   Partido Nacionalista Vasca (Basque Nationalist Party)

Northern Ireland

APNI   Alliance Party of Northern Ireland

DUP   Democratic Unionist Party

IIP   Irish Independence Party

INLA   Irish National Liberation Army

IRA   Irish Republican Army

IRSP   Irish Republican Socialist Party

MORI   Market and Opinion Research International

NILP   Northern Ireland Labour Party

NIO   Northern Ireland Office

OIRA   Official Irish Republican Army

OSF   Official Sinn Fein

OUP   Official Unionist Party

PD	People's Democracy
PIRA	Provisional Irish Republican Army
PSF	Provisional Sinn Fein
PTA	Prevention of Terrorism Act
RUC	Royal Ulster Constabulary
SDLP	Social Democratic and Labour Party
SF	Sinn Fein (We Ourselves)
UDR	Ulster Defense Regiment
UMS	Ulster Marketing Surveys
WP	Workers' Party

1

Unconstitutional Means to Constitutional Change: Dilemmas of Violence and Politics

Setting the Stage

In October 1984, the Irish Republican Army (IRA) captured the attention of the world press when it bombed the Brighton Hotel and very nearly succeeded in assassinating Margaret Thatcher and the Tory cabinet during the annual Conservative Party Conference. In May 1985, Sinn Fein, the political party that represents the interests of the Irish Republican Movement, pushed the IRA off the front page when it secured almost 35 percent of the nationalist vote in its first nonabstentionist campaign for seats on local government councils in Northern Ireland. Quite symbolic of this dual bullet and ballot strategy was a photograph that appeared in numerous press accounts of the elections. This photograph showed Sinn Fein supporters in Derry, Northern Ireland, carrying their newly elected representatives down the stairs of the Derry Guildhall where the returns had been tallied. The photograph's caption indicated that the Sinn Fein supporters were chanting "I, I, IRA, I, I, IRA" as they exited the hall. Pictured among the five Sinn Fein representatives was Gerry Doherty, whose prior connection with the Guildhall included carrying bombs into the building while on active service as an IRA volunteer. When asked in an interview how he felt about taking his seat in the same building he was convicted of bombing in 1972, he responded,

> In 1972 I made a political statement by carrying a bomb into this building, and today, as a Sinn Fein councillor, I am making the same political statement. The attack in 1972 on the Guildhall was highly

acclaimed by the people of Derry. The Guildhall was a symbol of gerry-mandering, discrimination, loyalism, and British rule.

The situation has changed, the republican struggle has evolved, and I am proud to be involved with it, now in the role of a Sinn Fein councillor.[1]

Challenged by both Margaret Thatcher and Garret Fitzgerald to prove their popular mandate for violent resistance to British rule in a democratic and legitimate forum, Gerry Doherty and the other elected Sinn Fein representatives proved false the premise behind that challenge, that is, that the electoral support given in the 1981 Westminster by-election to hunger strike candidate Bobby Sands was merely an ephemeral expression of sympathy with the plight of the Irish republican prisoners. Both British and Irish governments were compelled to acknowledge that the goals and tactics of the IRA were espoused by more than a "small band of terrorists," as Thatcher had proclaimed. Indeed, both governments were forced to confront the prospect that democratically elected representatives of a legal political party would now use their public, political positions to endorse armed resistance and actively engage in political opposition to British rule in Northern Ireland with the aim of establishing a united, democratic, socialist, Irish republic.

In August 1994, almost a decade after the Brighton bombing, the IRA once again struck a surprise blow against British rule in Northern Ireland that captured the attention of both its supporters and opponents, the media, and foreign governments. But this time, it was neither bombs nor bullets that seized the headlines of the world press, but the IRA's announcement of a complete cessation of operations to begin as of midnight of 31 August 1994.

Then, on 30 May 1996, in elections to the Northern Ireland forum from which negotiators for the Irish peace talks would be chosen, Sinn Fein, facing the prospect of exclusion from those talks because of the collapse of the IRA cease-fire, achieved its greatest electoral success to that date, securing approximately 15.4 percent of the total votes. Eighteen months after its initial cease-fire, the IRA, giving voice to the frustration of the Irish republican movement with the glacial pace of the peace process, once again rocked the center of London with a massive bomb at Canary Wharf in February 1996. The subsequent eighteen months would witness a dramatic rise in the Sinn Fein vote in the Westminster (16.1 percent) and Northern Ireland local government elections (16.9 percent). By August 1997, the IRA had renewed its cease-fire, and Sinn Fein prepared to enter into public, political negotiations with the British government for the first time since 1920.

In 1986, at the Sinn Fein *ard fheis* (party conference) where the historic decision that would initiate the radical shift in the Republican Movement's political strategy and electoral fortunes was taken, that is, the delegates' decision to drop the party's long-standing constitutional prohibition against its candidates taking seats in the Irish Parliament,[2] another historic statement was being made. However, despite the sizeable contingent of international journalists present in Dublin's Mansion Hall throughout the *ard fheis,* the presence of José Luis Enparanza ("Txillardegi"), one of the founders of the radical Basque nationalist organization Euskadi ta Askatasuna (ETA) went largely unnoticed by the media. Indeed, the only published account of his address to the conference delegates appeared in the Sinn Fein party newspaper, *An Phoblacht/Republican News (AP/RN).*

While the international media focused on the abstentionist debate and the tension between Ruairí Ó Brádaigh, former IRA chief of staff, Sinn Fein president, and leader of the Sinn Fein "old guard," and Gerry Adams, leader of the new northern-based leadership, they failed to note that Txillardegi, former *etarra*[3] and Senator to the Spanish Cortes for the radical Basque nationalist party Herri Batasuna (Popular Unity), had announced major changes within his own party regarding its participation in the autonomous Basque parliament. Like Sinn Fein, Herri Batasuna, since its founding in 1978, had refused to participate in either the Spanish Cortes or the autonomous Basque parliament on the grounds that they were illegitimate political institutions, imposed on Basques against their will. However, in February 1987, Herri Batasuna, following an intense internal debate, had decided to present a candidate for the position of *lehendakari* (president) in the autonomous Basque Parliament.[4] The Herri Batasuna candidate, Juan Carlos Yoldi, was under arrest for suspicion of ETA activities. He was chosen to symbolize the dual strategy of armed struggle and electoral mobilization that the Movimiento Liberación Vasco Nacional (MLVN, Basque Movement for National Liberation) endorsed and Herri Batasuna (HB, Popular Unity) was prepared to implement. Indeed, when asked why Herri Batasuna had nominated Yoldi, Iñaki Esnaola, a member of the party's national executive and spokesperson, replied,

> We elected him as a political prisoner to illustrate the contradiction which reveals that in 1987 there were political prisoners in Euskadi. In our country there are people who believe in the right to take up arms because they see no other means possible to advance their political objectives. This is the important contradiction which was made quite clear in Yoldi's speech in Gasteiz.[5]

The demonstration by thousands of Herri Batasuna supporters outside the parliament building in Gasteiz during Yoldi's address gave notice to both the

Spanish government and the party's Basque competitors that Herri Batasuna was not only intent upon radicalizing the Basque electorate but that they had the ability and resources to do so.

Following an intensive electoral campaign for the 15 June 1987 elections to the Spanish and European parliaments, Herri Batasuna secured a seat to the European parliament, despite a massive propaganda campaign against its candidate by the Spanish media and the other Basque parties. Herri Batasuna also unseated the Basque Nationalist Party (PNV) as the most popular party in the Basque provinces of Spain. The González government, like that of Thatcher and Fitzgerald, would be forced to acknowledge that ETA had more than a marginal base of support.

A decade later, however, the MLVN, although it has succeeded in maintaining the core electoral support for HB within an extremely hostile political environment, has been unable to secure the commitment of either the Basque regional government or the Spanish government to initiate a negotiated political settlement of the violent conflict between ETA and the state security forces, which continues to claim the lives of agents, activists, and innocents.

From Belfast to Bosnia to Bilbao, and from Sri Lanka to South Africa, these and other nationalist movements actively engaged in armed struggle have successfully adopted electoral intervention as a strategy for furthering movement goals while continuing their use of armed struggle. Defying any neat organizational characterization, these movements reflect the intersection of three distinct forms of political action: participation in democratic, institutional, political processes, participation in extrainstitutional forms of nonviolent direct action that may or may not be illegal, and participation in illegal acts of violent direct action. They are agents of both violent and nonviolent political protest and of parliamentary politics. Employing each of the three basic types of collective action—violence, disruption, and convention— they are truly multiform movements whose power to sustain their struggles rests in part, as Tarrow (1994, 15) has noted, in their ability to combine a variety of forms of collective action.

Specifically, the military organization, through armed attacks on government forces and institutions, seeks to delegitimize the incumbent regime by denying it its most important symbol of authority and legitimacy, the monopoly of coercive violence. At the same time, the political wing operates to undermine the legitimacy of the incumbent regime through mass agitation on social, economic, and political issues, seeking both to erode the ruling government's claim to authority in the eyes of its constituents and to convince the international community of the regime's illegitimacy by establishing its own "legitimacy of numbers." Finally, through selective (non)participation in political institutions, elected representatives seek to establish formal access to the formal institutions of the state, to translate movement aspirations into policy, and ultimately to create new state institutions.

Although political mobilization and armed struggle,[6] according to classic guerrilla theory,[7] should be complementary and pursued jointly in order to force an incumbent regime to relinquish its rule, reconciling the conflicting demands of a strategy of armed struggle and one of political outreach and mobilization has often proved more contentious in practice than in theory. To ensure the successful coordination of these two distinct forms of struggle, revolutionary movements have adopted a variety of structural combinations.[8] For example, the political wing may create and direct an underground movement, as did the Communist Party of Chile with the Movimiento Izquierda Revolucionario (MIR) and the African National Congress with Umkonto we Sizwe. Conversely, the military organization may direct an independent but subordinate civilian wing to carry out the work of disseminating propaganda and mobilizing local support for the insurgents, as did the Monteneros in Argentina. The military organization may also be divided into different fronts (i.e., military, political, trade unions, cultural, etc.), as was ETA in the late 1960s and early 1970s.

Finally, as is now the case in Ireland and the Basque Country, the military and political struggle may be waged by distinct but allied organizations. But despite these variations in structures, attempts to pursue a joint military-political strategy have more often proved to be a source of disagreement and disintegration than one of success for these organizations. In particular, internal debates regarding the question of whether the bullet or the ballot box should take priority in the struggle for national liberation have repeatedly resulted in organizational splits and internecine warfare.

For those who favor an electoralist strategy, elections provide a vehicle by which to expand the popular struggle and to expose the "sham democracies" of the governments in power.

> Politics in the Free State, as in most bourgeois democracies, takes place only at election times—at least insofar as political action visibly affects the mass of the people. There is no social revolutionary potential in the Free State at present. It must therefore be in the superficially reformist area of advice clinics and elections that we build our base, and in principled and patient work in other organizations. . . .We cannot get around this gradualist process under the conditions that exist. . . . The fundamental necessity which appeared at the time of transition from a

fascist regime toward a democratic regime was the need to create an exclusively political organization, an organization which could participate in the political dynamics of Euskadi. . . . It is necessary to participate in the legal framework of bourgeois democracy. . . . However, . . . a revolutionary strategy cannot limit itself to this path . . . to fall into electoralism is to suppress political principles for the sake of securing a certain number of votes.[9]

For those opposed to an electoralist strategy, participation in elections only legitimates the institutions of the incumbent regime and leads not to victory but to mere reformism.

A revolutionary movement in being true to its own nature either succeeds or fails badly. Involvement in parliamentary elections is certainly its most dangerous activity; everything is put at risk; but electoral defeat and temporary disillusionment for some is always preferable to and easier overcome in the long run than the political surrender which is the proper description for being diverted into reformism.[10]

It is impossible to justify the position of parties, revolutionary until today, which have fallen into the parliamentary game. Experience teaches us that it is utopian to believe that in playing the game we will receive any real advantages; and little is it possible to use those institutions as a tribunal in which to denounce them because we are there. It does not appear to us either honorable or logical that Herri Batasuna should engage in a politics of electoral negotiation for fear of remaining isolated.[11]

In the case of the IRA and Sinn Fein, internal debates regarding the respective role of armed struggle and electoral politics resulted in disastrous splits in 1922, 1926, 1933, 1945, and 1969. Similar splits occurred within ETA in 1965, 1974, 1978, and 1981. So damaging was the 1969–70 split within the Irish Republican Movement that, following the regrouping in the Provisional IRA and Sinn Fein of those who rejected participation in parliamentary politics, the question of participating in elections was not raised again until 1983, when delegates to the annual Sinn Fein *ard fheis* passed a motion proposing that "no aspect of the constitution and rules be closed to discussion."[12]

Both Sinn Fein and Herri Batasuna, however, despite their historic opposition to participation in parliamentary politics, have successfully adopted electoral intervention as a strategy for securing political goals while continuing to support the armed struggle of their military counterparts. Yet, despite the concern of many analysts regarding the potential impact of these organizations on the political development of their respective regimes, relatively few studies have offered insights into such questions as, Why do these organizations flourish in some political environments but not in others? Why and under what circumstances do organizations shift strategies? Why are similar strategies adopted by organizations active in very different political environments or, conversely, why are different strategies adopted by similar organizations active in the same political environment?[13]

In view of recent debates regarding the resurgence of nationalism and the rise of new parties with close affiliations to religious and/or ethnically based social movements in Eastern Europe and the former Soviet states, parties such as Sinn Fein and Herri Batasuna would appear to offer fertile areas for scholars of both social movements and political parties. Yet despite the electoral inroads made by these and similar parties in the past decade, and the potential importance of this shift in strategies for the demilitarization of these conflicts, existing research on these organizations, particularly of a comparative nature, has been rather limited and, in general, has focused on the clandestine wings of these movements.[14] This overarching concern with the military operations of revolutionary organizations has resulted in a significant theoretical gap in our understanding of the political wings of these movements and their impact on democratic politics within societies whose political systems exhibit many, if not all, of the characteristics ascribed by Sartori (1976, 132–39) to polarized political systems.

Certainly, the presence of an armed insurgent organization represents a significant challenge to the legitimacy of an incumbent regime and indicates a highly polarized regime at risk of serious political disorder and likely disintegration. Given the central role that such movements play in the politics of such societies, I argue that we should invert the question of why political organizations adopt armed struggle as a strategy and ask as well, Why, and under what circumstances, might movements already committed to a militarist strategy opt to abandon often long-held policies of abstention from and opposition to electoral politics and adopt an electoral or a mixed political-military strategy?

Too Long a Focus on Violence

While an ever-growing number of studies of political violence and terrorism have focused on the issue of why individuals or political movements adopt violence as a tactic, fewer have sought to examine why and under what circumstances armed insurgent organizations adopt alternative, nonviolent strategies.[15] For those organizations confronted with overwhelming repressive force, the answer is perhaps obvious. In many cases, however, organizations that have succeeded in achieving some movement goals through the use of violent tactics and that do not face physical annihilation, have chosen to abandon violence, or to employ alternative tactics in conjunction with armed struggle. Yet, despite the obvious importance of this question, the literature on political violence has had far less to say.[16]

Perhaps this is because, as Clark (1990, 90) points out, most violent insurgencies tend to end in one of two ways: (1) the government in power combines a vigorous policy of repression with a judicious program of reforms to isolate the insurgents from their base of popular support and ultimately to defeat them both militarily and politically, or (2) the government loses its legitimacy with the people and then the support of its army and police, and the insurgents either sweep away the existing regime or separate from that regime. In many conflict situations, however, neither government nor insurgent forces are capable of defeating the other, either militarily or ideologically. In these cases, stalemate, not victory, is the more likely outcome. Success for insurgents and incumbents alike often becomes synonymous with enduring, while "acceptable levels of violence" are often substituted for legitimacy. For these conflicts, a third route to resolution is necessary: one of negotiated cease-fires and political compromises. It is clearly within these cases of protracted conflict that political organizations such as Sinn Fein and Herri Batasuna play a crucial role in the conflict process. As the history of abandoned cease-fires and failed negotiations in Northern Ireland, the Basque Country, and many other countries shows, this route to peace is perhaps the most difficult of all.

Clearly, the choice of strategy by a revolutionary movement confronted with political and military stalemate has significant implications for the ultimate resolution of violent political conflict. To date, however, comparatively few works have sought to determine what factors facilitate or constrain shifts by such movements from violent to nonviolent forms of political mobilization and participation.[17] No doubt such research has been impeded by the obvious difficulties faced by researchers who want to "get inside" these revolutionary organizations, which often inhabit a very gray and narrow political space between legality and proscription.[18] Certainly it has been limited by the practice, common to most scholars of political violence, of subsuming both the political organizations and the armed organizations of revolutionary movements under the general rubric of "terrorist" organizations. Also, as Robert White (1993, 10) has noted, such scholars often promote the idea that "violent activists are so close-mouthed and unstable that interaction with them is pointless." This attitude, which has its origins in the works of theorists of violent collective action such as Lasswell (1930), Hoffer (1951), LeBon (1960), and Goodspeed (1962)[19] continues to inform the work of some contemporary analysts of political violence.[20]

Although potentially intriguing, analyses of political violence that focus primarily on the psychological "neuroses" of participants in collective violence are beset by a number of drawbacks, the most damaging of which is their inability to specify how or when the relationship and interactions between regimes and significant social groups might produce actors willing to engage in acts of violence.[21]

Aside from the work of these analysts, acts of violence, particularly those perpetrated by dissident minority groups, are often publicly portrayed, if not always viewed in private, as irrational. Clearly, the presumption of irrationality on the part of revolutionary organizations who reject participation in institutional politics in preference to a campaign of armed struggle or terrorism is heavily influenced by the pluralist paradigm, with its assumptions of open access to the political arena, procedural consensus, crosscutting solidarities, and shifting majorities. But as many contemporary social movement theorists have demonstrated,[22] the pluralist model extends only to competition by organized interests that are not challenging the status quo. For, as Gamson (1975, 17) notes, while members may bargain with other members, "with persistent challengers they are prepared to fight and destroy or ultimately to yield if the fight proves more costly than the stakes warrant."

Militant nationalist movements are radical challengers with radical goals. They seek not only to displace the members of the regime but to change the regime itself. To assume, therefore, that these organizations use the same political calculus that is used, for example, by parties of the status quo is to ignore the reality that many of these organizations operate in societies where some or all of the conditions conducive to the consolidation of pluralist democracies are absent. Thus the obvious, rational, political strategy for these organizations cannot simply or always be presumed to be participation in the legal, institutional political process.

Indeed, the right to participate in the electoral process can pose considerable ideological as well as tactical dilemmas for these movements. As Hirschman (1982) has noted: "When the vote was granted, it became enthroned, in effect, as the only legitimate form of expressing political opinion. The vote represented a new right for the people but it also restricted its participation in politics to this comparatively harmless form." (112)

The enthronement of the vote as the primary form of expressing political opinion has thus often served to limit other, more active forms of expressing political opinion and has virtually excluded revolutionary change. Indeed, in his examination of the opposition to the vote by some British trades unions' representatives, Hirschman (1982) finds a hostility to the electoral process based on arguments that are echoed in those of some contemporary movement organizations:

> One fundamental reason for hostility to the vote as a false gift, a hostility born of the feeling that the resolute opponents of the existing social and political order had been tricked into a poor bargain: the vote was a mess of pottage for which they had inadvertently bartered away their birthright, Lockeian or otherwise, that is, the right to give vent to their discontent by any means whatsoever. . . . The trouble with the vote . . . is not so much that the outcome of voting is stacked, because of the way in which the economic and political power is distributed in society; rather it is that the vote delegitimizes more direct, intense, and expressive forms of political action which are both more effective and more satisfying. (112)

In particular, since the legitimacy of and popular support for revolutionary movements is often a function of their abstention from and opposition to existing government institutions, their participation in those institutions could have negative consequences for the organization, as the following remark by a member of Herri Batasuna's national executive makes clear:

> In our opinion, the best political option for Herri Batasuna has been not to participate in the institutions of parliament because, thanks to that attitude, they have not been legitimated. We are not considering participating in the parliamentary process because that would serve to reinforce those institutions and would be contrary to our interests.[23]

Indeed, the use of institutionalized tactics, even in the pursuit of "radical" goals, implicitly conveys an acceptance of the established, or "proper," channels of conflict resolution and acknowledges the authority of the existing institutions. Such tactics are thus more likely to be viewed as less threatening by elite groups, both because they leave unchallenged the structural underpinnings of the political system and because the power disparity between incumbents and challengers is greatest within these "legitimate" channels.

Reliance on noninstitutionalized tactics thus represents the converse of the above situation and poses a distinct challenge to elite groups for at least two reasons. At the symbolic level, it communicates a fundamental rejection of the established institutional mechanisms for seeking redress of group grievances. It also deprives elite groups of their recourse to institutional power. For both these reasons, elites are likely to view noninstitutionalized tactics, especially violence, as a much more serious threat to their interests.

For movements that have developed outside the parliamentary arena and depend on their ability to mobilize mass street demonstrations and campaigns of direct nonviolent action to demonstrate their popular support as well as the armed struggle of their military wings, a shift to the use of institutionalized tactics often has the perverse effect of reducing their ability to mobilize supporters for mass demonstrations and hence diminishing their visibility and traditional source of strength:

> To enter into a dynamic of electoral campaigns could limit the mobilization of the masses. Participation in elections could distract the people from the objectives for which, until [the] present, it has been fighting for, reducing its level of combativity. . . . Elections are a means of demobilizing protest by filtering it through the ballot box once every year or so. People begin to get the idea that politics is synonymous with elections. Once the people come to believe this, then it is far easier for the state to mold the people's thinking and actions. We must continually work to make people aware that real political power lies in our ability to effect change, and we believe we can do that better through popular mobilizations and armed struggle.[24]

Similarly, Mitchell McLaughlin, Sinn Fein's national chairperson, has made the following points in reference to Sinn Fein's electoral success:

> I think there has been a wasting of the organization to some extent in that there is an attitude within Sinn Fein, as within the community generally, that having elected representatives means that those representatives should take responsibility for those things which ordinary Sinn Fein members previously would have seen as being their responsibility prior to the emergence of the electoral strategy. There is certainly a tension there, and that was an unforeseen difficulty for the movement when we began considering the electoral option. In fact, it has actually changed our movement. We are less now, in 1989, a movement of the streets than we were prior to the 1985 local government elections. We have discovered that on one or two of the campaign issues there has been a certain backstepping in terms of being able to mobilize people, to get them back onto the streets. Now people are saying, "What have we got councillors for? Why don't they put forward a motion in council?" So, that's one of the factors and consequences of electoralism we should think seriously about.[25]

Thus, although granting formerly excluded revolutionary groups access to the electoral arena is often considered sufficient for the demilitarization of violent political conflict, this study illustrates that the opportunity to participate in the legal political process does not inevitably mean that insurgent organizations will participate in that process. Access to the electoral arena, therefore, though certainly a necessary condition for the demilitarization and demobilization of the military wings of movements, is clearly not a sufficient one.

Understanding Strategic Change: Theoretical Approaches

The militant nationalist movements discussed in this study are part revolutionary political party, part popular protest organization, and part military organization; thus, their analysis is informed by extensive bodies of literature on parties, on social movements, and on political violence. The theoretical framework adopted here to analyze the internal dynamics primarily of the political wings of the Irish Republican and Basque Nationalist movements draws on both instrumental and behavioral models of revolutionary movements.

The Instrumental Approach

According to the instrumental approach, the behavior of revolutionary movement organizations is rational and purposive. They choose their strategies by calculating the benefits to be gained from an action, the costs of the attempt and of its failure, the consequences of inaction, and the probability of success, which is measured in terms of the movement's ability to secure its stated political goals. Any decrease in the expected cost or benefit of any particular strategy would then be expected to result in shifts in strategy. These shifts or innovations in strategies by the movement are viewed primarily as responses to government actions, that is, as being exogenously rather than endogenously generated. Indeed, variations in strategies are explained almost entirely in terms of external constraints, such as the level of repressions, organizational resources, and so on, while endogenous changes in the distribution of the beliefs and preferences of activists are largely ignored. As Crenshaw (1988, 26) notes, "Because the intentions of the actors are inferred from their behavior according to logical rules, [this approach] is both intellectually satisfying and relatively undemanding in terms of information requirements." Since empirical data on clandestine organizations and, at times, those related to them is problematic to obtain, there is clearly a practical advantage to adopting this method of inquiry. Instrumental explanations, however, come close to structural determinism. While the actions of revolutionary movement organizations are conditioned by specific configu-rations of existing resources, structures, and institutions, if all actions were deducible from those structures, then we could predict what strategic op-tions a paramilitary organization would adopt by understanding those struc-tures. But numerous studies of playoffs of the well-known prisoner's dilem-ma, in which the actor's strategic options are completely determined by the preexisting payoff structures, have shown that the predicted, "rational" op-tion is not always chosen. Similarly, there have been many revolutionary "games" in which the actors have not adopted the predicted strategy, often winning or losing suddenly and unexpectedly. Explaining the dynamics of movement organization behavior, therefore, cannot be reduced simply to surveying the political situation and identifying the strategy that accom-plishes the most; nor can imperatives of effectiveness alone explain the dy-namic of movement organization and strategic choice. As DeNardo (1985, 145) has written, "If we proceed on the assumption that political effective-ness alone governs the dissident's choice of strategy, their strategy-making organization fades into a neverland of theoretical irrelevancy. The game boils down to surveying the political situation and identifying the strategy that accomplishes the most."

Indeed, despite the widespread characterization of violent revolutionary movements, especially their military wings, as closed systems, isolated and sealed off from their environments, they clearly do not exist in isolation from the political, economic, social, and cultural life in which they are em-bedded. Rather, they emerge, evolve, and dissolve in reaction to and in com-petition or cooperation with other groups that advocate or contest similar or opposing goals. They are open to and dependent on flows of personnel and resources from outside their own system. Thus, rather than viewing revolu-tionary movement organizations as coherent systems of relations oriented to the pursuit of specific goals, it may be more accurate to view them as an op-portunistic collection of divergent interest groups, temporarily banded to-gether to pursue goals that are developed through internal political discourse.

Activists in these movements, therefore, should not be assumed to rep-resent a homogeneous group; rather, they are individuals with different in-terests and motivations. They join or leave the movement, switch from one wing to another, depending on the relative advantage to be had from staying or exiting. Movement recruits also bring with them different cognitive inter-pretations of the external political environment, which they employ to assess the rationality of any given strategy. Which strategy a movement ultimately adopts is, therefore, conditioned not only by external constraints but also by a process of internal debate and negotiation among activists whose own preferences are variable and shaped by the collective process of internal debate. Any adequate explanation of strategy, therefore, must also include an analysis of microfoundations, that is, the internal politics of an organization that can explain how movement activists respond to structural constraints and alter their behavior and organization.

Attempts by rational-choice theories to reconstruct organizational and strategic change within movements have, in general, focused on internal power struggles between radical elites and more moderate grassroots activists for control of the organization's political agenda. While radical elites are concerned with maintaining the organization's integrity and securing its long-term goals, rank-and-file activists are more concerned with the short-term benefits that the organization can provide. To ensure the organization's commitment to their ideological goals, radical elites seek to limit the influence of the dissenting voices of the more moderate and pragmatic rank-and-file through coercive control of the internal decision-making bodies and by isolating the strategy-making process from the corrupting influence of the "reformist" rank-and-file. Thus, strategies as well as organizational form, according to these models, represent the preferences of the radical elites.[26] Such an argument is, however, inadequate, as Kitschelt (1990, 43) has noted, because it cannot explain why and to what extent grassroots activists allow elites to pursue policy and strategic options that diverge from their own preferred positions; that is, it provides no mechanism by which to reconstruct the internal debates that shape the formation of strategy. Further, it ignores the reality that when competing organizations are present, elites must often bargain with members in order to prevent their exit to competitors.

To explain the authority and control of elites within revolutionary movement organizations, the theoretical literature on these organizations has proposed at least three different views of the behavior of grassroots activists. In the first view, grassroots activists unquestioningly accept the leaders' views, statements, and judgments and give them unqualified support and devotion because they identify emotionally with the leaders, who compensate them with solidary rather than material benefits.[27] According to the second view, grassroots activists are compliant and cooperative because they believe that only the leaders possess the skills necessary to determine appropriate strategies and goals. Activists, therefore, leave complex decisions to leaders because they are perceived as being too difficult to understand. The third view claims that elites coerce activists into pursuing strategies very different from those they would have adopted themselves. According to this Leninist orthodoxy, grassroots paramilitary activists are less committed than the leadership to the radical, long-term, political goals of the organizations, and since they are therefore more willing to compromise principles for concessions, only an internal oligarchy can maintain the purity and radicalism of the organization.

Empirically, however, these perspectives encounter many inconsistencies. First, many activists clearly support militant revolutionary organizations for purposive reasons. Second, many activists are highly intelligent, skilled, and politically sophisticated individuals. Third, activists have often adopted more radical positions regarding political goals and strategies than movement elites, and splits have repeatedly occurred precisely because elites were unable to impose their preferences on the rank-and-file.

The behavior of revolutionary movement organizations cannot, therefore, be adequately explained by the simple dichotomous categorization of an organization's membership into a radical "vanguard" and reformist rank-and-file. Thus, while rational-actor models of revolutionary politics are perhaps the most intellectually satisfying in regard to their logical completeness, they too often fall short on empirical content.

The Behavioral Approach

In contrast to the image of revolutionary movement organizations as rational, purposive, organizations with relatively formalized structures, composed of distinct but homogeneous groups of zealous, ideologically pure leaders and passive, reformist supporters, behavioral models represent these organizations as collectivities composed of subgroups of activists with varying interests and objectives.

As an alternative to the selective incentives or by-product motives for participation, numerous scholars have suggested other bases of member motives and organizations' incentives that cannot be reduced to utilitarian cost-benefit calculi. Among these alternative models of behavior are the instrumental-expressive dichotomy (Gordon and Babchuk 1959); Clark and Wilson's (1961) material-purposive-solidary incentive typology; Etzioni's (1975) utilitarian-normative-coercive bases of organizational compliance, and Knoke and Wright-Isak's (1982) rational-choice, normative-conformity, and affective-bonding motivations. These typologies recognize that activists vary enormously in their preferences for and responses to a variety of incentives provided by collective-action organizations. As Knoke (1988, 314) has demonstrated, adherence to equity norms, standards of fairness, altruism, and emotional ties to persons and groups may all play some part in individual decisions to become involved in a collective-action association. Reducing such complexity to simple utilitarian calculi of net benefits minus costs distorts the reality and ignores organizations' capacities to tailor their inducements to fit the diversity of members' interests.

In her review of clandestine, violent movement organizations, Crenshaw (1988), for example, claims that such organizations, in order to ensure a continuing supply of recruits, must offer a mixture of incentives. But despite her focus on the material/expressive incentives that militant organizations may provide for their members, she maintains that the purposive goals will always remain strong, since the collective goals of the organization appeal to the activist's sense of satisfaction at contributing to a worthy political cause and because members sincerely identify with the organization's purpose. She does, however, argue that conspiratorial organizations in which a premium is placed on group solidarity and cohesion will, over time, tend to substitute group solidarity for political purpose as the dominant incentive.

In contrast, therefore, to the instrumental model of social movement organizations as a coherent system of structures and relations oriented to the pursuit of specific goals, behavioral theorists argue that it is more accurate to view these organizations as loosely coupled systems composed of coalitions of shifting interest groups, with each attempting, as Pfeffer and Salancik (1978, 36) have noted, "to obtain something from the collectivity by inter-acting with others, and each with its own preferences and objectives." Thus, rather than being oriented to the pursuit of specific consistent and shared goals, these coalitions "change their purpose and domains to accommodate new interests . . . and when necessary become involved in activities far afield from their stated purposes" (Pfeffer and Salancik, 1978, 24). Only rarely, ac-cording to these models, can effectiveness in securing the stated ideological goals of the organization adequately explain an organization's behavior.

Further, as an alternative to the dominant emphasis of incentive analy-sis, which has been a market orientation that views members' concerns about the benefits as preconceived instrumental interests, these approaches view interest formation as a dynamic process shaped through political strug-gle. As Bowles and Gintis (1986, 138) note, both individuals and groups, in general, "participate not merely to meet preexisting ends, but also to consti-tute themselves, or to reaffirm themselves, as persons and groups with par-ticular and desired attributes." Preferences for various types of incentives and collective-action objectives, therefore, "are not simply imported into an associational marketplace but are continually formed and reformed through mutually determining interactions among leaders and members" (Knoke 1988, 327).

Indeed, as Scott (1987, 83) has stated, one of the most valuable insights provided by this perspective is that individual activists are "never merely 'hired' hands but bring along their heads and hearts: they enter into the organization with individually shaped ideas, expectations, and agendas, and they bring with them differing values, interests, and abilities."

The strategic choices of organizations are therefore intimately linked to the internal organizational discourse, a discourse that I maintain is significantly conditioned and constrained by cultural and organizational symbols and mythologies.[28] For nationalist organizations such as Sinn Fein and Herri Batasuna, commonly agreed-upon historical truths often serve to justify the existence and actions of a group. Events that occurred in the distant past are frequently endowed with symbolic meanings, and a reification of these events in the form of myths or legends that support the organization's goals is developed. Indeed, as Horowitz (1985, 218) notes, the use of cultural symbols and myths is particularly effective in ethnic conflict because "it clothes ethnic claims in ideas and associations that have acknowledged moral force beyond that particular conflict, thereby masking something that would otherwise be controversial; . . . symbolism permits the purposeful confusion of meaning, so as to conflate segmental claims with a wider political morality."

Particularly within ethnically divided states, symbolic rewards produced by government action or inaction are matters of great public sensitivity, in that "official" sanction of an ethnic group's demands lends legitimacy to the group and improves its chances of securing its share of the material benefits of politics. Exclusive control of cultural symbols is therefore of utmost concern and importance to the leaders of nationalist movement organizations, since they seek to use these symbols to mobilize their constituency and expand their movement.

These organizational symbols and "mythologies," however, serve more than merely as a means to justify the existence of the organization or to mobilize supporters. Internally, they can be used to manipulate and influence the behavior of individuals; hence, they have a significant impact on organizational and group behavior. Also, the ritualistic use of symbols by elites serves to reinforce allegiance to the organization;[29] when they can, leaders will use symbols and myths to legitimate their position within the organization. By interpreting complex political situations in terms of the group's ideology and by translating abstract beliefs into existing concrete situations, leaders are able to define the procedural and substantive concerns of the organization and to legitimate the proposed responses to specific events. Certainly, common agreement on particular beliefs by the membership facilitates the ability of individuals to work collectively toward a desired goal.

The indoctrination that characterizes an individual's entry into a nationalist movement organization, particularly a clandestine wing, entails a socialization of the individual into the community of activists, and that person's experiences with members of that organization may effect shifts in preferences regarding strategy and perhaps final goals. Ideology, then, is intimately linked to strategy and tactics as it constrains the organization's repertoire of tactical alternatives.

Behavioral models thus provide a much richer and more detailed description of movement dynamics than the rational-choice model's reconstruction of revolutionary organizations as dominated by elites who formulate the organization's goals and strategies, with which grassroots activists either agree or to which they acquiesce. But these models are unable to explain why certain subgroups dominate in some organizations but not in others; nor can they explain shifts in the size and influence of subgroups within the same organization over time.

Toward a More Comprehensive Understanding

While each of these models contributes to our understanding of militant nationalist movements, I suggest that neither model is sufficient to provide an adequate understanding of the dynamics of these movements. To provide such an understanding requires a theoretical model that can identify how the various actors' ideas and preferences interact with the existing political structures to determine the adoption of a specific strategy in preference to another. Such a model requires a synthetic approach that facilitates not only an understanding of how historical changes in the socioeconomic and political opportunity structures affect the development of militant nationalist organizations, but also of how the political experiences and ideas of individual activists mold the ideological discourse, internal debates, and organizational practices of the organizations.

Drawing on the insights of both instrumental and behavioral models of social movement strategies and organization, the next chapter introduces a theoretical model that attempts to combine the logical precision and theoretical strengths of rational-choice studies of revolutionary politics with the rich, descriptive analysis of behavioral studies. Adopting as its structural underpinning the political-process model (Tilly 1978; McAdam 1985; Kitschelt 1986; Tarrow 1989, 1994) of social movement mobilization, and complementing that model with a detailed examination of movement ideoculture and internal discourse, it attempts to demonstrate that a militant nationalist movement's choice of strategy and structures can best be understood as the outcome of a process of debate and coalition-building among three distinct subgroups of activists: ideologues, radicals, and politicos. The relative size and influence of each group within the organization are held to be affected by external conditions and strategic situations in the political environment. Which strategy dominates, therefore, is determined by the relative strength and interactions of different subcoalitions of activists. I examine three factors—regime responsiveness, competitive environment, and organizational resources—that are of primary importance for the empirical investigation of the internal balance of power among the groups.

2

Splits in the Ranks: A Theory of Militant Nationalism

There have always been three tendencies within the republican movement: a militaristic and fairly apolitical tendency, a revolutionary tendency, and a constitutional tendency. Throughout the history of the movement, one or the other of these has been in ascendancy.

Gerry Adams, The Politics of Irish Freedom

Actors and Objectives

The chronicles of innumerable militant nationalist movements, including those that are the focus of this study, show that disparities in the political aspirations and the intensity of political preferences expressed by activists can easily fuel violent disagreements about strategy. Although activists in both of these movements have generally agreed on final goals, they have often had markedly divergent perceptions of the existing structure of political opportunities and their core base of support. For some, nationalism represented the appropriate guiding ideology and all members of the ethnonational group were a potential support base. For others, revolutionary socialism was the correct path to follow, and workers, regardless of their ethnicity/nationality, were the proper base of support. The political objectives specified in the programs of two factions of ETA, which would become known as ETA-Fifth Assembly (V) and ETA-Sixth Assembly (VI) illustrate this division.

ETA(V)

1. The unification of the Basque ethno-nation by separating its two halves from Spain and France, and the creation of a new political entity.

2. The sovereign independence of this new Basque state from both France and Spain.

3. The restoration of the Basque language to the status of an official and functional language (without necessarily eliminating Spanish from the Basque country).

4. Democratization of basic industries.

5. Nationalization of basic industries.

ETA(VI)

1. The violent destruction of the Spanish state and the imposition of popular armed councils of workers.

2. The right of separation and reunification of the Basque nation, exercised through a Basque people's government composed of people's councils of workers.

3. Socialization of the goods of the oligarchy, of the imperialist, and of other counter-revolutionaries without compensation.

4. Effective equality of the Basque and Spanish languages and the encouragement of Basque popular culture.

5. Political and trade union freedom.[1]

Within both the IRA and ETA, widely varying perceptions have existed regarding resources, opportunities, and threats, as well as much uncertainty and disagreement about which strategies would maximize the organization's potential to secure its goals. Activists in both organizations have not only disagreed about the effectiveness and correctness of particular strategies and tactics, they have also held very different views of how ultimate goals and the strategies for obtaining them were causally related. Some activists saw the clandestine struggle of a vanguard militant organization as the only way to wrest concessions from the existing regime. For others, this represented pure adventurism, which did little to win popular support from the masses and even less to encourage the existing regime to negotiate potential gains. The following selections from documents of three ETA factions reveal distinct positions regarding the role of armed and mass struggle. The first criticizes armed struggle as antirevolutionary adventurism. The second relegates armed struggle to mass struggle. The third asserts the primacy of the armed struggle in the Basque struggle for national liberation.

1. ETA(V) has initiated an activism seduced by a contemporary "blanquismo" which has envisaged the creation of an armed group before having created a political movement tied to the masses. ETA has adopted numerous texts which stress a certain "cult" of action which is seen as something that overcomes ideological differences; "action unites us; action is our guiding principle." This is their thesis. This is how ETA(V) functions, without a clear political ideology, without a political program, without a single proposal developed on how to deal with the major problems confronting the Basque popular movement.[2]

2. The initiative in the struggle for the total liberation of the Basque people must reside in political activity since the Basque working class now has many more opportunities to effect a direct protaganism than it ever had before. The armed struggle, which in no way do we intend to renounce, passes to a secondary role, serving as the guarantor of the peoples' victories and as a guard against the aggressions of the dominant classes.[3]

3. ETA intends to carry forward an armed struggle against the apparatus of the oppressor states in the service of the working class and the Basque people. Armed struggle is the supreme form of class struggle. Only the armed insurrection of the workers and the ordinary Basque people can create an Euskadi, a homeland free of all exploitation and oppression.[4]

Even those activists in Sinn Fein and Herri Batasuna who fully support the armed struggle of the IRA and ETA have differences of opinion regarding the extent to which the armed struggle should figure in their electoral campaigns. The following excerpts from a transcript of a video of a Sinn Fein internal party conference held in 1987 illustrate this tension:

1. Now, we must say that the issue of explaining the armed struggle split our group down the middle with some people seeing the armed struggle as a stumbling block and others holding the totally opposite view.

2. There was some discussion about whether the armed struggle was something around our neck. . . . I think there was a general consensus that it wasn't difficult to explain, but the problem was that we didn't explain it.[5]

To the extent that the distribution of collective incentives depends on the official goals that reflect the organizational ideology, such conflicts clearly represent a potential threat to the existing leadership's legitimacy, the organization's identity, and its ability to compete effectively for popular support (see Panebianco 1988). Further, to be considered credible, official goals must be accompanied by an indication of the means for achieving them; that is, they must be translated into a political strategy. A close relationship between the performance of a political strategy and a leadership's legitimacy is therefore inevitable. An excellent example of how an organizational failure was used to discredit the legitimacy of a former leadership is contained in the speech by Martin McGuinness to the 1986 *ard fheis* delegates. To refute the legitimacy of the charges by the former Ó Brádaigh leadership that the Adams's leadership was once again "selling out," Sinn Fein by advocating that the party drop its policy of abstention from participation in the Irish parliament, McGuinness turned the tables and accused the Ó Brádaigh faction of never having come to terms with the fact that its strategic choices during the 1970s had very nearly destroyed the organization.

> The reality is that the former leadership of this movement has never come to terms with this leadership's criticisms of the disgraceful attitude adopted by them during the disastrous eighteen-month cease-fire in the mid-1970s. Instead of accepting the validity of our case, as others who have remained have done, they chose to withhold their whole-hearted support from the leadership which replaced them.[6]

As this example illustrates, the leadership (dominant coalition) often becomes a prisoner of the political strategy it has adopted. Indeed, the leadership's ability to recruit members depends on the application of the strategy: if it loses credibility, both the leadership and the organization are vulnerable to defections.

A review of the histories of both the IRA and ETA reveals that justifications for the expulsion of members or factional "walk-outs" have often been couched in terms of a betrayal of the founding principles upon which the organization's identity has been based or as attempts by "dissidents" to sow confusion among the party faithful. For example, the Provisional IRA and Sinn Fein leadership, which had walked out of the 1970 party conference over the issue of participation by elected Sinn Fein representatives in the Irish parliament, issued a press release that stated,

> We call on them [those who remained] to cease describing themselves as Sinn Fein. That honored name has never belonged in Westminster, Stormont, or Leinster House. Let them join with their new found friends in their National Liberation Front or whatever they wish to call it and leave the Republican Movement alone.[7]

Similarly, when a group of ETA founding members who had been forced into exile challenged the legitimacy of decisions taken by de facto leaders of ETA within the Spanish state, they did so on the grounds that these activists were in the process of "liquidating" the organization:

> ETA, Basque Revolutionary Movement of National Liberation, cognizant of the current situation of confusion in the Basque patriotic camp created by the enemies of the Basque revolution, directs the attention of all the Basque people to this National Manifesto. . . .
>
> Following the elimination of the Spanish liquidationist elements and the withdrawal of the right wing of the organization in the year 1966–1967 . . . we found ourselves once again in a situation where our organization was becoming a brake on our journey toward national liberation and socialism. We have no doubt that from the autumn of 1968 the Basque people expected much more from ETA. . . .
>
> Once again, diverse foreign forces, especially Spanish, have tried and are trying to create divisions among the Basque political forces, including supposedly patriotic forces who are attempting to use our Basque youth in a new adventure to solve the French or Spanish problem. Before these dangers of the liquidation of the Basque revolution which deliberately ignored the reality of the Basque people who are oppressed culturally, politically, and socially. ETA wishes to declare that it was born and exists for the purpose of securing the national and social liberation of all Euskadi. . . . This resistance, united with that of the various Basque popular organizations which are fighting for Basque national independence, is the nucleus of a Basque National Front which will lead Euskadi to its final and definitive liberation. The fundamental goals of such a front should be the independence of all Euskadi, [and] the establishment of Euskara as the sole official language of Euskadi. ETA reminds all the people of our country, natives as well as those who have come from other places, that the struggle for national and social liberation cannot be the struggle of a small minority but must be a mass struggle. In that struggle there are patriots and traitors. Who is not with the Basque people and its resistance is against us. We, Basques, will make our revolution in Euskadi, for Euskadi.[8]

Discourse on strategy is clearly not governed simply by its presumed effectiveness in securing movement goals. Ideology and movement principles intervene to shape the internal debate on strategic options. In this chapter, I attempt to explain the strategic choices of Sinn Fein and Herri Batasuna by recourse to a model of revolutionary nationalist politics that integrates several variables, institutions, individual motivations, and ideology. It assumes that a revolutionary nationalist organization's choice of strategy is the outcome of the internal dynamics of the organization, that is, a decision-making process that links collectively held values and goals to perceptions of the environment. It focuses on the relationship between the existing structure of political opportunities, the composition of subgroups of activists within the organization, and the adoption or rejection of the strategy of electoral struggle. It suggests that the set of opportunities, constraints, and resources within which the activists define their goals and select the strategies to pursue their demands will be affected by (1) regime responsiveness; (2) organizational resources, both domestic and international; and (3) the absence or presence of competing political groups willing to cooperate with the incumbent government.

The interaction of these variables is hypothesized (1) to influence the respective size and influence of three subgroups of activists: "ideologues," "radicals," and "politicos," each of which is defined according to its ranking of specific programmatic, strategic, and organizational concerns; and (2) to set the strategic context within which the activists must choose among alternative, competing strategies of mobilization via terrorism,[9] armed struggle, mass nonviolent direct action, and/or institutional politics. My first step, then, is to identify theoretically the three groups of activists that compose the organization. The activist subgroups are empirically identified in chapter 5.

Ideologues

Ideologues are often the "hard" men and women of militant nationalist organizations. They are drawn to action more than to political discussion, and they are committed to the belief that organizational goals can only be obtained as a result of the armed struggle of their military wings.

Drawn, in general, from the most "traditional" areas of support for the nationalist struggles, ideologues are unwilling to compromise the organization's ideological principles even to secure concessions from the incumbent regime. For this type of activist, as Darby (1990, 154) notes, "All that goes on around him, even internal disputes, confirms in him the uncompromising purity of his position." Ideologues argue that armed struggle is necessary to maintain a constant pressure on the sources of colonialist exploitation and imperialism. Without this pressure, they claim, any liberation struggle is doomed to failure. So long as the colonial power or incumbent regime controls the apparatus of domination—the government and its bureaucracy, the educational system, the mass media, and the economy—ideologues argue that nonviolent struggle will always fail. For ideologues, only insurgent violence directed against the agents of colonialism and imperialism is capable of raising popular consciousness about the aims of the liberation movement. Although these activists recognize that insurgent violence is likely to provoke the state into increasing repressive actions against their supporters, ideologues view that repression as one of the costs of prosecuting the struggle and as a potentially mobilizing force for those previously uninvolved in the struggle.

For ideologues, any participation by the movement in institutional politics legitimates the incumbent regime and thereby diminishes the legitimacy of armed struggle as a strategy for political change. Isolation, not participation, is the key to revolution and eventual victory. Participation in parliament and other institutions of government, they claim, leads not to victory but to reformism and considerably diminishes the effectiveness of the military wing. Indeed, these activists argue that participation in government institutions is not only ineffective but counterrevolutionary. Most important, participation in electoral campaigns diverts significant resources, both human and material, from the armed struggle, which is viewed as the ultimate guarantor of the success of the revolution.

Ideologues are opposed to strategic alliances with other radical organizations composed of different ethnic groups. They consider cooperation with such groups both undesirable and potentially damaging to the movement, since it would very likely require the subordination of the national struggle to other dimensions of the liberation struggle. The preferred mass revolutionary organization of ideologues is, therefore, a broad nationalist front composed of all members of their ethnic group, regardless of their social class. Recovery of the national identity and the liberation of the nation must be secured before any meaningful actions on specific social and political questions can be implemented.

Ideologues are unimpressed with the effectiveness of the slow political work of base-building and prefer the action and quick results of armed operations. They reject as counterrevolutionary any strategy that necessitates cooperation with the incumbent regime. When, as a result of extreme repression or lack of popular support, these activists are unable to implement their preferred strategy of armed struggle, they will choose to withdraw from the political arena rather than compromise the organization's principles or demands. Unwilling to compromise on strategy or tactics, they severely limit the strategic options of a revolutionary nationalist movement and restrict the ability of the popular organization to expand its mass base and to diversify its political appeal.

Internally, ideologues prefer a closed, highly disciplined, efficient organization and place the needs of the military organization first. Although internal organizational debates and decision-making processes among the hard core of activists are often democratic, the directives of the leadership (and sanctions for failure to obey) are rigidly enforced.

Ideologues, in sum, prefer maintaining the organization's ideological purity to political concessions if those concessions require abandoning core principles, and they value ethnic/national concerns over those of class. They reject cooperation with other ethnic groups, even those with whom they share common ideological goals, preferring a broad nationalist alliance. They prefer active and violent strategies to the slow work of political base-building, and closed, efficient organizations to more ideologically diverse and participatory structures.

Radicals

Radicals, like ideologues, prefer an active strategy to a passive one, but although radicals support the active strategy of armed struggle, they believe that physical force alone will not be sufficient to secure movement goals. While quite willing to employ armed struggle as a strategy when perceived as likely to be effective, these activists clearly acknowledge the contradictions involved in supporting the armed struggle of the military wing and expanding its electoral base of support. The following comment by former IRA and Sinn Fein leader Daíthí O'Conaill addresses this issue:

> It's very difficult to reconcile the two—the constitutional and the unconstitutional. In the Northern context it is understood, and where you have good military operations, it generally enhances one's prospects in elections. In the Southern context, however, it can be the other way around, unless you have, for instance, a good strike against the British Army—that can have a good effect. But the shooting of a few UDR [Ulster Defense Regiment] men can have a negative effect, and the further South you go, the greater the negative effect. So you are caught in a bind in the sense that we are trying to combine two forms of action—military action and political action—which at times work against each other. It makes our task more difficult.[10]

Radicals acknowledge the necessity of political base-building and education as a means of transforming the political landscape. Unlike ideologues, radicals value tangible concessions more than doctrinal purity. They are more willing, therefore, to compromise, though not necessarily to abandon, movement principles if those sacrifices appear likely to win real concessions from the incumbent regime. In contrast to those who choose ethnicity over

class, radicals choose both and attempt to prosecute the revolutionary struggle on both fronts simultaneously. For radicals, the only way to free themselves and their ethnonational group is to wage a war of national and social
liberation that targets as enemies those members of other ethnic groups unwilling to cooperate and all members of the bourgeoisie of their own group
who do not cooperate with the struggle.[11] Radicals also favor participation
in electoral campaigns and tactical participation in existing political institutions. They argue that electoral activity and the close contact with the organization's supporters that such mass mobilization entails ensure the popular
support necessary to sustain the armed struggle of the military wing and that
the failure to participate in elections enables competing organizations to
reap the benefits of the political gains secured by the military organization.

In negotiating alliances with other organizations, radicals choose allies
opportunistically. Unlike ideologues, they are willing to trade a limited degree of control to other groups so long as they can make progress in redress-
ing the grievances of their own particular constituency and so long as the
core values and ideology of the organization are not threatened. Radicals,
since they seek to expand the movement's base, will tend to prefer a democratic and participatory organization. Also, to radicalize and mobilize the organization's grassroots constituency, these activists will devote considerable
attention to the development of the organization at the local level.

Although often drawn from the same traditionally nationalist subculture as the ideologues, these activists, because of their experiences in other
political organizations such as trade unions, human-rights campaigns, and
environmental or feminist organizations, are less fearful of ideological conta-
gion through contact with other organizations than ideologues. They also
are familiar with a wide repertoire of tactics. While cognizant that an overly
heterogeneous membership can weaken the organization through factionalism, radicals are more likely to see strength, rather than weakness, in a controlled degree of ideological diversity.

In sum, radicals prefer tangible gains to doctrinal purity, and a democratic and participatory organization. They value class and ethnic concerns equally, and employ a mixed strategy of armed struggle and political mobilization.

Politicos

Rejecting the notion that violence can be used successfully to mobilize the
masses, politicos are far more willing than their more "militarist" counterparts to acknowledge that acts of political violence, particularly those in
which noncombatants are killed, invite both crippling repression and the
organization's alienation from all but its core base. Though politicos reject

violent forms of direct action, except under the most extreme circumstances, they do not limit themselves to participation in the electoral arena. Rather, they support "parapolitical" strategies of nonviolent direct action.[12] Politicos support a strategy of base-building and political education as a means of transforming the ideological preferences of an immature political base.

These activists are most concerned with securing tangible gains and do not view incremental reforms as counterrevolutionary. As DeNardo (1985, 98) notes, to the more pragmatic activists of revolutionary organizations, "nothing seems more doctrinaire or more hopelessly impractical than clutching to an ineffective if principled strategy when real gains can be made by responding flexibly to the political alignment of forces." Like radicals, politicos prefer an inclusive membership that extends the political boundaries of the organization and dilutes the power of the ideologues. They measure organizational strength not in terms of ideological purity, but in terms of real political power. Isolation from the institutional struggle for political power, they claim, will lead either to disintegration or violence, which may or may not result in success. Parliamentarism, far from representing an organizational "sellout," is viewed as another arena in which to challenge the incumbent regime's authority and legitimacy. In particular, electoral campaigns are seen as an opportunity to present the public with their image of an alternative political structure and society, to develop the personnel capable of implementing those changes, and most important, to demonstrate their capability to administer the new society. In situations where constitutional nationalist parties who espouse similar class goals or radical socialist alternatives exist, politicos are likely to defect if they perceive the competing party as credible.

In sum, politicos are opposed to the use of violence to secure political goals. They prefer tangible gains to ideological purity, and open as opposed to closed memberships. Also, they are least likely to come from the movement's traditional subcultures. In general, nationalist objectives are supported by nonethnic party members because of the organization's identification with the desired social and economic objectives. Concerned with securing personal political goals as well as real gains for their constituency, these activists are likely to join only when the organization has achieved some political power.

Table 2.1 summarizes the preferences of each subgroup of activists as well as the empirical patterns of political experience I predict to be associated with each type of activist. It does not yet reveal (1) the relative strength of each group, (2) what coalitions may form among them, and (3) which group(s) will dominate the leadership. Merely identifying different types of activists is not sufficient, however, to explain or predict the size and influence of a particular group in a specific situation. Nor does it provide us with much analytical understanding of why certain coalitions emerge, dominate, or decline within the organization.

Table 2.1. Three Ideal Types of Activists and Their Pathways to Activism

Type	Political Objectives	Strategy and Tactics	Organization	Pathway to Activism
Ideologues	Independence and social reform	Armed struggle Terrorism Limited electoral/ abstentionist Broad national front	Vanguard party Closed membership (ideologically heterogeneous)	Armed groups Cultural groups Nationalist family
Radicals	Independence and social transformation	Mass mobilization Armed struggle Terrorism Electoral politics Limited institutional participation	Mass party Open membership (ideologically homogeneous)	Armed groups Trade unions Social movements Nationalist family
Politicos	Social transformation Self-determination	Nonviolent direct action Electoral politics Full institutional participation	Mass party Open membership (ideologically heterogeneous)	Other party Limited prior activism

Although the skills and choices of individual activists play an important role in the formation of internal coalitions, strategic situations clearly influence not only the relative strength of each subgroup of movement activists but also their propensity to form coalitions and to shape the movement leadership. Indeed, the central hypothesis of this study is that the internal composition of militant nationalist movements, that is, the relative proportion of ideologues, radicals, and politicos, and their propensity to coalesce with each other, is influenced by the internal discourse and by the external environment, which both offer opportunities and impose limitations for collective mobilization on behalf of the aggrieved minority. Three factors, (1) regime responsiveness; (2) organizational resources; and (3) the competitive environment, are held to condition the strategies and tactics adopted by militant nationalist organizations.

Regime Responsiveness and Political Violence

As numerous scholars (Gurr 1970, 1993; Tilly 1978; McAdam 1985; Gamson 1975; Oberschall 1973; and Kitschelt 1989) have demonstrated, differences in regime structures affect participation in rebellious collective action because they influence the extent to which dissident groups are able to develop strong organizations, the dissidents' belief in the probable success of collective action, and the range of political opportunities available for achieving their goals. In democratic regimes, relations between party elites and interest groups, competitiveness of political participation, competitiveness of executive recruitment, electoral rules, and state institutional structures (e.g., centralization of public administration, autonomy of the courts, etc.) clearly influence the openness of a regime. For ethnically divided societies, how the state distributes benefits and enforces rules that determine cultural status and allocate economic resources and opportunities can also have a significant impact on mitigating or exacerbating the collective mobilization of ethnic groups.

In a relatively open system, it is more likely that authorities will attempt to deflect, coopt, or mitigate ethnic claims, and that violent tactics will neither command the support of most members of the ethnic community nor be required to secure group goals. In relatively closed systems, however, violent tactics may appear to be the only recourse available to aggrieved groups. But as Esman (1990), Horowitz (1985), and others have noted, even in relatively open systems ethnic extremists may succeed in outbidding moderate leaders who are prepared to compromise with the state or with competing ethnic groups.

The more open a regime is, however, the more likely it is to recognize the legitimacy of grievances and demands lodged against it and the more willing it may be to negotiate some of the demands. In open regimes, public demonstrations of dissent are apt to be viewed as legitimate expressions of political dissatisfaction, and acts of protest regarded as political, not criminal. Protest, therefore, is more likely to be confined to the civil arena.

Conversely, a closed regime will tend to characterize dissident demands as illegitimate and the actions of those who make those demands as criminal. Such a regime vigorously resists attempts by dissident organizations to participate in the political and policy-formation processes and is characterized by extreme levels of coercive force and the use of extensive special "emergency-powers" legislation. Given that collective mobilization will therefore be

extremely difficult, nationalist movements active within such an environment will tend to adopt terrorism as a strategy to compensate for reduced
support and internal security demands.

The worst strategy, therefore, for preventing regime-threatening rates of
mass violence would seem to be to attempt to suppress opposition movements through the imposition of emergency-powers legislation and reliance
on coercive force while at the same time maintaining a semirepressive regime
structure that permits some organization and expression of discontent but
does not give dissident groups genuine opportunities to participate in political decision making.

Muller and Seligson (1987) in their study of cross-national variations in
political violence similarly concluded that a combination of semirepressive
regime structures and intermediate levels of coercive force could be expected
to produce high levels of violence, since peaceful protest may no longer be
possible, and deterrence should not yet work; that is violence is "neither effectively deterred by the inability of dissidents to mobilize for collective action nor rendered superfluous by the availability of effective peaceful forms
of collective political action" (445). Any increase, from the authors' perspective, either in regime repressiveness or the use of negative sanctions, would
be expected to reduce the likelihood that an individual would choose to engage in rebellious collective action.

However, in their review of Hibbs's (1973) seminal cross-national study
of mass political violence, Muller and Seligson, contrary to their predictions,
found that of all the variables in Hibbs's causal model, the variable with the
strongest impact on political violence was current negative sanctions: *high
costs* were *positively* associated with political violence. Hibbs's finding that
governmental acts of coercion exacerbated violence in the short term but
reduced it in the longer term was also viewed as being inconsistent with a
rational-actor model of political violence. This perceived inconsistency in
the relationship between costs and the willingness to engage in political violence is, I argue, partly a function of the overemphasis placed by economic
models of behavior on the individual as an "isolated" actor. By dismissing
the group as a source of rationality and ignoring the historical situation of
the group, these models are less able to account for the historically conditioned reactions (often undetected in the objective analysis of an event) of
an actor to a particular situation. But if, as Muller and Opp (1986) suggest,
the strict economic model is expanded to allow for collective rationality,
then the perceived inconsistency between costs and action may be resolved
through appeal either to the "unity principle," which stipulates that the participation of each member of a community is necessary for group success,

and/or to the "duty principle," which stipulates that each member of the community has a moral duty to participate in acts of collective action undertaken on behalf of the community. The following excerpts from interviews with Basque and Irish nationalists graphically illustrate the preceding theoretical arguments:

> I think most everyone who joins in an HB protest march knows that there is some degree of risk involved. Sure, some people might perceive that risk to be lesser or greater than others, but after a while you don't really focus on the risk because it's always there. Now, that's not to say you aren't conscious of it, because I bet almost everyone pays attention to where the police are and where they would run if trouble broke out. I guess what I'm saying is that if you're involved with HB, you're in a risky business, and you just deal with it. I started to say people just learn to accept it (the risk), but that's not so. In fact, that's why we show up for the marches, because we believe we should be able to march peacefully in our streets to protest a government decision we don't agree with. I know that's why I, and many of my friends, make the effort to participate whenever we can. Also, we know that the more people that turn out for a march, the harder it is for the police to stop anyone, and that anyone could always be me. It also makes it more difficult for the establishment press to ignore our protests, so, in a way, we are responsible to each other for showing up, because each of us is important to the success of the march. And, if violence breaks out, and if people are injured, well that more or less makes our case about the repressive nature of the Spanish state for us, doesn't it?[13]

> I think the most frightened I have ever been was the day of the funeral for the three IRA volunteers killed in Gibraltar. I had a funny feeling about that whole day, what with all the delays of the bodies even getting to the cemetery, and then there not being any police or soldiers around. . . . Then, just all of a sudden people were screaming and there were shots and explosions everywhere. I only remember falling over my child trying to protect her. . . . I knew there would be a march the next day to protest the killings and honest-to-God for the first time I seriously considered staying home. I mean all the times before, even after the RUC came round the small shop where my husband had finally found some work with photos of him marching behind a Sinn Fein banner in order to get him fired and then had come here to threaten to do the same to me, I never thought about not marching unless I was sick or something. But the day after the attack in the

cemetery I decided to stay in, especially because my husband was away visiting relatives, and I thought about how I might have lost my own child the day before. But, then, once I started thinking about the cemetery again, I knew we all had to get out and march or the "Brits" and the loyalist murder gangs would know we'd been scared off our own streets, and if they ever think that, we might as well call it quits. Besides, if those three young people were willing to die so me and my family could live in peace in our own country, well, who am I not to do what little I can to make sure their deaths and the deaths of so many of my friends haven't been in vain?[14]

From these comments, which were similar to those of the majority of interviewees, it is clear that activists in both Sinn Fein and Herri Batasuna feel a sense of moral obligation to participate in acts of protest organized by the parties.

From this perspective, well-integrated individuals in communities with a high percentage of Sinn Fein or Herri Batasuna supporters will receive extensive rewards for participation in protests, while those who abstain will likely face extensive social costs. An interesting avenue for future research, particularly in situations characterized by long-term violence, would be to explore the relationship between the use of violence and community support for the agents of the violence. Such an approach might provide some responses to the following question: Has the Irish Republican Movement or the MLVN, for example, continued to employ violence only because they believe that violence can secure greater benefits than other forms of protest, or might they continue to use violence because, in a social context in which the costs of engaging in acts of nonviolent direct action (i.e., marches or even campaigning as a candidate for Sinn Fein and Herri Batasuna) have often been as high as those of engaging in violent acts, a violent strategy receives the greatest support within those communities that provide its popular support base? This relationship might help to account for the adoption by ETA and the IRA of strategies that are certain to provoke state repression.

As numerous studies of aggressive behavior have revealed,[15] physical assaults and verbal insults are among the most potent elicitors of aggressive responses. Within tightly integrated communities that have been subjected to verbal and physical assaults over long periods of time, it would not be surprising to find high levels of support for violence as a counterresponse to such regime-sponsored violence. As the following excerpts from conversations with Sinn Fein and Herri Batasuna supporters illustrate, the violent attacks by ETA and the IRA are often viewed as the collective expression of individually impossible yet desired retribution against the enemy:

> According to the British media, you'd think you'd hear everyone in West Belfast cheering whenever a "Peeler"[16] or a "squaddie" is wounded or killed. I'm sure there are many who would, but most everyone, myself included, would probably first be thinking how senseless it was for another person to have to die in this bloody conflict and how some family must be suffering terribly the loss of a loved one. That reaction is natural for everyone here because we have all experienced or known others who have suffered the same loss. At the same time, the ability of the IRA to carry out operations despite having everything thrown at it the British security forces can muster does give the nationalist community a big lift. For the young lad who is constantly harassed by the Brits as he walks home from a pub, for every woman who has had her house wrecked in a search or been insulted by a Brit, for the family who has a loved one in prison or who has had a member of their family injured or killed in the conflict, the IRA's success is a personal triumph, and for some even more an act of personal revenge experienced vicariously. In many ways, the IRA provides this community with a feeling of self-worth, of personal efficacy, which if this were a normal society, people could find in their schooling, in their jobs, etc. . . . But here, the social, political, and economic inequalities and the war itself have distorted people's lives. [17]

The answer to why ETA persists is quite simple. It is because Euskadi is not Spain. Until Spain accepts that and agrees to allow the Basque people themselves to choose the form of relationship, if any, they wish to retain with the Spanish state, then ETA will continue to be the voice of those who rejected the Spanish constitution in 1978 and who continue to deny Spain's right to dictate the politics of our country. You ask why we don't participate in parliament? I would ask you, how can you think that Basques could expect justice at the hands of Spain? Has any country willingly dissolved itself? Look at Ulster, the Irish must fight like us because the political system is loaded against them. As an individual, I can't do much to fight Spain, but by supporting HB and ETA, I can. And you can't forget that for many Basques for very many terrible years, ETA was their only voice, the only expression of their anger and resistance and most importantly their ethnicity. Every ETA operation affirms the existence of a distinct nation fighting for its right to self-determination.[18]

I do not mean to suggest that the IRA or ETA would not consider the potential costs and benefits of any action it proposes to engage in, but perhaps knowledge of the popular support that its armed operations elicit within its core support base might well play a role in its cost-benefit analysis.

If we consider that 930,000 Basques were affected by the violence of the civil war period,[19] and that some 16 percent of the population (238,000 Basques) in 1985 had suffered from that violence,[20] both the breadth and depth of the Basques' exposure to state violence become quite clear. Since the experience of violence that Basques had endured as a result of the civil war was extended throughout Franco's regime, it is not surprising that the experience of violence, for Basques, became intimately identified with Spanish rule. Perez-Agote (1984), Zulaika (1988), and Zulaika and Douglass (1996), for example, have argued that one cannot adequately understand the phenomenon of ETA without reference to the development of a subculture of violence within Basque society as a result of its experiences under the Franco regime. The pervasiveness of fear and violence within Basque society, even ten years after the death of Franco, was clearly revealed in de Olabuenaga's (1985, 52) study of violence in the Basque Country, which indicated that 30 percent of the respondents believed that they or a family member would be beaten at some point by a member of the Spanish security forces, with another 23 percent indicating fear of arrest, and 18 percent indicating a fear of being tortured if arrested. Interestingly, only 7 percent of the respondents believed they would at some point be the target of a terrorist attack, thus indicating a strong connection between the state and terrorism, rather than one associated with ETA.

Another means by which the experience of state-sponsored repression, particularly long-term exposure to state violence, might affect the cost-benefit analysis of an individual's decision to engage in political violence is alluded to by Muller and Opp (1986). Having found, contrary to their predictions, that high expected costs were positively associated with participation, they suggested that high expected costs might be closely related to a high public-good value of rebellious action. It is quite reasonable to expect that communities that have been exposed to long-term, state-sponsored violence would represent the most alienated segments of society and that the individual members of those communities would be the most likely to regard regime changes resulting from rebellious behavior as public goods. Since many of these individuals have already incurred considerable costs as a result of participation in acts of nonviolent direct action or merely as a result of their membership in a particular community, the question of whether the benefits of an action outweigh the costs of inaction becomes, "Are the costs of an action likely to exceed the costs experienced with inaction? If anticipated costs are not expected to exceed the costs incurred normally, then the costs of participation roughly equal the costs of nonparticipation, and since the benefits of change clearly outweigh the benefits of inaction, rebellious collective action is undertaken.

Finally, in attempting to understand why the IRA and ETA continue to employ a strategy of armed struggle, even though the electoral option is now available to Sinn Fein and Herri Batasuna, it is important to analyze their use of violence from a symbolic as well as an instrumental perspective.[21] From a purely instrumental perspective, it is perhaps reasonable to argue that the IRA and ETA's strategy of armed struggle has been ineffective, at least in terms of securing their final objective and that any continued use of violence would be irrational.[22] But if we examine the symbolic relationship between the strategy of armed struggle and the goals of both ETA and the IRA (i.e., an independent Ireland and Basque Country), then regardless of the number of opposition forces killed or injured, violence remains a rational option for ETA and the IRA as long as they can mobilize support for their goals.

To explain, consider Weber's characterization of the defining quality of a state, that is, its monopoly over the use of coercive force within its territorial boundaries. If one makes the argument that a state cannot be considered legitimate if it cannot maintain the monopoly of force over its territory, then it must, de facto, be an illegitimate state. The ability of the IRA and ETA to execute an armed struggle against the state thus represents a continuous reminder of the inability of the state to legitimize its authority in Northern Ireland and the Basque provinces through the use of violence, and at the same time it forces the state to continue to use violence. To the extent, therefore, that the IRA and ETA are capable of mounting operations against state agents, they are capable of reminding the members of their broad support base of the illegitimacy of the state and, perhaps, of reinforcing their commitment to the goal of Basque and Irish independence. As Agote (1984) has stated,

> In the Basque country, the nation of the Nation state is continually being contested by the inhabitants of the territory although it is maintained by the apparatus of the state with a violence much greater than that which maintains the idea of the Basque nation. The Francoist state will never secure a legitimacy among the minority by its violence and yet cannot stop using it continually. The Spanish state was never able under Franco to establish a Spanish "Us" which was legitimate.

This is the real social problem which hides under the political formula
of the Spain of the autonomous regions. (83)

The IRA and ETA's ability to reinforce public recognition of the inability
of the central governments to exercise complete authority over Northern
Ireland and the Basque provinces, and thereby to portray their struggles as
just struggles for a legitimate government, is particularly valuable in an
international environment where claims to state power are regarded as legitimate only if they are couched in the form of national self-determination.

In sum, in order to understand why the IRA and ETA continue to pursue a strategy of armed struggle, we must consider both the subjective as well
as the objective environments in which that violence is exercised. Violence,
both symbolic and physical, has contributed to the formation of dense social
networks within the communities in conflict and has reinforced two distinct
social realities: the world of "them" and the world of "us." In both Northern
Ireland and the Basque Country, the continuing violence succeeds to the
extent that it perpetuates the concept of two contending social, as well as political, realities. We might argue, therefore, that the armed struggle of the
IRA and ETA represents a permanent crisis of legitimation for the British
and Spanish governments and that the efficacy of their violent struggle lies
as much, if not more, in its symbolic attack on the legitimacy of the state as
in its physical attacks on the agents of that state.

Hypothesis 1
In semirepressive regimes characterized by intermediate levels of negative
sanctions, nationalist movements will primarily attract militant activists, both
ideologues and radicals, who will opt for a strategy of violent confrontation
with the regime.

Organizational Support
A conducive political environment, however, only affords an aggrieved population the opportunity for successful insurgent action. What enables insurgent groups to exploit those opportunities is the resources of the minority
community. In the absence of those resources, "the aggrieved population is
likely to lack the capacity to act even when granted the opportunity to do
so" (McAdam 1985, 43).

Similarly, Levi and Hechter (1985), in their examination of the emergence and decline of ethnoregional parties, conclude that although threats to
the vital interests or established expectations of an ethnic community (i.e.,

its political positions, cultural rights, livelihoods, or neighborhoods) may account for why people support ethnoregional parties, the continued existence of those parties depends on their ability to mobilize the resources necessary to support staff, attract party workers, and mount campaigns. Given that regions vary in their natural resources, they maintain that the amount of resources available to an ethnoregional party is important in accounting for variations in its size both over time and between regions.

Among the resources most crucial to a militant nationalist movement is the availability of an accessible sanctuary. If the military wing is to wage a successful struggle, neighboring countries or relatively inaccessible rural areas within the country must be able to provide the militants with a secure area in which to train cadre and experiment with political appeals and insurgent organization. Sophisticated weapons are of little value if militants are unable to train in their use.

Among the factors conditioning the availability of a secure base is the extent to which the organization is integrated with the minority community. Oberschall (1973) and McAdam (1985), for instance, assign paramount importance to the degree of organization in the minority community. They suggest that the ability of an organization to generate an insurgency is ultimately dependent on the presence of an indigenous infrastructure that can be used to link members of the aggrieved population into an organized campaign for political actions.

In addition to domestic resources, international support, both political and material, can often affect the competitive position of movement organizations and thereby influence their choice of strategies, tactics, and occasionally even their goals. Of particular importance is the (un)willingness of the governments of states bordering the areas of conflict to extradite movement activists accused of criminal activity by the petitioning state.

In ethnic conflicts, external support is likely to come from countries facing domestic pressure to intervene based on the ethnic affinity of their populations with the organizations engaged in conflict. But movement elites are well aware that external support often implies external constraints; therefore they will attempt, whenever possible, to mobilize resources sufficient to carry on their struggle from domestic sources or from sources that attach as few strings as possible to their support. We should also note that the imposition of sanctions, military or economic, unless overwhelming or linked to an explicit political settlement that meets the minimum demands of the ethnic community, will tend to reinforce the sense of siege and threat to the ethnic community and strengthen the power of the ideologues.

Hypothesis 2
The greater the availability of resources, particularly weapons and skilled personnel, and the accessibility of domestic and/or international sanctuaries, the more likely it is that a coalition of ideologues and radicals will prefer an active strategy of armed confrontation and mass mobilization.

Competitive Environment
Wilson (1973) argues that the vulnerability of an organization stems from its inability to attract followers rather than its failure to secure its political goals. Similarly, Hirschman (1970) notes that organizations struggle to prevent decline through the loss of members or internal factionalization. He also suggests that organizations behave very differently in competitive than in noncompetitive environments. In competitive environments, organizations find it much more difficult to defend their own identity. The internal stability of organizations is threatened, therefore, both by the number of competitors and the extent to which those competitors threaten the organization's control over its "hunting ground" (Panebianco 1988, 53).

For ethnonationalist organizations, the increase in the number of competing ethnic organizations is particularly threatening because, unlike non-ethnic organizations, they depend exclusively upon the ethnic group for its support. Should an ethnic organization be discredited and lose the support of the group it represents, the loss would be difficult to recoup. This is partly because the ethnic cause has an element of sacredness to it. Indeed, "the charge of neglecting it may carry an indelible stigma" (Horowitz 1985, 344). The inability of ethnic organizations to defray a loss of support by diversifying its clientele means that any competitive threat is likely to appear as a genuine threat to the organization's survival.

Like any organization, then, militant ethnonationalist organizations will attempt to prevent the emergence of competitors. But unlike most political organizations, they face competition from military as well as electoral competitors. Each dimension of competition has significant implications for the internal politics and external strategy of the organization.

The Military Dimension
To preserve organizational unity in the face of rival organizations, Hirschman (1970) suggests that leaders will stress commitment to group goals and attempt to strengthen group solidarity in order to encourage dissatisfied members to choose the "loyalty" option rather than the "voice" or "exit" option. The appeal to loyalty in militant nationalist organizations is particularly important, given that the survival of the organization and the security of its

members is heavily dependent on group solidarity. For this reason, leaders of the military wings of ethnonationalist organizations will attempt to avert internal dissent and the development of factions when at all possible.

Among the methods frequently adopted by military organizations to instill loyalty are ideological indoctrination and the imposition of high initiation and exit costs. Although these measures are often successful at reducing internal dissension, the combination of high initiation and exit costs is likely to ensure that "discontent serious enough to surface is likely to be explosive . . . and often leads to bitter factionalism" (Crenshaw 1985, 485). Whether the dissatisfied member will choose "exit" or "voice" is often influenced by the absence or presence of rival organizations. When an already established rival organization is available, "exit" is clearly simpler, but when no competitor exists, dissatisfied members are likely to use "voice" to effect change within the organization. In either case, the absence or presence of paramilitary competitors can affect the survival of the organization and influence the leadership's choice of strategy.

Violence as Competition

Because ethnonationalist organizations face difficulty in cooperating and coalescing with potential supporters from across ethnic lines, the presence of intraethnic competitors is likely to be the result of one of five conditions. The first is the existence of strong differences of opinion regarding the relationship of armed struggle to political struggle, that is, whether the armed struggle is to be subordinated to the political struggle or vice versa. The second involves the definition of "legitimate" targets, that is, the inclusion or exclusion of categories of people and places as potential military targets. The third relates to leadership rivalries within the more militant segment of the ethnic group. The fourth is the effect of regime repression, both structural and behavioral, on organizational proliferation. For ethnonationalist organizations with leftist orientations, the fifth condition relates to differences of opinion regarding alliances with radical organizations drawn from other ethnic groups.

If any of these conditions exist, a militant nationalist organization is likely to be faced with a challenge to its control of the armed struggle. Because, by definition, these organizations are dedicated to the use of violence to secure their political goals, one of the principal dimensions in which they compete is armed struggle. Consequently, both intramilitary and intermilitary organizational conflict is likely to be characterized by an escalation of violence, as the following hypothetical examples illustrate.

Case 1

In the case of moderate intraorganizational conflict, the leadership, in order to prevent defections, may attempt to increase the level of armed struggle as a way of deflecting attention from the internal debates. By escalating the level of violence, the leadership can effectively restrict internal communications, inhibit participation in political debates, and perhaps restore group cohesion and solidarity.

Case 2

If exit to an alternative organization is possible, dissatisfied members may try to persuade others to join them in the rebellion against the organization's leadership. Once on the outside, these critics will be extremely hostile to the parent organizations. Competition between these organizations is likely to inspire an escalation of violence as each group tries to outdo the other in the military struggle not only in order to retain existing members, but also to attract recruits.

Case 3

In situations where no possibility of exit exists, and when voice is prohibited or ineffective, dissidents, if they are too few to form a new organization, may choose to "fight harder," thereby challenging a more moderate leadership to escalate the level of military activity or negotiate internal settlements with the dissatisfied members.

In sum, a militant nationalist organization's stability depends on its ability to defend its own identity, and that identity is threatened by the existence of competitors. The leaders of these organizations must therefore adopt hostile and aggressive stances toward competitors in an attempt to reassert their own credibility and to preserve the organization's control over its support base. Further, given the close relationship between the leadership's legitimacy and the success of its chosen strategy, elites will attempt to prevent the development of internal factions. In an attempt to retain the loyalty of more militant members, leaders may agree to a collective radicalization of the organizations.[23] Should dissident members remain dissatisfied, they may opt to exit to rival organizations if they exist, or to create new organizations if necessary. In either case, competition between organizations is likely to result in an escalation of the level of violence as each attempts to outperform the other in the armed struggle.

Militant Nationalism: The Social and Electoral Dimensions

The popular fronts of militant nationalist organizations, including labor, cultural, and electoral groups, are developed to expand the boundaries of the struggle, to serve as ideological transmission belts to the broad masses. These mass organizations perform two particularly invaluable functions. First, they mobilize the broad support and resources necessary for the military wing to continue its armed operations. Second, they challenge governmental authority, often substituting alternative centers of authority, and erode its claim to legitimacy.

In seeking to maximize support for the military wing, however, the popular organizations may "stumble into a dilemma common to other movements of social transformation: ideology must be reworked to fit the practical exigencies of successful mobilization and legitimation" (Hannigan 1985, 31). But by tampering with its ideology, the popular organization risks compromising broader movement beliefs and political goals. Therefore, the need to win external support may ultimately clash with the ideological leanings of the membership base and create internal conflicts that require the solution of a number of strategic and organizational dilemmas. Among the most complex issues confronting militant nationalist movements are the relationship of armed struggle to electoral struggle and the issue of participation or abstention by representatives of the political wing in the institutions of the state.

The political party or electoral coalition that represents the interests of an insurgent nationalist movement is, if not an explicitly antisystem party, at least a "challenging" party.[24] As such, its participation in the electoral arena is oriented at a minimum to replacing the government in power and, more generally, to changing the system of government that it opposes. Its political influence resides primarily in its continuous challenge to the legitimacy of the existing regime. So long as the party persists, the polity faces a crisis of legitimacy. Further, to the extent that a movement has defended its use of violent force as a legitimate response to the illegitimate exercise of coercive force by the existing regime, participation in the formal institutions of government by its representatives would erode the military's claim to the justness of its actions. Therefore, in a monopolistic environment, or one in which its competitors are weak, the political wing of a militant nationalist movement will eschew parliamentarism in an attempt both to delegitimate the incumbent regime and to defend the legitimacy of its own armed struggle. However, for ethnonationalist organizations confronted with strong rivals competing for support from the same social or ethnic groups, such a strategy becomes increasingly untenable. In this situation, it is likely that the political wings of the movement will be compelled to participate in order to prevent rival organizations from filling the political void created by their nonparticipation in the institutions of government.

Hypothesis 3

The leadership of a revolutionary nationalist movement in a strong competitive position in both the military and civil arena will likely be dominated by ideologues or by a coalition of ideologues and radicals who will opt to abstain from electoral politics and attempt to prevent the emergence of military competitors by increasing their level of military operations.

Table 2.2 indicates the predicted influence of each of the independent variables hypothesized by this study on the choice of armed struggle, joint struggle, or electoral politics as the primary movement strategy by militant nationalist organizations. The impact of these variables should be evident in both cross-national and longitudinal analyses. Where regimes are nonresponsive, the boundaries of organizational support are narrow, and competitors are weak or nonexistent, militant nationalist organizations will be dominated by a "militarist" coalition and will pursue a strategy of armed struggle or terrorism.

Table 2.2. The Impact of the Political Environment on Insurgent Nationalist Strategy

Strategy	Regime Responsiveness	Organizational Resources	Competitive Position
Terrorism	Low	Low/moderate	Weak
Mass Armed Struggle	Low	High	Strong
Paramilitary (Mixed)	Moderate	Moderate	Moderate
Institutional	High	High	Strong

In a longitudinal perspective, as regime responsiveness, organizational resources, and the number and relative influence of competing organizations increase, the relative influence of the radicals within a militant nationalist movement will rise at the ideologues' expense. Radical-dominated organizations will pursue a mixed strategy of armed struggle and electoral mobilization. As the movement becomes more involved in electoral politics, it will attract greater numbers of politicos, who will coalesce with radicals to isolate the ideologues and pursue an increasingly electoralist strategy. The adoption of a purely electoralist strategy is indicative of a politico-dominated leadership and, in general, represents the transformation of a militant nationalist movement organization into a legitimate political party that may or may not retain its revolutionary goals.

Thus far, I have treated regime responsiveness, organizational resources, and competitive environment as independent variables affecting the internal balance of power in revolutionary nationalist organizations and their external strategies. To present a model that truly reflects the dynamic interaction between movement strategies and their external environment, one additional variable needs to be included: tactical performance. Both the movement's hard-core militarist base and its more moderate political sympathizers evaluate the success of a strategy with regard to the political consequences they attribute to the organization's actions. In particular, I propose the following hypothesis.

Hypothesis 4

Revolutionary nationalist movements will adopt strategies designed to maximize popular support for the military wing as well as the movement's organizational goals. The following hypothetical cases illustrate how such a dynamic link between a movement's internal discourse and external environment might be created.

Case 1

If a coalition dominated by ideologues devotes most of its resources to armed struggle, it will increase the level of social control exerted against it and alienate its marginal supporters, who will be available for annexation by the organization's nonviolent competitors, thus reducing support for its core base. This leads to high internal cohesion and highly ideological internal and external behavior reinforcing the sectarian nature of the organization. As it attempts to realize its original goals through armed struggle, hostility continues to grow, and the organization becomes further isolated. The more isolated it becomes, the more the strategy of armed struggle will be perceived as impotent. If the movement's military wing does not secure any tangible concessions from the government through the use of violence, the failure of its pure militarist strategy will increase the internal influence of the radicals and politicos, who will devote more resources to political education and outreach programs. However, if a competing organization is able to secure tangible concessions by participating in institutional politics, a coalition of ideologues and radicals will choose to participate in electoral politics but on an abstentionist basis, as parliamentarism is shunned as an appropriate strategy for organizational advancement, and elections are used only as a means of registering support and counting the enemy. If the intensity of armed struggle and repression declines as a result of the movement's increasing attention to electoral politics, more marginal political sympathizers will be drawn to the popular movement organization. An increase in the number and influence of politicos will contribute to an intensification of factional conflict as they attempt to form a coalition with radicals to disengage the movement from armed struggle and adopt a fully participatory electoral strategy. At the same time ideologues will attempt to persuade the radicals to pursue a joint strategy of armed struggle and electoral politics. While the movement's political wing continues to advance electorally, a coalition of radicals and politicos is likely to remain dominant and to increasingly politicize the broader movement. Increasing support by politicos and increased domestic and international resources and legitimacy will encourage this process, as will a more open and less repressive response by the regime.

Case 2

If a dominant political coalition devotes most of its resources to political struggle, it will attract more marginal supporters and slowly expand its boundary of support, thereby increasing its electoral competitiveness with its nonviolent competitors and diminishing its reliance on its military wing for legitimation. The more tangible concessions a political strategy can secure from government, the greater the influence of the politicos in the organization and the greater the isolation of the ideologues, which permits a de-escalation of the armed struggle. But abandonment of the armed struggle threatens the identity of the movement and hence will be pursued only if the concessions obtained through political struggle enable an organizational transformation. During this period of increasing participation in institutional politics, the military organization's interests will strongly resist any tampering with its ideological foundations. Therefore, the initial phase of movement electoralization will be accompanied by revolutionary rhetoric and public assertions by the leadership of its fealty to the revolutionary ideals of its predecessors. To the extent that political struggle fails to deliver policy results, it will antagonize the organization's radicals, reinforce radicalism within the organization, frustrate the politicos, increase the influence of ideologues, and result in an escalation or resumption of armed struggle, a decline in the organization's electoral support, and a contraction in its membership.

Summary

In this chapter I have presented a theoretical framework to explain militant nationalist movement behavior that focuses on the relationship between the external political environment, the composition of subgroups of activists within movements, and the movement's choice of specific strategies and structures. In particular, shifts in regime responsiveness, organizational resources, and competitive environment are hypothesized to affect recruitment into the movement. These shifts in recruitment are themselves held to effect changes in the dominant coalitions of revolutionary nationalist movements and the adoption of more or less violent strategies. I have contrasted my approach to existing instrumental and behavioral models of social movement behavior. These models are, by themselves, incomplete because they fail to recognize the multiplicity of the interests and motivations of movement activists, and they are unable to explain why certain subgroups of activists dominate within specific militant nationalist organizations or why the balance of power between subgroups increases or declines over time.

The empirical study of Sinn Fein and Herri Batasuna that begins in the next chapter proceeds in two parts. In chapters 3 and 4, I examine the events leading to the initial decisions by the IRA and ETA to support the choice of their political wings to participate in electoral politics. I also analyze the positions of Sinn Fein and Herri Batasuna within the Northern Irish and Basque party systems during this transitional period.

In chapter 5, I identify the three types of activists in Sinn Fein and Herri Batasuna, and in chapter 6 I demonstrate in a comparative static analysis how the composition and strategy of Sinn Fein and Herri Batasuna reflect variations in the degree of regime responsiveness and organizational support in their respective political environments.

3

Resurgent Nationalism in Ireland and the Basque Country: The Historical Context, 1950–1976

Social Reforms: National Revolutions

By the early 1960s, the social reforms set in motion in Northern Ireland by the introduction of the welfare state fifteen years earlier were beginning to have a noticeable impact on Catholic class composition. Perhaps the most significant of all the welfare state measures for the Catholic community was the provision of access to a free higher education. A young Catholic intelligentsia was now taking shape as a result of that reform. In the job market, however, the situation was much less positive. Catholics continued to have great difficulty finding work, and throughout the 1960s their rate of unemployment was much higher than that of Protestants. According to the 1971 Census of Population, the overall rate of unemployment for Catholics was 14 percent compared with 6 percent for Protestants.[1]

In Spain, Franco's industrial development strategy placed a double burden on the Basque working class. On the one hand, Basque industry was pushed to increase production, and thousands of Spanish workers were attracted into the Basque region to compete with Basques for scarce employment. At the same time, Madrid failed to supply the resources necessary to deal with the ills of industrial growth, including urban decay, inadequate housing and schools, and severe air and water pollution. The consequences were the radicalization of the Basque working class and the emergence of a movement centered on Basque ethnicity and revolutionary socialism.

In both Northern Ireland and the Basque Country, the anti-imperialist struggles in Cuba, Algeria, Bolivia, Vietnam, and Prague, as well as the civil

rights protests in the United States, inspired the post–World War II generation to challenge the authority of the existing regimes. The old colonial em-
pires appeared to be breaking up, while protest and resistance were spread-
ing. For those who wanted political, social, and cultural change, things no
longer seemed hopeless: imperialist powers could be beaten or forced to re-
treat after all.

To explore the dynamics of this critical pre-electoral period for both the
IRA and ETA, I describe the major military and political actions that each
organization engaged in during this period and relate these actions to internal debates and to events in the external environment. Both organizations
would inflict considerable costs on the governments they opposed. However,
their success would, in turn, impose considerable strains on their own organizations and supporters. Each would fall victim not only to external pressures but to internal disputes. They would be declared dead on several occa-
sions only to arise stronger from each defeat.

The Border Campaign: The Resurgence of Republicanism

The period from 1956 to 1962 witnessed the last military campaign by the
IRA before the outbreak of the present "Troubles." The IRA took the
150,000 votes for Sinn Fein candidates in the 1955 Westminster election as
a mandate to renew the armed struggle in Northern Ireland.[2] Operation
Harvest was put into effect on the night of 11 December 1956. Sinn Fein
quickly made clear its support: "Irishmen have again risen in revolt against
British aggression in Ireland. The Sinn Fein Organization says to the Irish
people that they are proud of the risen nation and appeal to the people of
Ireland to assist in every way they can, the soldiers of the Irish Republican
Army."[3]

Within the leadership of the IRA, many had been unenthusiastic about
the resumption of military activity, arguing that the army did not have
enough weapons to justify the campaign. Those in favor argued that action
was necessary to renew support against partition and, as so many times before, the optimism of young men and the preference for uncertain action to
that of cautious inaction won the day. It was now the task of their generation
to take up arms to secure that goal. For these men, the Irish Republic, proclaimed in 1916, was "not a formula to be dispensed at ballot boxes once in
every five years."[4] Indeed, that was "a deceit . . . founded by the Free
State . . . and used by clever men to cloak the surrender of 1922 as a stepping
stone to the Republic."[5] Their republic was the Republic declared in 1916, a
thirty-two-county, united Ireland, and the only sure path to that Republic
was the path of armed struggle.

On 12 December 1956, approximately one hundred and fifty men took part in the opening night of the campaign, which would cost the British government approximately 1 million pounds in damages and approximately 10 million pounds for increased police and security patrols. Although the renewed campaign appeared serious to foreigners and poisoned relations between Dublin and Belfast, most Irish men and women were inclined to view the campaign as "the IRA at it again, without any clear appreciation of why they should have been at it again."[6] But on New Year's Eve, 1957, the deaths of two young IRA volunteers provided another great boost for the IRA and the Republican Movement. Killed in a raid on an army barracks, Sean South and Feargal O'Hanlon became martyrs overnight. Their deaths triggered a huge wave of emotion and sympathy in most of Ireland. People began to wonder, once again, what had prompted two young, affable, bright, and capable Irishmen to join in a fight for their country that so many others had forgotten or tried to ignore.

On 28 January 1957, Irish Prime Minister Seamus Costello, whose government had declared that it would do everything necessary to "bring unlawful military activities to an end," lost a vote of no confidence partly on the grounds of his "failure to formulate and pursue any positive policy calculated to bring about the reunification of Ireland." New elections were called for 5 March. With popular support for the IRA at its highest level in the postwar years, an Irish economy in shambles with seventy thousand unemployed, a large trade deficit, and the highest emigration rate since the 1880s, the leadership of Sinn Fein believed that a very large protest vote was likely against the ruling political parties. Sinn Fein, therefore, prepared to participate in its first Twenty-Six-County General Election in thirty years. On the eve of polling, over fifteen thousand people gathered in Dublin to hear the Sinn Fein leadership's appeal. Sinn Fein nominated nineteen candidates and received 5.8 percent of the total vote. The vote was sufficient to elect four candidates who had stood on an abstentionist ticket. Among those elected were Ruairí Ó Brádaigh and John Joe McGirl, who would remain key figures in the IRA and Sinn Fein throughout the next three decades and find themselves on opposite sides of the historic 1986 Sinn Fein debate on participation in Dail Eireann.

Although satisfied with their results, the Sinn Fein leaders realized they could have done better. They recognized that Sinn Fein's share of the protest vote could have been larger if they had placed more emphasis on social and economic issues, rather than focusing exclusively on the nationalist issue, and if they had fielded more candidates. They made plans, therefore, to increase Sinn Fein's attention to the economic crisis and to increase the number of candidates to stand in the next election. But the actions of the IRA in the next six months would result in Sinn Fein's being declared illegal in Northern Ireland. It would not have the opportunity to stand candidates there until 1974.

By the time of the 1961 general election in the twenty-six counties, Sinn Fein, which had watched its fortunes grow with the IRA, had seen them decline. As the campaign wore on, the emotional tide of protest subsided, and support for violent struggle fell away. Improvements in the economy and a rise in the standard of living in the twenty-six counties pushed the issue of partition further into the background where the Dublin government could more easily ignore the social, cultural, and economic effects of the physical division of the country. Sinn Fein would lose its four seats and see its vote drop by over 50 percent. Then, on 22 November, the new minister for justice, Charles Haughey, announced that the government was again setting up the Special Criminal Court and that it was ready to take the most drastic steps necessary to defeat the IRA once and for all.

Rethinking the Republican Struggle

By January 1962, the campaign that had generated so much enthusiasm in its early stages had failed. External support and internal morale were at an all-time low. On 16 February the IRA announced, "The Leadership of the Resistance Movement has ordered the termination of the Campaign of Resistance to British Occupation." The statement added that one of the reasons for the army's decision was the attitude of the public: "Foremost among the factors motivating this course of action has been the attitude of the general public whose minds have been deliberately distracted from the supreme issue facing the Irish people—the unity and freedom of Ireland."[7] No blame was publicly attached to the IRA; instead, the Irish people were blamed for their lack of support. As 1962 ended, "the IRA was a husk—its strength eroded, its purpose lost, its future unclear. Sinn Fein lay shattered on the far shore of Irish politics, its future unclear, without power or prospects, still a captive of the principle of abstentionism."[8] Once again, a juncture had been reached in Irish history where the IRA appeared to have been defeated once and for all.

The aftermath of the campaign saw much dissension within the Republican Movement regarding the future of the struggle, but everyone agreed that if the Republican Movement was to have a future, it had to take decisive action. For the next eighteen months, republicans would carry out a painful self-assessment. Their conclusions were that both Sinn Fein and the IRA were small, ineffective, elitist, largely rural organizations that offered no consistent political program and that arrogantly saw it as the responsibility of the Irish people to support them without question whenever they decided it was time to resume the war for Ireland's independence. To remedy the situation, they decided that both Sinn Fein and the IRA needed to increase their popular support. Thus, both organizations would increase their involvement with the nationalist communities and concern themselves with the social and economic issues affecting those communities.

Such conclusions were difficult for organizations "steeped in tradition and ritual and constantly paying homage to past heroes" (Kelley 1982, 85). Finding fault with the campaign verged on heresy for many traditional republicans, who believed that it was the duty of the IRA to wage war against Britain when, where, and how it saw fit and that it was the duty of the people to support it. Combined with this assumption was the belief that entry into politics was a betrayal of the Republic, that "no one ever went into politics except a failed revolutionary."[9] This was not an entirely unfounded view. From the republican viewpoint, many former comrades—Arthur Griffith, Michael Collins, Eamon De Valera, Seán MacBride—had indeed sold out and opted for politics rather than rely on physical force.

In 1963, the bicentennial of the birth of Wolfe Tone, one of the founders of Irish Republicanism, was marked by the Republican leadership with the founding of a Wolfe Tone Society as a means to reevaluate principles and strategy following the failure of the border campaign. In 1965, Sinn Fein announced that while it would continue to sit on local government bodies in the Free State, it would maintain its boycott of Stormont, the Dail, and Westminster. Nevertheless, the party decided idealistically that if Sinn Fein were to win an overall majority that would enable it to take over the Dail, the party would do so.

Reinvigorated by the emotionalism of the fiftieth-anniversary celebrations of the 1916 Easter Rising, Sinn Fein increased its strength, openly in the South and in the North under the guise of the Republican Clubs, although as one Sinn Fein activist told me, "Very few people within SF would have said that they were members of the Republican Clubs. If you like, SF was banned at the time, and Republican Clubs were meant to be banned as well. It was still SF though, and so the party had continued to exist."[10] During 1966, individual members of the IRA began to undertake actions again, the most notable being the celebrated destruction of Admiral Nelson's pillar in Dublin. In general, however, the leadership of the IRA, which had changed hands from Ruairí Ó Brádaigh to Cathal Goulding in 1962, was devoting most of its energies to cultivating links with people through political action in order to ensure that the next time it engaged in military struggle it would have the proverbial "sea" in which to swim. Within Sinn Fein and the IRA, a slow redefinition of the role of militarism and political action was taking place. They were now to be combined in a much more subtle and complementary blend. There were no longer to be two different types of Republicans, physical-force men and politicians. Rather, according to the leadership, "We in the Republican Movement must be politically aware of our objectives and must also be prepared to take the appropriate educational, economic, political and finally military action to achieve them."[11] But many in the movement were uneasy with the predominance of political matters over military ones and with the new emphasis on political agitation regarding social and economic issues. While the vast majority of those uneasy with the new leadership came from the older generation of more traditional republicans, there were also some radical members who followed the Leninist critique of parliamentarism and argued that participation in the political protest would deradicalize the movement.

By 1967, the activities of the resurgent Sinn Fein had once again increased enough to warrant attention from Stormont, and on 7 March Republican Clubs were also banned. Stormont was soon to face a much greater challenge to its authority from the Northern Ireland Civil Rights Association (NICRA), which had been formed on 29 January. Its members included both Protestants and Catholics with a wide variety of political experiences. The demands of NICRA were (1) one person, one vote in local elections; (2) the removal of gerrymandered boundaries; (3) laws against discrimination by local government and the provision of machinery to deal with complaints; (4) allocation of public housing on a point system; (5) repeal of the Special Powers Act;[12] and (6) the disbandment of the B-Specials.[13]

The Civil Rights Campaign: Reforms Are Revolutionary

On 24 August 1968, the first Civil Rights march took place, with over twenty-five hundred demonstrating to protest housing allocation. On 8 September, NICRA notified the police (Royal Ulster Constabulary, RUC) of its intention to stage a march in Derry on 5 October. One of the NICRA activists present would state in an interview that "our conscious, though certainly our unspoken strategy was to provoke the police into over-reaction and thus spark off mass reaction against the authorities."[14]

On the day of the march, the RUC responded to NICRA as anticipated. Using batons and water hoses, they forced the demonstrators off the streets. Unlike previous confrontations, however, this display of brutality against unarmed civilians was photographed by the international media. In the aftermath of the march, support for the Civil Rights Campaign grew even stronger, and over fifteen thousand people took part in another march in Derry on 16 November. On 22 November, Stormont Prime Minister Captain O'Neill announced a five-point reform program. For many Irish republicans, it appeared that "the Civil Rights movement [had] done more in a few weeks to damage the Unionist structure than decades of IRA activities."[15] The IRA leadership appeared to agree:

> What can we in the republican movement learn from these happenings? The obvious thing is to leave the Civil rights people alone. . . . For Republicans or any other group to attempt a takeover would bring about its downfall. . . . The next twelve months will tell the story of the North—whether rights can be gained through nonviolence or through the use of stronger weapons.[16]

For the traditionalists within the IRA, this decision was further proof of the erosion of the military role of the IRA.

The 4 January attack by hundreds of Protestants on Civil Rights protestors as they attempted to cross the Burntollet Bridge would be the first of many actions in 1969 to convince militarists within the IRA that nonviolent direct action would never secure civil rights for Catholics.

As the confrontations between Protestants and Civil Rights protestors grew increasingly violent, a group of Belfast IRA leaders traveled to Dublin in May to ask the Army Council for large supplies of arms. The northerners were to discover that the IRA was essentially demilitarized, having sold most of its weapons to Welsh nationalists. The northern leaders returned empty-handed and determined to set up their own Northern Command. The conflict between the demands of the politically oriented leadership and the concerns of the militarist traditionalists was, once again, about to produce a split within the Republican Movement.

August 1969: Republicans Divide
As the "Battle of the Bogside" raged in Derry and thousands of Catholics were driven from West Belfast as Protestant mobs set fire to their homes,[17] divisions within the IRA would be brought to a head by the needs of the besieged northern nationalists. Without support from Dublin, it was left to a handful of Belfast IRA men with no more than six guns between them to hold off the Protestant mobs, led by the B-Specials, as they attacked the Catholic areas.[18] Indeed, when the initials IRA were found spray-painted on walls following the riots, they were usually accompanied by the text, "I Ran Away."

Meanwhile, the principal response of the Dublin IRA leadership to the pogroms and the introduction of British troops on the streets was to issue a statement saying that units of the IRA were active in the North and ready to take any and every action in defense of Catholics and the liberation of the North. The statement may have been true, but the active units were not those of the Goulding IRA. Those who defended the Catholics in the North came from the physical-force camp, which had never stopped believing in the necessity of armed struggle to secure Ireland's freedom and security for Catholics.

Following the events of August, tension between the politicos and militarists increased still further when the IRA leadership failed to respond to the new conditions in the North. What finalized the split was the Goulding leadership's call to remove abstention from the constitutions of the IRA and Sinn Fein. For the orthodox, physical-force republicans, this was rank heresy. Abstentionism was not a tactic but a principle. To sell principle for power, as Griffith and Collins had done in 1921, as De Valera had done in 1927, and as MacBride had done in 1948, would not bring the Republic any closer; it would only split the faithful.

For the traditionalists, the IRA was the legitimate heir of the Second Dail, making it the caretaker government of an Irish republic. The insistence that a de jure Republic did exist or would exist again had been the IRA's justification for the use of force for many generations and would remain so for yet another. To abandon the abstentionist policy and enter the Dail or Stormont would therefore be the first step in recognizing partition and British involvement, and in denying the historical authority of the IRA. Participation in the Dail would be not only an invitation for disaster, but an outrageous and immoral act. Any decision to abandon the policy of non-participation in the parliaments, North and South, was viewed as nothing more than a tainted tactic that would wrench the movement away from its ideological foundations and, perhaps most important for many republicans, would betray all those who had given their lives for Ireland or had spent years in prison. As Coogan (1994, 255) has written, "The I.R.A. tradition is one of physical action and separatism. . . . Deaths, commemorations, holding firm with the past—these are and will be the preoccupations that nourish the I.R.A."

For the Goulding faction, however, abstentionism was a major stumbling block to the implementation of their "stages" approach to Irish reunification. Although contoured to fit the Irish case, the strategy resembled its Stalinist antecedents. Basically, socialism would be achieved in Ireland in three distinct stages. First, as a result of internal forms relating to civil liberties, a capitalist democracy would be established in Northern Ireland. The campaign for civil rights would be conducted by and for Protestant as well as Catholic workers, thus promoting interdenominational working-class unity. Second, the newly united proletariat in the North would gradually link up with its southern counterpart, which would have been mobilized as a result of agitation led by Sinn Fein in the South. With the border now largely irrelevant, the proletariat would turn its attention to defeating their real class enemy. The third stage, therefore, would result in militant, coordinated action by Ireland's now nonsectarian proletariat to overthrow capitalism throughout the island.

Under Goulding's instruction, a motion to end abstention was put to Sinn Fein delegates at the party's annual *ard fheis* on 11 January 1970. Although a simple majority voted for the motion, it fell short of the necessary 67 percent needed for approval.[19] Undeterred, the leadership, determined to proceed with a strategy of political agitation and electoral politics, moved that "this *ard fheis* support the decisions of the Army Council." Since the council under Goulding's control had voted to drop abstention, and as this motion required only a simple majority to pass, the militarists realized there was nowhere to go but out. Under the leadership of Seán MacStiofáin and Ruairí Ó Brádaigh, the Provisional IRA and Provisional Sinn Fein were born. Those who remained behind would be known as the Official IRA and the Official Sinn Fein. Once again, the Republican Movement had divided as a result of deeply held and opposing views of the identity of the movement, the nature of the enemy, and the appropriate tactics and strategies needed to defeat the enemy.

The Provisionals were intent on exposing the irreformable nature of the Stormont regime; the Officials were dedicated to pursuing a gradualist approach to the reform of the state. The former was apolitical and militarist, the latter intensely political and increasingly antimilitarist. As Gerry Adams (1986) would later note,

> [T]he split in 1970 [was] a major set-back for the republican cause. It also ensured that the reinvigorated republican struggle which emerged then was an inadequate one because the only republican organization which arose from the ashes was a military one: it had little or no proper educational process, no formal politicization courses, and there was scant regard paid by the leadership to such needs. (35)

As the Officials turned their attention to politics, the Provisionals turned their attention to rebuilding the IRA in the North and providing for the defense of the Catholics as the level of confrontation between Protestants and Catholics escalated.

The IRA: From Defense to Offense

As 1970 progressed, the Civil Rights marches increasingly began to end in open confrontation and riots, and even the most supportive members of NICRA were forced to admit that the northern state, rather than becoming more democratic, was becoming more coercive. Major Chichester-Clark, who had been elected Northern Ireland Prime Minister in May 1969, largely as a result of Protestant dissatisfaction with O'Neill's concessions to NICRA, was determined to end the protests and rioting.

On 3 July, the British army imposed a thirty-four-hour curfew on the Falls Road area of nationalist West Belfast. During this period, still referred to as the Rape of the Falls, over sixteen hundred canisters of CS gas were fired, and three civilians were killed in gun battles between both IRAs and the British forces.[20] The neutrality of the British forces was discredited, and the Provisional IRA prepared to move from a defensive to an offensive campaign.

In August, as the Civil Rights Campaign became increasingly provocative in its actions, many of the more moderate members, including John Hume, Austin Currie, and Seamus Mallon, opted to form a new constitutional nationalist party, the Social Democratic and Labor Party (SDLP), which drew its support largely from the emerging Catholic middle class. Rejecting the violent strategy of the IRA as contrary to the interests of the nationalist community, the SDLP's stated goal, then and now, was the reform of the Northern Ireland state and the eventual reunification of Ireland by consent:

> The SDLP's basic political view is that the Irish people as a whole have the right to national self-determination and that the Irish people should be defined as those people domiciled in the island of Ireland. This is a view shared by Sinn Fein. It is also shared by a majority of the people of this island. However, the SDLP has pointed out that since there is a very deep division among the people of this island as to how that right is to be exercised, it is the search for agreement on the exercise of that right that is the real search for peace in this island. Since this is a search which involves ourselves—all the people of Ireland—it is self-evident that it should not be pursued by armed force and cannot be won by armed force. The agreement of the unionist people is essential. Such agreement is obviously a task of persuasion and not a task of coercion.[21]

Empirical analyses of the Sinn Fein and SDLP voters some two decades later would reveal that the divisions between two segments of the Catholic community present at the founding of the SDLP continued to distinguish the two electorates.[22]

As 1970 drew to a close, the SDLP's decision not to participate in a NICRA rally scheduled for 19 December in Enniskillen, on the grounds that street demonstrations at the time could only do more harm than good, revealed the two quite distinct approaches that would continue to character-ize Irish nationalism in the North of Ireland. Competition between the IRA and Sinn Fein, on the one hand,[23] and the SDLP, on the other, for the "hearts and minds" of the Catholic communities in Northern Ireland would henceforth condition all attempts to secure a resolution to the conflict. In fact, the British Labour government, with Roy Hattersley as minister of de-fense, actively encouraged the establishment of the SDLP as a means of shifting the center of nationalist politics back from the streets, which the re-publicans had effectively captured, to the corridors of Westminster, which the constitutionalists could control. By supporting the SDLP, the British had, in essence, selected the nationalist leadership with whom they would (more important, could) work in their attempts to isolate the more militant and intransigent republicans.

On 6 February 1971, the first British soldier to die in the "Troubles" was killed in a gun battle with members of the IRA. On 7 February, Prime Minister Chichester-Clark declared, "Northern Ireland is at war with the Irish Republican Army Provisionals." The actions of those within the Republican Movement who argued for armed struggle were now clearly jus-tified. On 20 March, Chichester-Clark, having failed to achieve the security measures he desired from the Heath government, resigned and was replaced by Brian Faulkner. The IRA, now on the offensive, initiated a major bomb-ing campaign: thirty-seven explosions in April, forty-seven in May, and an-other fifty in June. On 9 August, Faulkner introduced internment and gave the IRA its largest recruiting boost prior to the hunger strikes of 1981.[24]

The IRA leadership had received advance warning of internment, and thus the majority of those picked up were Catholics who happened to be in the wrong place at the wrong time. As one Sinn Fein member told me,

> I don't think anyone in my family was politically involved prior to internment, certainly not with republican politics anyway. But on August 9 that all changed. Most of my family and several friends had gathered at our house because of my sister's wedding. So in the midst of all this joy, the army arrives, busts down the door, and without real-ly bothering to determine who was who, simply swooped up all the men, young and old, who were in the house. Two of my brothers were savagely beaten, and my dad, who had a bad heart condition, did not receive his medicine for over a day. As it was, everyone was back home within three months, but you can imagine the impact that internment

had on my family. All my brothers joined the IRA, and the rest of us did whatever was necessary to support them. We knew that if completely apolitical, innocent Catholics were going to be treated in this way, it was clear that the Brits had to go. Now multiply this experience by hundreds of families, and it's easy to see why and from whom the IRA receives their support.[25]

On 24 October, as gun battles raged in the North, Sinn Fein President Ruairí Ó Brádaigh in his *ard fheis* address declared that the most desirable prelude to a thirty-two-county Republic would be to make the North ungovernable and to destroy Stormont. Ó Brádaigh and republicans would receive their wish on 24 March 1972, when Stormont was prorogued, and direct rule was imposed by Westminster. Armed struggle had conclusively secured this Irish republican goal.

The IRA now enjoyed an influence on politics unparalleled in the past fifty years and quite unthinkable only three years before. The republican "victory," however, had come at the great cost of the lives of thirteen protestors shot dead by British paratroopers on 30 January.[26] The events of what became known as Bloody Sunday would swell the ranks of the IRA, whom the British had again proved right. Those events would resonate far beyond the walls of Derry and prompt the entry into the struggle of many apolitical people who had previously turned a blind eye to the events in the North. The patriot game would once again be played by the Irish, North and South, emigrants and refugees. As one Sinn Fein activist who had been living in England at the time told me, "I would say that Bloody Sunday was the watershed for me and a lot of nationalists. I was aware of and had read a lot of Irish history, but I would say that Bloody Sunday was what got me active in the movement."[27]

By summer, the Officials (IRA and Sinn Fein), who had never called for the abolition of Stormont but rather its democratization, found their support slipping away, and on 29 May they declared a unilateral cease-fire, retaining only their responsibility to defend Catholics under attack from British or sectarian forces.[28]

By June 1972, violence had escalated to an all time high,[29] and as Pat McGeown, blanketman, hunger striker, and Sinn Fein Belfast City Councillor, has stated,

[N]ationalist Ireland was almost completely alienated from the British and it was recognized that—as opposed to "containing" the situation, and allowing it to evolve towards a climate in which a political settlement could be initiated to isolate the insurgents (another cornerstone of counter-insurgency strategy)—the opposite was happening.[30]

On 15 June, William Whitelaw, the newly appointed secretary of state for Northern Ireland, met with John Hume and Paddy Devlin to discuss the possibility of a cease-fire. The emerging British strategy focused on isolating the IRA, fragmenting the unionist bloc, and consolidating the support of the moderates in the SDLP and the Catholic middle class.

After discussions with leading Provisionals, Hume told Whitelaw that the IRA would probably agree to a cease-fire if two conditions were met: (1) the release from internment of Gerry Adams, and (2) the granting of political status to IRA prisoners. The first was relatively easy for Whitelaw. The second condition was much more difficult to agree to. The British government was well aware that conflicts such as that in Northern Ireland were more often won through appeals to public opinion than on the battlefield,[31] and it was reluctant to portray the IRA as anything other than criminals. However, given the escalating levels of violence, the British government decided that securing a cease-fire was paramount. Thus Whitelaw announced on 20 June that a "special category status" would be available for both republican and loyalist prisoners. On 22 June, the Provisional IRA announced that it would suspend operations at midnight on 26 June. Mindful of the errors of the 1956–62 campaign, and sensitive to the increasing influence of the SDLP, this leadership wanted to demonstrate that they were much more than mere gunmen. As part of their peace proposals, therefore, the Provisionals introduced their *Eire Nua* document. *Eire Nua* proposed the establishment of a federal Ireland with four provincial parliaments, including a nine-county Ulster Parliament, Dail Uladh. According to the Provisionals, Dail Uladh would be representative of "Catholics and Protestants, Orange and Green, Left and Right."[32] It would be "an Ulster parliament for the Ulster People." For a moment, guns were silenced and politics placed fore and center. It was now up to the British to respond.

Testing Enemy Resolve

In response to the IRA cease-fire, the British government sought to extend its contacts with the leadership of the IRA.[33] On 7 July, six leading republicans were flown to London for talks with William Whitelaw,[34] giving the IRA an influence on Irish politics unparalleled since the Anglo-Irish treaty of 1921–22.[35] The IRA had bombed its way to the negotiating table.

The goals of the two delegations were opposed: republicans sought British withdrawal, independence, and reunification, while the British sought an end to IRA operations and a reformed but still British Northern Ireland. Nevertheless, the two delegations eventually agreed on a four-point program to structure further interactions:

1. A bilateral suspension of offensive operations would continue until July 14.

2. In the event hostilities should resume, a twenty-four-hour notice would be given.

3. On 14 July, another meeting would be held during which the British government's submissions and documents in reply to points one and two of the republican submission would be discussed.[36]

4. In the event the British documents were unacceptable to the Irish, they would be at liberty to resume military operations without notice.

British intentions[37] with regard to the IRA proposals were quickly made evident two days later when Whitelaw failed to return calls from Seamus Twomey, who was attempting to negotiate a resolution to a standoff between Catholics who had been displaced from their homes by loyalist gangs and were now seeking access to their new homes in a "mixed" housing estate, and loyalist paramilitaries intent on keeping them from those homes. Declaring that the British had broken the truce, the IRA returned to offensive operations.

On 21 July, twenty-two bombs went off in Belfast, killing 9 civilians and injuring over 130. The IRA had given Protestants their Bloody Friday, and on 31 July, the British government responded with Operation Motorman,[38] which sent British troops into existing "no go" areas deep within the nationalist communities. Not only did this action severely restrict the IRA's ability to carry out its operations, it also deprived the organization of a powerful propaganda weapon. As Mallie and Bishop (1987, 181) have noted,

> The disappearance of Free Derry was a serious setback. The existence of a Republican mini-state inside the North was good propaganda which the leadership exploited to the hilt, going up there frequently for press conferences. . . . Losing it dispelled the notion that the Provisionals still held the military initiative.

Operation Motorman, however, was an informative lesson in British counterinsurgency strategy for the republicans, who now recognized that British meetings with the IRA leadership were designed not so much to resolve issues as to identify the strengths and weaknesses within the republican support base, as well as to bring republicans into the institutions of the state without handing them any real power.[39]

Following Operation Motorman, the IRA, which had operated freely in those areas, would be forced to act clandestinely, sheltered by a community growing increasingly weary of war. The year ended much the way it had begun, with armed attacks. By now, however, the tolerance shown by the Dublin government to the IRA in the wake of the 1969 pogroms was beginning to dissipate in proportion to its renewed campaign of violence. Then in December, while the Dail was considering a new, antiterrorist Offenses Against the State Act, loyalist paramilitaries carried out two car bombings in Dublin, killing two and injuring over eighty. The bill, previously anticipated to fail, passed by an overwhelming majority. The Republic now had its own antiterrorist legislation that was as harsh as the Special Powers Act in the North. Under its provisions, suspected terrorists could be convicted on the evidence of a senior member of the Irish police (Garda) in a juryless court presided over by three judges. December would also witness the publication of the Diplock Report, which recommended the abolition of jury trials, an act that, when implemented in 1974, would have serious consequences for the IRA as conviction rates soared.

In March 1973, the British government, in consultation with the SDLP and Faulkner, proposed a plan for the SDLP to share cabinet power with the unionists in a new Northern Ireland Assembly. The proposal was for a seventy-eight-member parliament, elected by proportional representation, which would in turn choose a prime minister and cabinet that would include a proportion of members from the leading opposition party (i.e., the SDLP). The plan also recommended a Council of Ireland, which would act as a link between the Government of Ireland in the South and the new assembly in the North. The plan was seen as a way to build consensus between moderate Catholics and Protestants and to isolate both the Provisionals, who were still opposed to any participation in electoral politics, and the hardline unionists, led by Ian Paisley. As the violence continued to rage, there were indications that many within the nationalist community were eager for a political solution. Elections for the Northern Ireland Assembly were set for 28 June. The IRA was extremely perturbed by Whitelaw's initiative.

While the public IRA line was that the new assembly would establish a Northern "Free State" that would never work, privately the Provisional leadership was deeply troubled by the amount of support the agreement was generating for the SDLP. As Ó Brádaigh was later to admit, "[T]he SDLP was able to grow more and more and claim that they had a mandate from the nationalist people and the IRA was only carrying on a military campaign with no political dimension to it."[40] The large vote given to the SDLP in the elections, despite the Provisionals' call for a boycott, confirmed the leadership's fears.[41] The British counterinsurgency strategy of containing and wearing down the IRA while bolstering the reformers (SDLP) appeared to be on the verge of success.

On 21 November, after talks between Whitelaw and representatives of the Unionist parties, the SDLP, and the Alliance party, an agreement to form a new Northern Ireland Executive was announced. The Provisionals announced that they would bring down this Executive just as they had brought down Stormont. In 1974, however, it was to be militant Protestants under the leadership of Ian Paisley and William Craig who would bring down Stormont if the Sunningdale Agreement were enacted. On 14 May, after the new assembly endorsed the new agreement, the Ulster Workers Council declared a general strike. On 28 May, the Northern Ireland Executive collapsed, and London was once again directly responsible for its governance. This reality was not lost on the IRA, which intensified its bombing campaign in England. On 21 November, 19 people were killed and over 182 injured by IRA bombs in Birmingham. In the aftermath of the bombings, the British Parliament passed the Prevention of Terrorism bill, which would greatly increase the special powers of the security forces. Indeed, throughout 1974 and 1975 the IRA would come under increasing pressure as the British both increased and refined their counterterrorism techniques.

In response to the escalating violence on both sides during the autumn of 1974, several leading Provisionals met with a delegation of Protestant clergymen to discuss proposals for peace. On 20 December, the Provisional IRA announced they would suspend operations during the Christmas holidays.

The year 1975 began with an announcement by the Provisionals that they were extending their cease-fire for another two weeks. On 19 January, Merlyn Rees, then secretary of state for Northern Ireland, met with two leading republicans to discuss another extension of the cease-fire. Although the full extent of the deal has never been revealed publicly, it is accepted that the British had assured the IRA that if it ceased all offensive operations, the army would slowly be withdrawn to barracks and then withdrawn from the North.[42] It was also agreed that internment would be phased out and prisoners released. In response, the Provisional Army Council announced that "hostilities against the Crown forces" would be suspended from 10 February. On 11 February, Rees announced that "incident centers" were to be established in various areas throughout Northern Ireland to monitor the cease-fire and to provide a center for contacts between representatives of Sinn Fein and the Northern Ireland Office (NIO).

The cease-fire provided the IRA with the opportunity to assess the heavy toll that the new security measures were having on its ability to operate.[43] The truce also coincided with the submission of a discussion document to the IRA by a group of republicans interned in Long Kesh. The internees called for the creation of "People's Councils" as a way of rebuilding mass participation in the Republican Movement. They also suggested an immediate implementation of parts of the *Eire Nua* program. They argued that the cooperatives and political institutions envisaged in the document should begin operation before the end of the war. According to the internees, it was vital that nationalists understand that a New Ireland would not and could not come into being solely as a result of elections or as the by-product of Ireland's reunification. Rather, as the following excerpt illustrates, they argued that a radical transformation of Irish society could only be accomplished with the full support, cooperation, and participation of the masses and that it did no good to postpone that kind of social and political awakening until the war was won.

> In the short term, we see People's Councils as a broadening of our War Machine, and in the long term we see it as the beginning of the implementation of our proposals for federal government—our national alternative brought down to local level, not as a diversion from the war, but as a necessary (especially in densely populated Nationalist areas), as a vital part of the war. An involvement of Republicans in social issues and an involvement by ordinary people in Republican issues [builds] community involvement in the war itself. . . . We believe it is vitally important for us to broaden our influence and to consolidate our gains. Our strength lies in our local areas. Our strength is our support and our base for operations. Our ultimate success relies on us retaining, solidifying, and strengthening that support. We see People's Councils, suitable to our needs and structured to suit our areas, our own abilities, and the war effort, as a way of doing this. We feel this needs active involvement by all Republicans with support, guidance, and directions from *Óglaigh na hÉireann* [IRA].[44]

For the British, the cease-fire provided the opportunity to focus on its political strategy, which included the formation of a new Northern Ireland Constitutional Convention that would prepare a proposal for a new Northern Ireland government. Elections were scheduled for 1 May. Although Sinn Fein had been legalized in April 1974, it called for a boycott of the Convention elections for the following reasons:

1. Under the present conditions, it is impossible to achieve justice by voting.

2. The Convention will only perpetuate the system in which we live if people vote.

3. The alternative, a thirty-two-county Convention, is the only solution to our problems.

4. The SDLP promised success in the Assembly but were unable to prevent the loyalists from wrecking it.

5. [The SDLP] when elected were as bad as the Unionists.

6. By boycotting [we] are exercising our democratic right.[45]

In particular, Sinn Fein feared that participation in the elections would give credibility to claims of normal democracy, which would merely legitimize the reestablishment of the status quo with minor modifications.

The boycott was also called to place pressure on the SDLP, which was increasingly filling the political space in nationalist politics left void by Sinn Fein's unwillingness to participate in "politics." Despite Sinn Fein's efforts, the boycott was largely ignored. The SDLP won seventeen seats and 23.7 percent of the popular vote.

Sinn Fein and the IRA were clearly weakened and demoralized by the election results and by the internecine feuding that had broken out in October between the two branches of the IRA and had left eleven people dead in a two-week period. By December, the relationship between the IRA and the nationalist community was seriously damaged. As a Provisional activist has commented,

> The people were turning against us as they had never done before. . . . [T]he feud coincided perfectly with British efforts to depict fighting in the North as a gangland murder spree. The criminalization strategy was advanced significantly as British propagandists pointed to the killings of young children and described the violence as a vendetta between two "crime" families.[46]

Similarly, Mallie and Bishop (1987, 218) have noted that the period ushered in by the cease-fire marked "the PIRA's darkest hours since its inception and brought it the closest it has yet been to collapse and defeat." Even major figures within the IRA would later refer to the period of the cease-fire as "the most critical stage in the last 16 years" and claim that "if changes had not taken place in a short time, the IRA would have been defeated."[47]

Ironically, however, the British had furnished Sinn Fein with the resources (i.e., the incident centers) to begin to reestablish its street credibility and to present itself as a real alternative to the SDLP. As a Sinn Fein activist would point out,

In 1974, 1975, and 1976, Sinn Fein was more or less a party of protest, or an organization of protest, that obviously had very strong, anti-
British, anti-imperialist sentiments. We were there to support our prisoners. We were there to psychologically support the nature of the
struggle, but to a large extent on very many key issues we were still
spectators. We also believed simply that the structure of the protest
movement would be sufficient to support the armed resistance; and, of
course, armed resistance would be strong enough to achieve withdrawal.
We also believed that many of the important political questions that
had to be faced on social, economic, and cultural issues could be dealt
with after the Brits had withdrawn, so there was no need at that stage
for us to develop a political analysis that was multifaceted. . . . What
happened in terms of 1976 onwards was the development of the incident centers, which increased our involvement with the community at
the grassroots level. That was very important both psychologically and
strategically. Although at first we dealt more with issues related to the
cease-fire, that began to change as we began to deal in a more organized fashion with a number of domestic complaints in terms of housing and welfare issues. The incident centers, after the collapse of the
truce, became community advice centers that were not there just to
serve republicans, but to serve the community. So we then consciously
began to pitch ourselves as an alternative political voice to the SDLP.[48]

Then, on 4 November, the British government announced that it would be
withdrawing special category status for IRA prisoners as of 1 March 1976,
which sparked the renaissance of the IRA and the Republican Movement.

Once again, by attacking the prisoners, the weakest link in the parami-
tary chain, it had attacked the very heart of the Republican Movement and, as
many times before, the republican community, war-weary or not, would not
abandon its family. As the mother of a prisoner, who at the time had not been
particularly involved in the movement except to support her son, told me,

I don't think the British will ever understand that they can portray IRA
volunteers as thugs, as criminals, as terrorists to the international
media, even to their own people, but to try and tell the families and
communities that raised those sons and daughters that they are anything other than people fighting for a better place in which to raise
their children is never going to work. I mean, even their own specialists
have said that if it weren't for the war, almost none of those in prison
would be there, and if their own believe that, you can imagine the sort
of response that their attempts to criminalize our sons and daughters

evoked here. I know lots of people have said the 1981 hunger strikes were what got republicans involved in politics again, but I'd say all that goes back to the blanket protest. Republicans never went to the polls because we believed elections would never free Ireland, but we would go to the polls to demonstrate that those criminals, thugs, and terrorists that the British government kept referring to were supported by their communities. Everyone in the British cabinet must have been blind and deaf not to have heard and seen that the pleas of one mother to let her child live like a human being in prison would not be echoed a thousand times over. But, then, again, I think that's part of the problem, and I'm not sure which is worse, that they don't see that reality or that they do see that reality and just don't give a damn.[49]

The blanket protest, the first of the "H-Block" protests,[50] began in September 1976 when Kieran Nugent, the first person convicted under the new regulation, refused to wear prison clothes or do prison work as part of his demand to be treated as a political prisoner. He was joined not only by incoming republican prisoners, but also by loyalist prisoners. Following the decision by prison guards to deny the "blanket men" access to toilets unless they wore prison uniforms, the blanket protest became the "dirty protest." Prisoners, almost four hundred at one time, smeared excrement on the walls, floors, and ceilings of their cells.

As conditions within the H-Blocks deteriorated, relatives of the prisoners, republican activists, and sympathizers mobilized in support of the prisoners. During this period Sinn Fein began the politicization process that would lead to its eventual reentry into electoral politics. It would be a process fraught with contradictions and impasses and intertwined with the strategic choices of republican prisoners. It would be forever linked to the lonely, agonizing deaths of ten young men. Both the external and internal political contexts in which these changes were effected are examined in detail in chapter 4.

Origins of Euskadi 'ta Askatasuna

In 1952, a group of young Basque university students formed a clandestine organization, EKIN (to do),[51] for the purpose of rediscovering the Basque language, history, and culture, which the Francoist regime had nearly succeeded in destroying. In 1956, EKIN merged with the youth organization, EGI (Euzko Gaztedi del Interior, Basque Youth) of the Basque Nationalist Party (Partido Nacionalista Vasca, PNV), the only organization that still carried out limited, clandestine political activity. From the beginning, however, the EKIN group disagreed with the PNV and the more traditionalist faction in EGI on three key issues: (1) the role and use of the Basque language, Euskara; (2) the timing and nature of the Basque Country's separation from Spain; and (3) the nature of that autonomous Basque society. The EKIN group argued that without the recuperation of the Basque language, the Basque nation would cease to exist. Thus they proposed making Euskara the sole official language of any new Basque republic, a proposition that the PNV found incredibly unrealistic, given the dramatic decline in the numbers of Basque speakers during the Francoist regime.

EKIN rejected the PNV's policy of limited, parliamentary-oriented political action while waiting for the restoration of the 1936 Autonomy Statute once Franco was dead and the Republic restored. EKIN argued that Basques had never received any concessions from Madrid that they had not fought for and that any deal made with Madrid or Spanish interests would result in the betrayal of Basque interests. While the PNV set as its objective the restoration of full autonomy within the Spanish state, the EKIN group envisaged an independent Basque state composed of all seven Basque provinces on both sides of the Pyrenees. Finally, while the PNV was largely middle-class and reformist, and supported a vaguely specified expansion of the public sector of the economy, the EKIN group was social-revolutionary and espoused the formation of a Basque socialist society, although the nature of that socialism would not be well defined for many years to come.

In 1958, the strain between the two factions would result in the division of EGI into two groups: one composed of the EKIN members and a portion of the more radical EGI members, and the other composed of those who remained loyal to the PNV. On 31 July 1959, after repeated attempts by EKIN members and representatives of the PNV in Spain as well as in the Basque government in exile in Paris to resolve their differences, the EKIN-EGI group created the new organization, Euskadi 'ta Askatasuna (ETA). As Clark (1984, 27) has noted, "Observers inclined to look for symbolism saw much in the choice of a date for the founding of the new organization. July 31, 1959, was the sixty-fourth anniversary of the founding of the Basque Nationalist Party by Sabino de Arana y Goiri." Despite its commitment to violent resistance against Spanish rule, ETA would not commit its first direct action against Spain until 1961. Its first years would be devoted to internal debate and organization.

The Ideological Struggle: 1959–1970
Although ETA was quite clear in how it differed from the PNV, it spent the first ten years of its existence struggling to define itself. This process led to

repeated splits within the organization, each of which appeared to have destroyed it. ETA, however, would not disappear, and the organization that
remained after each internal struggle exhibited a greater homogeneity of
thought and purpose and was increasingly radical and committed to armed
struggle. These early debates focused on questions pertaining to the relationships between class and ethnicity and between armed and popular struggle.
Three distinct factions, the culturalists, the *obreristas* (workers), and the
tercermundistas (third-worldists) struggled for control of the organization.[52]

The culturalists placed the greatest emphasis on the ethnic aspect of the
struggle for Basque freedom. The leading advocate of this approach, known
as "*Txillardegi*," argued that language represented the sole valid definition of
a nation. Basques were defined as a unique ethnic group by their language. If
Euskara were to disappear, the Basques would disappear as a nation. The
only way, therefore, to preserve Euskara and the Basque nation was to establish an independent, monolingual Basque state. To secure this goal, this
group advocated a Basque national front composed of all ethnic Basque political groups, regardless of their social class. Cooperation with Spanish organizations was seen as both unnecessary and undesirable.

The *obrerista* faction, led by Paco Iturrioz, in sharp contrast to the culturalists, maintained that social class was more important than ethnicity in
the struggle to liberate the Basque nation. This group shared many of the
same concerns as the group that became known as Official Sinn Fein. Both
were very much influenced by the Marxist writings of the European left
in the 1960s. Just as those in Official Sinn Fein had held that the key to
Northern Ireland's liberation was a joint struggle of the Protestant and
Catholic working class, the Iturrioz faction argued that a true liberation of
Basques could only occur in alliance with Spanish workers, who would
struggle against their class oppressors at the same time.

The *tercermundista* faction was influenced by the third-world revolutionary struggles of the 1960s, especially the Algerian revolution. This faction perceived the Basque-Spanish relationship as a colonial one, not unlike
that experienced by Cuba under the domination of the United States, or
Vietnam under the French. Basques, they held, under Spanish colonial rule
were exploited economically and oppressed culturally. Therefore, they argued, the only way to liberate Basques was to wage a war of national liberation. Inspired by Che Guevara, the *tercermundistas* adopted the position that
if the objective conditions for a revolution were not yet in place, then it was
the responsibility of a revolutionary vanguard to initiate the struggle that
would bring those conditions into being.

The concerns of each group were represented in one of the organization's five fronts: (1) cells and Euskara study groups; (2) internal publications and communications; (3) legal actions (mass organizing); (4) propaganda; and (5) military action. Following two years of debate and discussion, ETA was ready to assert publicly its opposition to Spanish rule.

On 18 July 1961, the twenty-fifth anniversary of the rebellion that began the Civil War, ETA attempted to derail a series of trains carrying Franco supporters to San Sebastián to celebrate his victory. Just as symbolism had played a part in ETA's founding, it had influenced its first direct challenge to Spanish authority. Although ETA's attempt was made with such precaution that it failed to derail a single car and no one was injured, Franco's reaction was swift and brutal. More than one hundred ETA members were arrested, tortured, and sentenced to jail for fifteen years or more, while a group of nearly equal size was forced into exile in France. ETA would be forced to spend the next year reorganizing.

In 1962, the exiles in France established an Executive Committee that convened ETA's First Assembly, which issued ETA's first formal statement of principles, *Los Principios.* ETA declared itself to be a revolutionary movement for national liberation, created in a patriotic resistance and independent of any other party or organization, and it advocated the proclamation of Euskara as the sole official language of the Basque nation. It also declared itself to be secular and opposed to all dictatorial regimes, both communist and fascist. It rejected the notion of the superiority of any one race over another, and it advocated the creation of a federated Europe based on ethnonationalities.

In 1963, a wave of labor unrest in the Basque Country forced ETA to examine its relationship to the Basque working class and, most important, to reexamine its position regarding the thousands of immigrants who had migrated to the Basque region since the early 1950s.[53] This examination deepened the conflict between the three ETA factions. These themes also figured prominently in the debate of ETA's Second Assembly, held in March 1963. During the assembly, the *tercermundista* faction began to assert its position as the dominant voice in the organization. The assembly adopted revolutionary war as its form of struggle against Spanish rule and set about restructuring the organization for that struggle. Rejecting the provincial divisions as inappropriate for guerilla warfare, ETA divided Euskal Herria into six geographic zones, *herrialdes,* better suited for an armed insurgency. ETA also designated its first *liberados,* that is, those who would be paid by the organization so that they could devote themselves to the struggle. However, a second wave of arrests and deportations in October 1963, which came as a result of ETA's participation in labor conflicts and strikes, virtually destroyed the organization.

In 1964 several events combined to reduce the influence of the EKIN "old guard" over ETA. Many of ETA's founders were forced to flee from France to Belgium and were increasingly isolated from events in the Spanish interior. ETA was left in the hands of Iturrioz and the *obreristas,* who wanted to turn the organization into a revolutionary workers' party that would join with radical Spanish forces to create a general socialist revolution in Spain. This assembly broke definitively with the PNV, which it defined as bourgeois and contrary to Basque interests. It declared ETA to be both anti-capitalist and anti-imperialist. The assembly approved and published a further statement of principles entitled *Carta abierta de ETA a los intelectuales vascos* (Open Letter to Basque Intellectuals), which announced that the national and social struggles were but two sides of the same coin. It was to be the most coherent and comprehensive document that ETA would publish during its first five years.

Although the document was ostensibly directed to the Basque intelligentsia, it was also a call to the middle-class Basques whose interests had been marginalized under Franco. Since 1958, ETA and the PNV had been competing for the leadership of the Basque nationalist movement, and that division would soon be reflected in the composition of the two organizations. ETA increasingly assumed a position as champion of the working class and lower middle class, and the PNV championed the upper middle class and elites who favored continued links with Spain.

The Tercermundistas *Rise to Power: 1965–1967*

In June 1965, ETA held its Fourth Assembly. It was the first to meet within Spanish borders. With the leaders of the old EKIN group and many of the *tercermundista* supporters in exile in Belgium, the *obrerista* faction was able to assert its control over the organization. This Third Assembly would implement important ideological, organizational, and strategic changes that would have a profound impact on ETA's future development. Ideologically, ETA would shift increasingly to the left. Organizationally, ETA replaced the former five-front system with five branches *(ramas)*: activism, information, external support, and political. Strategically, ETA approved and adopted the action-repression-action theory favored by the *tercermundistas.*[54] According to this theory, ETA could create the objective conditions for a spontaneous revolution by provoking Spanish security forces to overreact in response to its actions. ETA believed that the Spanish government in its attempts to stop ETA would aggravate the already high levels of Basque resentment to Spanish rule, inciting a popular Basque mobilization. ETA, however, failed to calculate whether the organization was strong enough to withstand the

Spanish counterinsurgency measures. This omission soon led to disastrous consequences for the organization.

Throughout 1965 and 1966, the Iturrioz faction, now in control of the Political Office of ETA, increased its attacks on both the culturalists and the *tercermundistas,* accusing the first of being ethnic chauvinists and bourgeois, the second of being adventurist. The culturalists responded by claiming that the Iturrioz faction was betraying ETA by attempting to link it with Spanish social revolutionary groups. They argued that participation in class-based fronts was intrinsically damaging to Basque nationalism because such fronts subordinated the national struggle to the class struggle. The *tercermundistas,* especially José Etxebarrieta, argued that the *obreristas* were too content to wait for the inevitable social revolution they anticipated and maintained that it was necessary to launch the armed struggle that would mobilize the Basque population.[55]

In the autumn of 1966, the Political Office urged all ETA militants to vote in the upcoming Spanish labor union elections. As all other Basque political groups had agreed to boycott these elections on the grounds that to participate in them would legitimize Franco's state-controlled union system, the culturalists and *tercermundistas* seized this opportunity to justify the expulsion of the Iturrioz faction in the first part of the Fifth Assembly held in December 1966. The first serious schism in ETA was now completed.

The Iturrioz group would, for a short period, reorganize under the name of ETA-Berri (New ETA). In August 1969, as the police increased their attacks on ETA, ETA-Berri, in order to avoid being identified with ETA, changed its name to Spanish Communist Movement (Movimiento Comunista de España, MCE). In this way, Clark (1984, 44) notes, "ETA served as the point of departure for a number of splinter groups that would occupy positions of radical intransigence throughout the Spanish and Basque political spectrum."

The second part of the Fifth Assembly convened in March 1967. It attracted all of the major figures who had been involved with ETA since its founding. Having succeeded in expelling the Iturrioz group, the two remaining factions now turned against each other in their struggle for ultimate control over the organization. As the debates progressed, it became clear that the radical *tercermundistas* were the dominant force. Many within the culturalist faction resigned from the organization, although they continued to play a significant role in the nationalist struggle, including the creation of Herri Batasuna. A new Political Office was elected to replace the expelled *liquidacionistas,* and ETA was defined as a "Basque socialist movement of national liberation." Members of the Basque working class as well as immigrant workers who wished to integrate into Basque society (i.e., learn Euskara) were assigned the central role in the liberation struggle. The assembly coined the phrase Basque Working People (Pueblo Trabajador Vasco, PTV) to illustrate the combination of social class and ethnicity that now guided its struggle. Basque members of the lesser bourgeoisie, if they accepted the principles of the liberation struggle, would also be considered part of the movement, although there were considerable reservations regarding the implications of their inclusion in a broad-front strategy supported by ETA.

> [I]t is only proper to recognize the fact that the entirety of social forces prepared and willing to participate in the struggle for national independence is not identical with the array of social forces whose task it is to establish socialism. The question is how to involve sections of the national bourgeoisie oriented to constitutional nationalism and opposed to armed struggle in a united national struggle to break the connection with Spain. . . . [T]he crucial question is not whether a broad front for national independence could unite disparate and conflicting class interests, but the terms on which it should take place. If the vanguard was compelled to forfeit its independence of action on matters external to such a broad front, or if the front threatened to undermine the armed struggle from within, then such a front would be neither viable nor desirable. Instead of sharpening the cutting edge of ETA, it would blunt it. If, however, the front was confined to agitation and propaganda around the right to self-determination for the Basque people and comments critical of the armed struggle were not allowed, then there would be some real benefit.[56]

In any event, ETA's attempt to launch a Basque National Front in September met with no success. Meanwhile, in response to the Iturrioz takeover of the Political Office, the assembly created a new central committee, or BT (Biltzar Txikia, or Little Assembly), to monitor the activities of the Executive Committee in order to ensure there would be no more deviations from the accepted ideology. The BT was to be composed of exiles who had no explicit decision-making power but who could convene a special assembly if necessary to prevent any deviations by the Executive Committee from the agreed-upon political goals and strategies. The assembly also reinstituted the four-front (cultural, political, economic, military) system and in 1968 added a Workers' Front. The assembly also reaffirmed its commitment to the action-repression-action spiral. With the conclusion of the Fifth Assembly, ETA, now more ideologically homogeneous and committed to armed struggle, appeared poised to launch its offensive operations. In April, however, ETA learned that events beyond its control could impede the best of plans.

Following a violent strike in Bilbao, Franco declared a state of exception in Bizkaia (Vizcaya) and a suspension of constitutional guarantees. The Guardia Civil and the Spanish police responded to the violence with counter-violence, and the period between April 1967 and June 1968 witnessed the first widespread activity by ETA, ending, almost predictably, with the death of Txabi Etxebarrieta, the first member of ETA to be killed. Despite prohibitions by the provincial government, funerals and masses for Extebarrieta were held in every major city and numerous villages throughout the Basque Country. As had occurred so often in the history of the IRA, the death of a patriotic young man, now a national hero and martyr for the cause, would renew support for the goals he had espoused. On 2 August, ETA exacted revenge for Extebarrieta by assassinating Meliton Manzanas, a police commissioner who had acquired a reputation as a sadistic torturer.

Franco reacted by imposing another state of exception on 3 August. More than six hundred arrests were made in August alone, and by the end of 1969 over two thousand Basques had been arrested, more than half of whom were detained, tortured, and imprisoned on a wide variety of charges of crimes against the state.[57] The most important prisoners among those arrested were the sixteen Basques charged with the murder of Manzanas.

By April 1969, virtually every key ETA leader on the Spanish side of the border had been arrested. ETA had gone through two entire generations of leaders in less than three years. What leadership remained was in disarray, and rank-and-file members were exhausted. Further, many ETA militants began to question the usefulness of the action-repression-action theory because repression had so often left the organization too weak to respond with further provocative actions. It was increasingly apparent that ETA had both underestimated the repressive capacity of the state and overestimated its ability to control the dynamics of the spiral. In particular, many ETA militants involved with the union movement criticized the action-repression-action strategy on the grounds that the repression fell mostly on the working class. Consequently, when the Sixth Assembly was convened in August 1970, many of the same questions regarding strategy and ideology that had divided the Fifth Assembly arose again, and the factions divided themselves along similar lines.

The group closest to the Executive Committee was the Red Cells (Células Rojas) faction.[58] They maintained that ETA and Basque nationalism in general were too contaminated by bourgeois thinking to meet adequately the needs of the Basque working class. They also believed that the

Basque Country could not be liberated as long as Spain remained a dictator-ship and therefore advocated joining with other radical forces to extend the revolution to all of Spain. The remaining factions joined forces. On this oc-casion, however, the Red Cells controlled the Executive Committee, and they expelled the *milis* group, whose members were most dedicated to armed struggle and emphasized Basque ethnicity as the key to ETA's struggle. However, the central committee, or Little Assembly *(Biltzar Txikia)*, which had been elected by the Fifth Assembly, responded by announcing that all participants in the Sixth Assembly were expelled from ETA. Thus, by the end of the year, ETA was in total disarray, and both ETAs, ETA-Sixth Assembly (VI) and ETA-Fifth Assembly (V), appeared close to extinction. Franco, however, would once again provide the impetus for its renewal and for international recognition of the plight of Basque nationalists.

On 3 December 1970, a military court-martial began for the Burgos Sixteen, as those accused in the Manzanas killing became known. The trial was greeted with mass demonstrations and repeated strikes resulting in vio-lent confrontations with the police throughout the Basque provinces. Franco responded by imposing another state of exception. Throughout Europe, Spanish embassies were attacked by ETA supporters, and many countries recalled their ambassadors for consultation.

Inside the courtroom, the defendants refused to address the court in Spanish. They admitted only to being members of ETA. Motion after mo-tion by the defense lawyers was rejected, and confessions presented to the court were denounced as having been extracted under torture. The verdict was never in doubt. However, the sentencing of the prisoners was greatly complicated by ETA's kidnapping of the West German consul, Eugen Beihl, in San Sebastián on 2 December. The kidnapping provided ETA with the opportunity not only to pressure Franco into reducing the sentences of the prisoners but to gain access to the international media. According to Basque sources, ETA's plan worked. ETA released Biehl on Christmas Eve. On 28 December, all of the accused except one were found guilty, and six were given the death penalty. On 30 December, Franco commuted all of the death sentences to thirty years in prison.

Reinvigorated by the Burgos trial, ETA-VI increased its labor activism, and ETA-V renewed its armed campaign. In the next two years, ETA-VI simultaneously increased its involvement with the workers' movement and reduced its commitment to the armed struggle. By 1972, as its members deserted in droves to ETA-V, it was clear that ETA-VI had badly misinter-preted the relationship between ethnicity and class that characterized its sup-port base. In 1973, ETA-VI dissolved and joined with the Revolutionary

Communist League (Liga Comunista Revolucionaria, LCR). Following the demise of ETA-VI, ETA-V was once again referred to only as ETA.

ETA, although weakened by this second split, was inspired by the resurgence of international armed insurgency in Latin America and the Middle East and began to resume operations on both military and social fronts. Also, just as inaction on the national front had led many to abandon ETA-VI, the failure of the PNV to participate more actively in the nationalist struggle once again led a section of its youth group, EGI, to defect and provide ETA with a new and much-needed influx of activists.

In January 1972, ETA initiated a period of intense activity unlike any ever seen before in the Basque provinces. It would culminate in the assassination of the Spanish prime minister and heir to Franco, Carrero Blanco, on 20 December 1973. ETA's first action was the kidnapping of Basque industrialist Lorenzo Zabala. This kidnapping became a major event in the history of ETA:

> [N]ot only was it the first kidnapping conducted as part of a labor dispute, but it was also the first ETA armed action directed against a Basque. With this dramatic blow, ETA not only demonstrated that it had survived the Burgos trial and the police suppression of the period 1969–1970 but also served notice that the final years of Franco were not going to be easy ones.[59]

Encouraged by their success with this operation, ETA continued to carry out operations at the rate of about one per day.[60] This activity, however, would not come without considerable cost to the organization, as numerous *etarras* were killed and imprisoned. ETA, from November to mid-December 1973, suffered its most serious blows since 1969. Over thirty *etarras* were arrested, and three were killed. Despite these blows, ETA managed to execute the most dramatic assault in its history, the assassination of Carrero Blanco. There is little doubt that ETA's assassination of Blanco influenced the development of Spanish politics and it significantly affected the role ETA would play during Spain's transition to democracy.

Following the assassination, the conflict between the Frente Obrero (Workers' Front) and the Frente Militar (Military Front) intensified, further separating the militarists from those members who were willing to adopt a more conventional political strategy to secure an independent Basque Country. In early 1974, the Frente Cultural (Cultural Front) officially separated from ETA and joined with dissident members of the moderate Basque labor union, Solidarity of Basque Workers (Solidaridad de Trabajadores Vascos, STV), to form the Basque Socialist Party (Euskal Alderdi Sozialista,

EAS). Meanwhile, on the French side of the border, other members of the Frente Cultural were forming the Popular Socialist Party (Herriko Alderdi Sozialista, HAS). These two organizations would eventually merge after the death of Franco in 1975 and form the new party, the Popular Revolutionary Socialist Party (Herriko Alderdi Sozialista Iraultzalea, HASI), which was to become one of the key coalition members of the radical Basque electoral coalition, Herri Batasuna.

The more significant split within ETA that year was initiated by members of the *Frente Obrero*. Accusing the *Frente Militar* of imposing its preferences on the rest of ETA, the leadership of the *Frente Obrero* declared itself to be free of the discipline of the organization. The Executive Committee of ETA responded by expelling the dissidents. Those expelled responded by creating their own organization, the Patriotic Revolutionary Workers Party (Langille Abertzale Iraultzalean Alderdia, LAIA) which in turn created its own labor union, the Patriotic Workers Committee (*Langille Albertzale Komiteak*, LAK). These organizations would also form part of the Herri Batasuna coalition during its early years.

Control of ETA was now roughly divided between the militants of the Workers' Front who had remained within the organization and the members of the Military Front. Numerous events, including the fall of the right-wing governments in Portugal and Greece, suggested the arrival of a more open and democratic political environment, and debates between the remaining factions regarding ETA's future and the role of armed struggle in a new political environment intensified.

For many within the Workers' Front, it appeared that ETA's assassination of Blanco had ushered in a new period of politics which, with the anticipated death of Franco, would make their struggle obsolete. This faction argued that to prepare for the new political environment, it was necessary to restructure the organization, eliminating the four-front system and providing for a joint political-military organization. In their opinion, the military struggle and political struggle would be mutually reinforcing.

For the militarists, the transition represented an opportunity to use violence to force Madrid to concede Basque independence. They argued that to avoid being seduced by the false appearance of Spanish democracy, ETA should remain a small, clandestine group dedicated to armed struggle. Although they saw the political struggle as supporting the armed struggle, they argued joining the two in one organization would expose the public political agitators to the same repression faced by those engaged in the armed struggle.

In October 1974, during the October meeting of the Biltzar Txikia, the final and most definitive split in ETA's history took place. Those who advocated a unified political and military organization and strategy became known as ETA (Politico-Militar), or ETA(pm). Those who supported the clandestine armed struggle and maintained the need for separate political and military organizations became known as ETA-Militar, or ETA(m). ETA(pm) emerged as the stronger of the two groups and proceeded to restructure the organization, eliminating the four separate fronts and establishing a unified political-military organization down to the regional level. According to the ETA(pm) leadership, the military struggle and the effort to promote a mass organization would be mutually reinforcing.

For its political program ETA(pm) set the following goals:

1. An independent and reunified Euskal Herria
2. The establishment of Euskara as the official language
3. The establishment of socialism and proletarian internationalism in the Basque Country

According to one of its former leaders, Mario Onaindia, the ETA(pm) was closer to a traditional Marxist-Leninist revolutionary organization because of its commitment to a joint political and military strategy that "combined an armed party at the head of a mobilized proletariat."[61] As its instrument for the radicalization and mobilization of the proletariat, ETA(pm) created the Patriotic Workers' Councils (Langille Abertzalean Batzordeak, LAB), which would be deeply involved with fostering the major general strikes that occurred in the Basque Country in December 1974 and June and September 1975.

Although ETA(pm) retained the majority of ETA militants, events in the final months preceding Franco's death helped shift the balance of power back to ETA(m). In particular, as ETA(pm) became increasingly committed to popular, nonviolent strategies of political mobilization, many of its more radical members grew restless and defected to ETA(m). By the beginning of the 1980s, ETA(m) members outnumbered those of ETA(pm) by almost three to one (Clark 1984, 81)

As Franco's death approached, tensions in the Basque provinces flared, and massive labor unrest combined with ETA actions to produce the most turbulent and violent year that Basques had experienced since the Civil War. The violence began with the arrests of twenty leading ETA activists in November 1974. That month over one hundred and fifty political prisoners began a hunger strike to demand amnesty, freedom for all political prisoners, and the return of all exiles. On December 2–3, over two hundred thousand

Basque workers participated in a general strike called in support of the prisoners. On 5 December, the strike spread to bank employees, and almost the entire financial system of the Basque provinces was brought to a virtual halt. ETA, meanwhile, increased its level of attacks against members of the police and Guardia Civil. By April 1975, Franco once again imposed a state of exception on the provinces of Bizkaia and Gipuzkoa. ETA, perhaps sensing that it was close to producing the collapse of the Spanish government it so desperately sought, kept up its level of activity. In early May, ETA killed a lieutenant in the Guardia Civil and a police inspector. On 22 May, the Spanish government declared a state of absolute press censorship and secrecy about events in Bizkaia and Gipuzkoa. The Basque Left responded with a massive general strike on 11 June, during which more than six hundred thousand workers walked off the job. The state of exception ended on July 25, but the violence and unrest continued, and Franco imposed a final state of exception that began on August 26 as two ETA members came to trial.

ETA: The Final Months of Franco

The trial and execution of ETA members "Txiki" and "Otaegi," the last prisoners to be executed under Franco, ignited support for ETA in much the same way as the blanket protest did for the IRA. It also led to the creation of the Patriotic Socialist Coordinating Council (Koordinadora Abertzale Sozialista, KAS), composed of EHAS (Basque Popular Socialist Party), LAIA, LAB, ETA(pm), and supported by ETA(m). From this group, the Basque Left began to develop an ideology that combined radical Basque ethnicity with revolutionary socialism in a parliamentary setting.

In the year following Franco's death and the legalization of political parties (except those such as HASI, which had explicitly separatist goals), ETA(pm) shifted increasingly toward the formation of a political party. This attempt by a faction of the organization to shift the organizational resources and strategy to one of political mobilization would, once again, split ETA into three distinct factions: those within ETA(pm) who wanted to distance themselves from armed struggle and adopt parliamentary politics; those within ETA(pm) who were determined to continue the joint political-military strategy (Berezi Commandos); and a resurgent ETA(m).

Conflicts between these factions would come to a head during the first half of ETA's Seventh Assembly, held in October 1976. At this meeting, the majority of ETA(pm)'s members agreed to break once and for all with the organization and to form a new political party, EIA (Euskal Iraultzale Alderdia, Basque Revolutionary Party), which defined itself as a revolutionary organization at the service of the working class. Arguing that the Basque working class could never be liberated so long as capitalism remained in either Euskal Herria or Spain, it called for the destruction of the oligarchy and the institutionalized violence employed by that class. Finally, it proposed a political structure to be developed within the framework of a liberal, bourgeois democracy that would be based on the power of autonomous organisms of the Basque popular classes. EIA would depend not just on a conventional political party structure but would attempt to involve the workers, students, intellectuals, artists, and other groups that perceived a need to achieve Basque independence. Radical Basque nationalists were now clearly divided into those who believed that the transition would bring with it opportunities to secure political goals through the political process and those who maintained a belief in the necessity of violent direct action.

Summary

During the period 1950 through 1976, new social and economic policies implemented by Britain in Northern Ireland, and Spain in the Basque Country, aggravated preexisting grievances, leading ethnic minorities to challenge the authority of the central governments. Influenced by the wave of anti-imperialist struggles in the 1960s, both the IRA and ETA adopted a strategy of revolutionary war. Within both the IRA and ETA, however, socialism and nationalism appeared as contending, rather than complementary ideologies. Debates among Irish and Basque nationalists regarding the primacy of nation/ethnicity versus class and the proper relationship between political and armed struggle led to repeated splits in both organizations. Likewise, despite claims by both organizations to be prosecuting a classic guerrilla campaign, armed struggle and electoral politics were viewed as competing rather than complementary strategies of political action.

As 1976 came to an end, both the IRA and ETA stood at a strategic crossroads. Their strategic options, located along a continuum of more to less violent, included a continuation of armed struggle by a small, clandestine army or expansion of the mass struggle through nonviolent direct action and popular mobilization through participation in electoral politics and the institutions of the state. Both organizations also faced competition for the leadership of the nationalist struggle from moderate, constitutionalist opponents, the SDLP and PNV, respectively, which had both the political and financial support of the opposition governments. They also had to confront challenges on their radical electoral flanks, Sinn Fein from the IRSP, WP, and People's Democracy, and Herri Batasuna from EE, MCE, and LKI. Further, the IRA and ETA also faced competition from other military organizations, the INLA and ETA(pm), respectively, which ostensibly shared both its social and its national goals.

Consistent with the model of revolutionary nationalist politics presented here, the application of extreme coercive force by the state against the ethnic minority resulted in the adoption of a strategy of armed struggle and terrorism by the IRA and ETA. Also, as hypothesized, competition among the Basque and Irish paramilitary organizations resulted in an escalation of violence by the IRA and ETA, while the increase in the political influence of their nonviolent electoral competitors resulted in the reentry by Sinn Fein into electoral politics and the creation of the radical Basque political parties allied with ETA.

4

Sinn Fein and Herri Batasuna: Parties to the Conflict

Transition and Consolidation: The IRA

During the two years following the death of Franco and the first H-Block protests, Basque and Northern Irish politics were a maze of intersecting forces. This was a period characterized by much experimentation with new political forms and strategies, with varying degrees of success. The history of the IRA and ETA during this turbulent time was a fascinating interplay of several key factors: a continuation of armed struggle and increasingly dramatic acts of violence, new attempts to establish mass-based organizations, including cultural associations and labor unions, and efforts to create or mobilize organizations that could compete effectively in electoral contests. It was a period characterized by a series of internal disputes and power struggles that were at once ideological and personal.

In this chapter, I first examine how these factors influenced Sinn Fein's increasing commitment to electoral politics as well as the formation and evolution of Herri Batasuna (HB, Popular Unity), the political party that represents the interests of ETA. Second, I provide a brief description of the Basque and Northern Irish party systems at the time that those electorates were provided with the opportunity to elect, respectively, a Northern Ireland Assembly in 1982 and an autonomous Basque Parliament in 1980. I then turn to an analysis of how the competitive environment influenced strategic changes within Sinn Fein and Herri Batasuna. To conclude, I identify the social bases of partisan support for the principal Basque and Northern Irish nationalist parties and focus on the images that voters hold of their own party, as well as of those with which it competes.

Protest and Political Mobilization: The H-Block Campaigns

Throughout the 1970s, Sinn Fein had functioned principally as a protest movement and a movement of support for the IRA. Further, due to their conspiratorial background Sinn Fein members were, as Adams (1982) has commented,

> temperamentally and organizationally disinclined to participate in any form of action with elements outside the movement itself. The movement had its origins in armed struggle, which had dominated to the extent of even being considered the only form of struggle; in such circumstances conspiratorial methods were, of course, essential. But what we were slowly and unevenly realizing was that one could not build a political intervention on the basis of conspiratorial methods and approaches. . . . Sinn Fein was at that time only beginning to discuss strategy and tactics, to assess what our attitudes should be in any given circumstances. (75)

The first indications that internal debates were taking place within Sinn Fein regarding its increasing isolation and that of the IRA and the prisoners surfaced in the 1977 Bodenstown Commemoration speech.[1]

In order to assure the rank-and-file members that this Sinn Fein, although it was "going political," was not going to abandon the armed struggle as the Officials had done in 1970, a highly respected republican activist, Jimmy Drumm, was chosen to deliver a speech that stands as a milestone in the history of the Republican movement.

> The isolation of socialist republicans around the armed struggle is dangerous and has produced the reformist notion that "Ulster" is the issue, without the mobilization of the working class in the 26 Counties. . . . The British government is not withdrawing from the Six Counties, and the substantial pullout of business and the closing of factories in 1975 and 1976 was due to world economic recession, though mistakenly attributed at times to symptoms of withdrawal. . . . Indeed, the British government is committed to stabilizing the Six Counties and is pouring in vast sums of money . . . to assure loyalists and to secure from loyalists support for a long-haul war against the IRA. . . . We find that a successful war of national liberation cannot be fought exclusively on the backs of the oppressed in the Six Counties, nor around the physical presence of the British army. Hatred and resentment of the army cannot sustain the war.[2]

That a decision had been reached to involve Sinn Fein more deeply in politics was now readily apparent, but it was also clear that there was still a lot of opposition to overcome, as evidenced by Sinn Fein's initial refusal to participate in the H-Block/Armagh Committee, which was formed in 1978 to campaign for the restoration of political status. Sinn Fein's demand that all the committee members express public support for the armed struggle of the IRA reveals how deeply republicans distrusted those from outside its narrow support base. Adams (1982) later noted that

> lack of experience and lack of preparation on our part resulted in . . . a lost opportunity to build unity because the price our representatives asked for that unity was that all within the front should express support for the armed struggle of the IRA. It was a price many of those who wished to unite in anti-Unionist action were not prepared to pay. . . . The IRA was constantly being denounced from all quarters and all standpoints. It was understandable that members of the movement had considerable difficulty in accepting the right of people with whom they were involved in joint action to attack the IRA. Members were increasingly coming into contact with organizations that expressed a position of "critical support" for the IRA, and any republican was bound to feel that one either supported the IRA or one did not; "critical support" seemed a contradiction in terms and a dishonest one at that. It took a maturing process on the part of republicans to appreciate that a position of "critical support" was better than one of not supporting at all. (75)

By 1979, the deteriorating conditions within the prisons, the stagnation of the military campaign, and the large crowds and publicity attracted by the H-Block/Armagh Committee protests had changed the attitudes of many within Sinn Fein regarding its participation in the broad-based committee. Consequently, Sinn Fein dropped its demand for the expression of public support for the IRA and threw its full weight behind the campaign. Participation in this campaign was to have a major influence on Sinn Fein's political development.

> During the period of H-Block/Armagh protests there was an influx of people into Sinn Fein as a result of the increased mobilization. Many of them had no republican ideas, no republican history. They certainly had no republican taboos. Those people began building the case that participating in electoral politics doesn't mean selling out. They fortified the position of those already inside Sinn Fein who were already

saying the same things but having a hard time making headway with the current leadership. Our participation in the campaign forced Sinn Fein into contact with people who were obviously not republicans. That started republicans thinking and forcibly broke down republican resistance to working with other groups, even those opposed to the IRA. We realized we needed to develop a working relationship with those people. From our experiences during this period came our drive to political maturity and electoral interventions.[3]

Despite the intensive lobbying and repeated attempts by the H-Block/ Armagh Committee to raise public consciousness and to mobilize support for the prisoners, it was unable to force the British government into movement on the issue. When this tactic failed, IRA prisoners began their first hunger strike in October 1980. The strike lasted fifty-three days, ending on 18 December, when it appeared that the basis of a reasonable compromise had been reached. Despite what the prisoners had taken to be an understanding that their demands would be accommodated in some manner,[4] it soon became clear that the British government would grant no new concessions. Within one week, the prisoners began preparing for a second hunger strike. On this occasion, as Adams (1982, 70) has made clear, much more than special category status was at issue: "[I]n resisting this move [criminalization] republicans were asserting the political nature of their struggle and contradicting the British attempt to suggest to the world that the political crisis in the six counties was not a political crisis at all but was merely a problem with a criminal element."

Although Adams wrote to Sands that those in Sinn Fein were "tactically, strategically, physically, and morally opposed to a hunger strike," all those involved knew not only that this time some of the prisoners would have to die, but also that they were engaging in a fight with the British government that went beyond the issue of prison conditions: "[T]hey were pitching themselves, with the only weapons at their command, against imperial power."[5] On 1 March 1981, Bobby Sands began the fast that would effect dramatic changes in the political strategy of the IRA and Sinn Fein.

Sinn Fein and the IRA: Electoral Strategy Reconsidered

On 5 April 1981, the H-Block/Armagh Committee, due to the death of the sitting nationalist MP, Frank Maguire, was presented with an unanticipated opportunity to demonstrate popular support for the hunger strikers when a by-election in the Westminster constituency of Fermanagh/South Tyrone was called for early April. Following an intense debate among the committee members regarding the possible consequences of either a successful or failed campaign, they agreed to stand Bobby Sands as the nationalist candidate. The committee also decided to focus the campaign on the single issue of special status for all political prisoners. "There is but one issue at stake," declared Sands's election manifesto, "and that is the right of human dignity for Irish men and women who are imprisoned for taking part in this period of the historical struggle for Irish Independence." The Sinn Fein members also agreed that there should be no discussion of armed struggle, on the grounds that "harping on the correctness of the IRA's fight would probably have alienated many potential supporters of the political status demands."[6]

Numerous Sinn Fein activists, including Jim McAllister, Jim Gibney, Joe Austin, Francie Molloy, Mitchell McLaughlin, and Fra McCann, discussed the concerns of the committee during this intense period in interviews with the author. The most important concern for the committee was clearly the negative effect that a unionist victory might have on the fate of the hunger strikers. While the committee was certain that Sands would attract a sizeable number of votes in the traditionally nationalist Fermanagh/South Tyrone constituency, they feared that other non-unionist candidates might also run and split the nationalist vote, thus allowing a unionist to capture the seat and deal a staggering blow to the hunger strike campaign. According to many of those interviewed, it had been anticipated that Noel Maguire, the brother of the deceased MP, would run and that they would be forced to withdraw Sands's name from the ballot papers. Maguire, however, after a personal appeal by the Sands family, withdrew his nomination papers, and Sands was left as the only nationalist candidate. Other concerns included the practical issues of running a campaign. As one Sinn Fein activist noted,

> While we recognized that Maguire's death presented us with an amazing opportunity, there were some doubts as to our ability to run an effective campaign. Remember a whole generation of republicans, including myself, had come of age with no experience of participating in elections. For example, I had never worked on an election in my life. I had never been in a polling station. I was one of the hardline republicans who didn't vote, who didn't believe in the electoral process. But what we lacked in experience we made up in our determination.[7]

The republican leadership and that of the H-Block Committee brought all of its resources to bear on the campaign, and soon many republicans discovered that fighting elections was, as an IRA leader noted to Bernadette Devlin McAliskey following her explanation of electoral procedures, "more complicated than stripping an armalite."[8]

The SDLP Stands Aside

During this period, the SDLP had also conducted an internal debate over whether to field a candidate against Sands. Although the party leadership was in favor of contesting the election, the Fermanagh members were strongly against an SDLP candidate running. Indeed, as one republican activist told me, "[E]ven the palest of greens in the SDLP were absolutely certain that if the party stood a candidate, it would face disaster in the local elections."[9]

Ultimately, the SDLP Executive decided to withdraw their candidate's nomination on the grounds that presenting a candidate would leave the party vulnerable to the criticism that it had deliberately undermined the prisoners' struggle and would seriously erode its support among its nationalist rump. Rather than risk appearing as "less nationalist" than either Sinn Fein or the Irish Independence party (which had also abstained from nominating a candidate) and face the possibility of conceding its "green" wing to either of those parties in future elections, the SDLP leadership merely suggested that "peace-loving nationalists" remain home on election day. As John Hume has stated, if the SDLP had contested the election,

> [it] would have been accused of lifting the siege of pressure on the British. That would have reverberated through other elections. It was a no-win situation. We would have drowned in the deluge. Politics are not only about principles but about the ability to put principles into practice. The second is as important as the first. There are times when it is more necessary to speak more quietly in order not to speak more often. The SDLP was being put in a situation that was not of its own choosing. It could have become one more victim of British policy.[10]

The nature of the dilemma the SDLP faced in choosing whether or not to stand a candidate was not lost on those within Sinn Fein who had begun to set their sights on challenging the SDLP's dominance at the ballot box:

> The SDLP leaders were quite aware that their party would have suffered irreversible harm had they contested a seat which they had no prospect of winning. With their eye on the local government elections, which were less than a month away, the prospect of being blamed for the defeat of a man on hunger-strike and the possible consequences this would have on their electoral prospects at local council level clearly steered them away from involvement in what would have been a definite defeat.[11]

Thus, in a dramatic reversal of roles, the most parliamentary of parliamentary nationalist parties was now calling for a boycott, while the most adamant of Sinn Fein boycotters were denouncing a boycott as a betrayal of Irish nationalists.

Elections: Results and Responses

On polling day, 9 April 1981, voter turnout was exceptionally heavy, and it soon became clear that SDLP supporters had not heeded the call for a boycott. Bobby Sands, at that time six weeks without food, became a member of the Westminster parliament with a majority of 1,446 votes. The National H-Block/Armagh Committee now had a singularly impressive centerpiece for its propaganda efforts in Ireland, Britain, and the international community.

The British government responded swiftly to Sands's election. Within hours, Tory Cabinet leader Francis Pym called a meeting of representatives of all parties to discuss the unseating of Bobby Sands. Following intense debates, they agreed that the potential threat that such an action might pose to the legitimacy of British parliamentary democracy outweighed any immediate benefits. It was also argued that any attempt to unseat Sands would probably cause the British government even more embarrassment than his election. Pym, however, did initiate legislation, passed three months later, that barred convicted felons from standing in elections.

In Dublin, meanwhile, Prime Minister Haughey, whose Fianna Fail government rested on a fragile majority, maintained that Sands's election was democratic and had to be respected. Despite massive international attention and attempts to resolve the conflict, the British government remained firm and refused to grant any of the prisoners' five demands. Sands died on 5 May 1981, the sixty-sixth day of his hunger strike. Sporadic rioting broke out throughout the North of Ireland, and it was soon apparent that the level of violence, which had been reduced in 1980 to facilitate negotiations, was now being increased in preparation for a renewed armed struggle that many within the H-Blocks and the IRA were again convinced was their only real chance for a successful outcome. According to Vincent Browne (1981, 5), a long-time analyst of the IRA, there was a "greater acceptance of the need for a military campaign than at any time since the present troubles [had begun] over a decade ago." As evidence for his assertion, Browne noted the "enthusiastic reception accorded to the firing parties at the hunger striker funerals throughout the North—the tens of thousands of people at these funerals *all* applauded when the firing parties appeared" (emphasis in the original).

The failure of Sands's election to produce a resolution to the hunger strike bolstered the position of the militarists within the IRA and Sinn Fein who had always rejected electoral politics as a strategy to secure political goals. The continued dominance of the militarists within the organization was illustrated by Sinn Fein's decision not to stand candidates in the May 1981 Northern Ireland Local Government elections. Maintaining that the party was officially bound by a resolution passed at the previous *ard fheis* not to participate in local elections in the North, the leadership of Sinn Fein called instead for a nationalist boycott: "Vote H not X."

The success of Sands's election campaign in mobilizing the nationalist electorate and reinvigorating the republican movement had, nonetheless, increased the influence of those within Sinn Fein who had been arguing for an expansion of the party's support base and its increasing involvement in social and political issues. The success of the H-Block candidates put forward by other parties, including People's Democracy and the Irish Republican Socialist Party, usually the purest of the pure anti-electoralists, provided the tangible evidence needed by the more political members of Sinn Fein to convince the doubters that there was substantial support for the prisoners that could be exploited not only to undermine the British claims that the hunger strikers had no popular support, but also to erode the position of the SDLP as the "official" voice of northern nationalists. Consequently, when the opportunity arose to participate in the June 1981 Irish parliamentary elections, Sinn Fein quickly moved to put forward nine prisoner candidates, four of whom were on hunger strike.

With only two weeks to campaign, it was widely said in the Dublin media that the hunger strike campaign would be doing extremely well if it could elect even one of its nine candidates. As it turned out, two "blanket men," Paddy Agnew and Kieran Doherty, were elected in the border constituencies of Louth and Cavan-Monaghan, and a third, Kevin Lynch, was defeated by a margin of 300 votes. The nine prisoners received a total of 40,000, or 2.3 percent of the votes cast, leading some of the campaign coordinators to regret openly that they had not put up a candidate in every Dail constituency. Both seats won by the prisoners came at the expense of Haughey's Fianna Fail government, which fell when it was reduced to seventy-eight seats as compared to the combined Fine Gael/Labor coalition total of eighty.

For the hunger strikers, however, the electoral success of the prisoner candidates failed to translate into any new concessions. The Fine Gael government merely maintained a posture of passive support for the prisoners, even though opinion polls revealed that 57 percent of Catholics in the North and 60 percent of those in the South agreed that "the British government should stop treating people convicted of crimes which they claim were politically motivated as ordinary prisoners."[12]

The IRA at the Polls: The SDLP Stands Down Again

On 20 August 1981, the H-Block Committee achieved perhaps its greatest victory. Owen Carron, who had made it quite clear that he was a member of Sinn Fein and the chosen candidate of the IRA,[13] not only won the by-election for the Fermanagh/South Tyrone constituency left vacant as a result of Sands's death, but actually increased the margin of victory by almost eight hundred votes. Carron's campaign was particularly significant because it announced Sinn Fein's commitment to a dual military/electoral strategy.

> There is no shift from armed struggle. An integral part of the Republican Movement's strategy is based on the use of armed struggle to remove the British military presence. Armed struggle backed by mass political struggle is the only way the British will be removed from this country. All wars—and this one is no different—are about determining political power and who should govern a country. Parallel with the use of physical force there must be a political program. What is being fought here is a political war, and therefore we must have a political organization, and we must engage in political battles, like the elections battles [that] have been successfully fought and won. Those elections have been significant in the overall context of the war.[14]

It also forced the SDLP to withdraw, once again, from electoral confrontation with Sinn Fein.

Although the decision to withdraw the party's candidate from the race drew widespread criticism, John Hume, the leader of the SDLP, has defended the decision on the grounds that if the SDLP had contested the elections, it would have been beaten in its first direct confrontation with Sinn Fein and that Carron's election would have provided the IRA with an even greater propaganda victory that would have further increased Sinn Fein's political momentum.

Despite this display of support for the prisoners, neither the British nor Irish governments, nor the Catholic church, chose to negotiate a response to the prisoners' demands. Consequently, on 3 October 1981, the six remaining hunger strikers announced that they were ending their fast. The hunger strike had lasted 217 days and had focused international attention on Northern Ireland as no other event had done in the course of the twelve-year conflict, and it had irrevocably altered the dynamics of the conflict.

Political Struggle, People's Struggle

Not everyone can plant a bomb, but everyone can plant a vote.

The popular mobilizations in support of the hunger strikers had taught both the IRA and Sinn Fein invaluable lessons that would henceforth influence the development of their struggle against British rule in Ireland. The foremost of those lessons was that popular mobilizations around emotive causes could serve as powerful propaganda campaigns. As one Sinn Fein activist stated,

> This is where it was at for a whole lot of people. We saw that for a whole range of people who we wanted to talk to that electoral politics was a good way of positively focusing their attention on issues that we were concerned with, without having to focus on the armed struggle. We also saw a new way to involve people in the movement who had previously been merely passive supporters. Whereas in the armed struggle only a few people can play active roles, in electoral campaigns everyone can do something, from canvassing to billposting.[15]

Another outcome was that republicans began to recognize that "winning" the war might well result in their losing the peace if they failed to establish a well-organized political party that would enable them to exercise political influence in a united Ireland. The third was the realization that it might be possible for Sinn Fein to unseat the SDLP as the dominant voice of Northern Irish Catholics if it committed itself seriously to electoral politics. Finally, Sinn Fein had apparently learned that fighting elections presented a practical way by which to make use of the support mobilized as a result of the hunger strike.

> Rather than placing our trust in a semi-religious belief in deserved victory, we should base our tactics on a realistic appraisal of what the future may hold for our struggle.
>
> The armed struggle is undoubtedly the central and most essential aspect of the national resistance against the British. Yet a number of false positions still exist among those who support it. . . . Perhaps the greatest error is the belief that the military effort is self-sustaining and that "politics" do not matter. This dangerous illusion is not only an elitist one, but it threatens the very base of the struggle. A guerrilla movement that discounts mass support, or which neglects the support which it has, leaves itself open to destruction. The war, therefore, must be a "war of the people" to succeed. Slogans in this regard will not

suffice. Hard work must be done to sustain and enlarge the existing base of support for the struggle to remove the British.

This active participation by a mass of people in pursuance of British military withdrawal is not confined just to a military role or a role in direct support of the IRA. . . . Force . . . cannot replace a mass movement, and only in particular circumstances can it be part of such a movement. Those circumstances exist in the North against military occupation. They may not exist in a Britless Ireland.[16]

Thus, with the experiences of the past year behind them, the delegates to Sinn Fein's 1981 *ard fheis* approved the following motion: "That Sinn Fein contest all local government elections both North and South." Sinn Fein's new strategy for securing Ireland's reunification was aptly expressed in Danny Morrison's now famous address to the *ard fheis* delegates, in which he asked, "Who here really believes that we can win the war through the ballot box? But will anyone here object, if with a ballot paper in this hand and an armalite in this hand, we take power in Ireland?" The resounding "No" from the delegates confirmed that the party activists now recognized the importance of the political as well as the armed struggle and that they were determined to advance on both fronts.

Strategy: The Armalite and the Ballot Box

As the following excerpt from an internal Sinn Fein discussion document, "Fighting Elections," reveals, however, the decision to contest elections would provoke considerable tensions between those arguing, respectively, for the primacy of the armed or electoral struggle. The arguments presented by each side reveal distinct strategic concerns. To illustrate more precisely the differences between the two factions on key issues, their arguments are presented together. The letters *M* and *E* are used to refer to the pro-military and pro-electoralist factions.

Costs and Benefits

M: Time, effort, money, there is a tremendous amount of all three put into fighting elections, especially national elections. Consider the time and effort put into deciding if we will stand, . . . where we will stand. Consider the time and effort spent planning tactics to be employed. Consider the time and effort spent gathering resources, i.e., people, cars, leaflets, posters, etc. Consider the time and effort spent at the polling stations on election day. And finally consider the time and effort that is put into analyzing the outcome, win or lose. All this of course takes a fantastic amount of money, and it's a fact we are still trying to pay off past elections. Would all this time, effort, and money not be better employed in the war effort? Is it not time we [threw] most of our resources into a sustained push against the Brits? The Movement has not got unlimited manpower, and if we spread this manpower over too wide an area, all sections will be weak. But if we concentrate say 80% of our resources on the immediate war effort, we should achieve better results. Allow the other 20% (these of course should be people with a flair for street politics) to get on with the job of building Sinn Fein and involving themselves in local affairs. We must remember that the last time the movement won an overall majority in Ireland was in the 1918 election. On that occasion people voted for the revolution, not for who had a lamp post shifted. I believe for us to gain power again we will have to win the war first, so most of our energies must be directed into pushing the Brits out. Allied to this of course we must have a manifesto for running the country when we achieve victory. . . .

I firmly believe that you cannot mix revolutionary and constitutional politics. They are like salt and sugar. They look compatible, but when you mix them you are left with a big heap of nothing. (2–3)

E: As for the point that election work takes people away from other work. If one had seen the coming together of people at the last elections: how it expanded and strengthened the movement and brought people into it, how it gave people a chance to take part in the struggle, one would see that they were not drawn away from any other work, but that people really found their place in the movement. The reality is, that if we are not fighting elections and winning seats, we will not be ready when the Brits leave. Our objectives should be the defeat of both the Brits and the Irish ruling classes by whatever means possible (be it military actions, elections, or whatever). . . . To make a statement that the political wing should develop its own leadership and to talk about political and military problems goes right to the root of one of our biggest problems. . . . [T]he very idea that the fight is not political hits a nerve end. The leadership of the Republican movement is the political leadership. To say we are fighting anything other than a political battle and that our actions are anything but political, puts us on the same level as the squadie with his political overlords. It smacks also of elitism, saying in fact, to let the best of us get on with the fighting and let the less capable do the less important work. . . . Political power comes out from the barrel of a gun. But the man with the gun must wield that gun with an understanding that it is to gain a political end, and he must play his part in all aspects of the struggle to gain that political objective. We all have a part to play in the fight, be it with a gun or a pen. Our work is, for all of us, the establishment of a Socialist country. We are not a physical force, we are a political force. We are going nowhere if we are anything else. (4–5)

M: First, let us examine why elections are held: elections are held to elect a government to govern the people, and to administer the country. We, as republicans, do not recognize any party or group of parties elected in either the "Free State" or the Six Counties. We deny them any legal right to govern. Now if we really believe that these assemblies are illegal, how can we justify to ourselves, our supporters, and the world in general our participation in their elections? . . . The Army Council of the IRA is the legal power, the only legal power of the 32 counties of Ireland. All the other assemblies are illegal. The people who work out of Leinster House, the people who worked out of Stormont Castle, the people of the Northern Ireland Office, are traitors and collaborators, and if we contest elections, and take part in their assemblies, then what does that make us? The Army Council of the IRA, at present, has the legal right to wage a war against the forces of occupation. The Army Council indeed has a duty to free our country. The Army Council has the legal right to take life in furtherance of that aim. The A.C. has the right to requisition from the people of Ireland any and all resources that the A.C. deems necessary to the war effort. The IRA has these rights as long as the IRA does not hand over its legal authority to another assembly. If we give recognition to the "Free" or Six-County states by fighting their elections, do we, the IRA, give up our legal right to wage war? People argue that if we have people in local councils, we have a voice that can be heard, thereby affording us publicity. Yes, that is true, of course, to a point. But it is also true that publicity comes from operations, and a lot more than will be reported about what councillor so-and-so said regarding any topic. (1–2)

E: The reasons for fighting the war in the north we all know, and there is no need to go into it. To say the governments north and south are illegal is firmly believed by us as republicans. But the fact is, that the southern government is firmly in place and is, in the minds of most people, their government. It is those minds that we must change, and if we can't through the ballot box, then how? We must have political power before we can shift the Brits, but, just as important, we must have the power to stop the Brits from setting up suitable gombeen men in political positions and then leaving. As for our enemies here in the Free State, they are not only our national enemies but they are also our class enemies and that is an area where we can carry the struggle here. I agree that, perhaps at the moment, there is no point in being in Leinster House, but if the day comes when we can gain the political support to win enough seats to change the system, we should enter hell if we have to. We can put the fires out once in. The people, in the end, will only put those in power who they think will take care of their interests. To make the statement that elections are wrong because they got us nowhere, is, in my mind, ridiculous. By that criterion, neither has military action. Bobby Sands's name still rings around the world and the fact that he was an MP (and we emphasized the MP) plays a major part in it. . . . When we look at what elections have done for the main parties and recently the Sticks, we have to wonder what effort we are putting into winning the people. Much as we may dislike the set-up, their position gives them a massive propaganda platform, while we are (I don't think anyone will disagree here) effectively silenced. As revolutionaries we must use every tactic that will gain us an advantage, and if elections do that, we adopt that tactic. It doesn't matter whether the last battle is won with a shot or a vote. We must keep an open mind. (4–5)

To mobilize support for the new "mixed" strategy, Sinn Fein and the IRA devoted the following year to assuring the rank and file that a commitment to the ballot box would not place any restraints on the armed struggle.

The Sinn Fein leadership viewed the presentation of its new electoral strategy with extreme concern for several reasons. Certainly the path followed by the Official IRA in the early 1970s, which had led the party from an involvement in a wide range of political activities to the complete abandonment of armed struggle, was a precedent that naturally prompted the question of whether the Provisionals were now going down the same "Sticky" road.[17] The following excerpt from an article in the Sinn Fein quarterly, *IRIS,* by a spokesperson "authorized to speak on behalf of the IRA" testifies to Sinn Fein's sensitivity to the 1969–70 split:

Generally speaking, what was wrong with the "Sticks" was not just that they had a totally incorrect analysis of the nature of British imperialism. They believed that the Six-County state could be reformed from within and that the so-called democratic process was one method by which this reformation could be made. . . . The Sticky attitude towards elections is one of complete involvement with the system and cannot be divorced from their collaborationist attitude towards the RUC, and loyalist paramilitaries, and reactionary elements within Fine Gael, and towards the whole national question, and the partitionist state, Leinster House, and the old Stormont. Similarly, the republican attitude towards elections cannot be divorced from our total rejection of the six-county state, our struggle for the last twelve years of unbroken resistance to the British government and to its crown forces, and our refusal to compromise with loyalism. Republicans have periodically contested elections in both six and twenty-six county states. In 1917, 1918, and 1919 before partition, and then again in the 1950s and in 1964 republicans contested elections on an abstentionist ticket. There is no reason now, where practical, as it appears in West Belfast, that republicans should oppose nationalist participation. If Sinn Fein contests this [NI Assembly] election, the IRA will obviously wholeheartedly support their decision. For those who would be concerned that such an intervention in the West Belfast election is a new tendency, or departure, they can be assured that the military struggle will go on with all the energy at our disposal, and, in fact, victory would actually be hastened with the development of a radical political offensive. . . . Our attitude to constitutional politics is quite simple and clear-cut. There is no such thing as constitutional politics in this country. The last legitimate constitutional forum in Ireland, Dail Eireann, was proclaimed illegal and subverted by the British and the Free Staters. Outside of a thirty-two county, sovereign, independent democracy, the IRA will have no involvement in what has loosely been called constitutional politics. . . .

There is room for republicans to examine if the struggle for independence can be improved by an intervention in the electoral process in order to show clearly that people support radical republicanism and resistance to the British presence more than they support any other collaborationist tendency. . . . There is a fundamental need for republicans to bring about conditions whereby the Irish people may seize political and economic control of their own destinies. Whether this can be assisted by an intervention in the electoral process should be the basis for discussion within republican circles. What should not be the basis for discussion is whether intervention means a run-down of the armed struggle. It patently does not. We must fight on many fronts, and the armed struggle has been historically and contemporarily shown to be the most important. It must be coupled, of course, with political and economic resistance.

Another strategic and organizational concern, especially for the IRA, was the possible defection of its most militarist members to the INLA if there were any doubts of the Army Council's commitment to armed struggle. Explicit calls were made to the IRA to maintain its level of activity in order to reassure republicans that its operations did not depend on the outcome of elections. There were, however, calls for the IRA to attempt, as far as possible, to gauge its actions in such a manner as not to affect negatively Sinn Fein's electoral campaign:

> The IRA needs to be especially careful. For just as a reckless Brit on the ground killing two or three civilians around polling day could conceivably take its toll on the vote of the collaborationist SDLP, so too could a commercial bombing accident hurt Sinn Fein. On the other hand it is important for Sinn Fein to defend the armed struggle for national liberation. It is also important for the IRA to maintain a level of activity to demonstrate that the war, regardless of the outcome of the election, goes on.[18]

For these reasons, Sinn Fein was particularly concerned with its presentation of any potential electoral breakthrough. If the British Government were to claim that Sinn Fein's success at the ballot box was wooing the party away from its commitment to the armed struggle, then the electoral strategy would no longer appear as a complementary strategy to the armed struggle but as a competing one. In such circumstances, the leadership of Sinn Fein recognized that it would lose its core support, which would defeat the original purpose of its dual strategy.

Consequently, in the year following the passage of the *ard fheis* resolution endorsing Sinn Fein's participation in elections, a massive propaganda campaign was undertaken by the IRA and Sinn Fein to allay fears of a sellout or running down of the military campaign. As the following excerpts from Sinn Fein publications demonstrate, the three principal tactics employed by Sinn Fein were (1) to emphasize the IRA's explicit support for the electoral strategy; (2) to present participation in elections as a means by which to enhance and support the armed struggle of the IRA; and (3) to reaffirm the necessity of armed struggle.

> Not for one moment should republican supporters consider the election as a verdict on armed struggle—that is not up for debate, so crucial and central an ingredient is it to the physical removal of the British from Ireland.[19]

Elections have nothing to do with the escalation or de-escalation of the armed struggle. The benefits in using it as another arm of the struggle are (a) the Brits don't want republicans to use electoral involvement, which proves that as a weapon it is very effective; and (b) it's a massive embarrassment to the Tories and the collaborationist political parties; . . . when we involve ourselves in the democratic process it's always shown up to be completely undemocratic and false. The electoral strategy wasn't forced on us. It was a conscious decision, and, to a large extent, the views of people throughout the Movement were canvassed and taken into account. Republicans must never allow themselves to be isolated. We must never depend on one facet of resistance alone. Our resistance must be military, political, cultural, social, and economic, at the same time. In that way we can involve all the people in our war against the British and collaborationist forces.[20]

For those who would be concerned that such an intervention in elections is a new tendency or departure, they can be assured that the military struggle will go on with all the energy at our disposal, and in fact, victory would actually be hastened with the development of a complementary radical political offensive.[21]

The IRA maintains its right to wage war on the basis that oppressed people in occupied countries anywhere have the right to fight back. . . . Peace in an occupied and oppressed land cannot, by any means, emerge from a ballot box, whoever is electorally successful. Peace, with its essential accompaniment of justice, can only come about when the occupiers depart and their allies are neutralized. Sinn Fein standing in these elections cannot immediately affect this matter of war and peace. But it may, if successful, bring that peace with justice somewhat nearer.[22]

Establishing a Republican Veto: The 1982 Northern Ireland Assembly Election

In April 1982, the secretary of state for Northern Ireland, James Prior, made public the white paper, "Northern Ireland: A Framework for Devolution," which envisaged elections for a new Northern Ireland Assembly sometime later in the year. Sinn Fein, although it was quick to dismiss the proposed assembly as an attempt by the British government "to promote the fiction that the democratic process continues to function in the six counties . . . and [to] bolster the SDLP,"[23] declared almost immediately that if the SDLP participated in the elections, it too would participate. "No longer," according to republican spokespersons, would the SDLP have a "clear field on which to compete."[24]

Throughout the summer, Sinn Fein, the SDLP, and the small IIP (Irish Independence Party) attempted to negotiate a unified nationalist response to the proposed assembly. Both Sinn Fein and the IIP declared that they would boycott the election if the SDLP did likewise. The SDLP, therefore, held the key to nationalist participation. It was not, however, a key that unlocked many promising doors. Within the SDLP there was a significant split at both the grassroots and executive levels regarding its participation in the election. Those who supported participation argued that only by doing so could the SDLP distance itself from Sinn Fein and the IRA. Only then, they argued, could the party move forward with its dialogue with the unionists, which was essential if the reconciliation necessary for eventual reunification was ever to occur. Those opposed to participation argued that by joining Sinn Fein and the IIP in the boycott, they could exert sufficient pressure on the British government to reintroduce the "Irish Dimension" and resurrect the moribund Council of Ireland, which had remained the SDLP's unique contribution to a potential resolution of the conflict. At a meeting of the party's executive on 24 August 1982, the leadership voted 25–14 to contest the election. Rather than risk a split in the party, the leader of the SDLP, John Hume, whose own preference was "to go into the Assembly, challenge the Unionists on power-sharing right away, and walk out, having exposed their intransigence," convinced the executive to adopt a compromise position of contesting the election on an abstentionist basis. The SDLP decision to contest the election thus put an end to the long-standing practice by the various Irish nationalist parties of formulating a preelection pact.

The following comments from a Sinn Fein councillor illustrate how deeply the republican leadership had taken to heart the lessons learned from the hunger strike elections and how they influenced the party's decision to stand candidates for the assembly.[25]

> By contesting elections, and taking our seats, when possible, we are giving ourselves the opportunity to show people that not only do we have policies which are meant to provide a better standard and way of living than what they have now, but we also, and more importantly, are showing that Sinn Fein representatives have the qualities of leadership needed in a national government, when the time comes. During the past ten years, our previous policy only enabled us to advise people on the daily problems that confront them. We often did all the groundwork, providing the necessary facts and figures, only to find ourselves dismissed as totally insignificant by the political bodies set up by the British due to the fact that we had no elected public representatives. By

refusing to participate in politics, we allowed the SDLP to take control of the political struggle. What happened was that although the war for national liberation was winning the hearts of the nationalist people, their minds were being won by the SDLP, who were seen to be doing all the work on the daily problems. The fact that many people saw no contradiction in, on the one hand, having an armalite under the bed while holding, so to speak, a ballot paper for the SDLP in the other hand, was an indication of our isolation. This is what elections have helped us to combat. People now see us as being interested in doing something practical which affects them here and now, not after the war is won. Had we not contested the 1982 elections, our isolation would have been further magnified.

The Army Council, then dominated by northerners who had been involved in the hunger strike mobilizations, quickly endorsed participation in the election as an effective means of challenging the SDLP for the leadership of the nationalist community:

In the North, especially where politicization is most intense, it is essential that the SDLP . . . be confronted. . . . Now that a contest is in the offing, it is imperative that the SDLP's monopoly on the leadership of the nationalist community should be broken. . . .

The struggle for the nationalist leadership should not be dogged by traditional republican hostility to what are termed "politicians." Sinn Fein will be fighting the election to consolidate republican support and build a revolutionary organization which will defend the struggle, not a constitutional party to replace it.[26]

Thus, with the legitimating approval of the IRA in place, Sinn Fein prepared its "ballot bomb" for the 20 October 1982 election.

The campaign for the assembly elections was also viewed as an effective means of mobilizing supporters who often felt isolated from the struggle because of their inability to participate actively in local party meetings. Electoral victories, of course, provided the party with internal as well as external momentum. Gerry Adams, for example, has stated that elections have provided an impetus for the consolidation of the party organization and, by harnessing the spontaneity often associated with the republican struggle, have helped to create a stronger political organization. The following excerpt from an interview with Adams expands on his analysis:

Electoral success in the Six Counties and in specific areas in the twenty-six has accelerated our development as a party political organization.

Admittedly, nothing concentrates the mind of a political party as much as an electoral campaign does, and while we do not restrict ourselves to electoralism—we participate as well in a many-faceted struggle of campaigns, including street agitation, education, cultural resistance, and, of course, publicity—our electoral campaigns have played a major role in changing the nature of Sinn Fein. Elections have helped to develop the party, and we have begun to develop a very committed and experienced bunch of political workers. The activists have had to think and to apply themselves to problems, issues, structures, and aspects of the struggle which they had never really had to consider before.[27]

The reversal of Sinn Fein's electoral policy was recognized by the more politically astute activists as an important step toward establishing a "republican veto" that could prevent the successful implementation of a purely "internal" political arrangement. In an interview with journalist Michael Farrell following the assembly elections and his election as MP for West Belfast in June 1983, Gerry Adams directly addressed this issue:

Our strategy has three main prongs. . . . We want to show clearly the degree of support for Sinn Fein and restrict the SDLP's freedom to manoeuvre—the British, in order to maintain the partition set-up, need the support of a party which appears to represent the nationalist population, and the SDLP has fulfilled that role admirably. We have now established a sort of Republican veto which I believe will grow. And we want to politicize our own organization. . . . Our longer-term objective is to become the majority nationalist party in the North as well as, of course, making considerable inroads in the 26 counties.[28]

A successful election campaign in the North was also viewed as a crucial first step toward the removal of the policy of abstentionism, a step that the activists knew could once again split the movement, yet recognized as a prerequisite to creating a political organization capable of exercising political influence in a united Ireland. Party elites who supported the electoralist strategy believed that without a credible political organization to present a realistic alternative to the existing systems of government, North and South, the party could easily be left sitting on the sidelines as political deals were done over their heads. The election of five Sinn Fein candidates with slightly more than 10 percent of the total vote would initiate significant changes within Sinn Fein and the IRA, and in the strategy of the British and Irish governments.[29] To understand more fully the consequences of the election for the development of Sinn Fein, we need to analyze the dynamics of the

Northern Irish party system and the differences in the bases of social support for Sinn Fein and its principal competitor, the SDLP.

The Northern Irish Party System

With Sinn Fein's entry into electoral politics, the Northern Irish party system in the 1980s came to represent a classic case of "polarized pluralism" (Sartori 1976). It was characterized by both the presence of an antisystem party, Sinn Fein, and bilateral oppositions, one predominantly British and unionist,[30] the other overwhelmingly Irish and nationalist. The former was composed primarily of the Democratic Unionist Party (DUP) and the Official Unionist Party (OUP), and the latter by the Social Democratic and Labor Party (SDLP) and Sinn Fein. Its center was occupied by a weak, nonsectarian bloc composed of the Alliance Party of Northern Ireland (APNI) and the Workers' Party (WP). Data from a February 1989 public opinion survey that solicited each party's preferred form for a future government of Northern Ireland[31] not only illustrates the distance that existed between the nationalist and unionist blocs, but also reveals significant intrabloc differences. For both parties in the unionist bloc, the preferred political solution (43 percent of the total unionist bloc) was a more complete integration within the United Kingdom. Among the nonsectarian parties, further integration with Britain received the support of slightly more than 34 percent of the total bloc. But although 26 percent of the Workers' Party voters indicated they would consider a solution with an Irish dimension, only 13 percent of the Alliance voters were willing to do so. Finally, within the nationalist bloc there was a clear division between support for the SDLP's preferred solution, that is, a power-sharing Northern Ireland government (19 percent of the total nationalist bloc), and that of Sinn Fein, that is, total integration in the Republic of Ireland (20 percent of the total nationalist bloc). Given the ideological distance between the preferred solutions of the major blocs, it is not surprising that virtually all competition took place within each ethnic bloc. Further, that competition is best described as a "politics of outbidding" that intensifies the system's centrifugal tendencies and promotes the enfeeblement of the center. Although the single, transferable vote method of proportional representation had been introduced in 1972 in the hope not only of maximizing the vote/seat ratio but also of encouraging transfers across the sectarian divide, Elliott and Smith's (1985, 33) analysis of the transfers in the 1985 Northern Ireland District Council election reveals a minimal level of *interbloc* transfers. All unionists, for example, transferred only 1.6 percent of their votes to nationalists; all nationalists transferred only 1.7 percent to unionists. Elliott and Smith's study also shows a high degree of intraparty cohesiveness, with over 75 percent of all transfers remaining within all the parties.

The picture was somewhat different for the small center parties, which transferred, respectively, 22 percent to unionists and 21.9 percent to nationalists. Data on the terminal transfers (e.g., transfers when candidates from the same party are no longer present) provides an even clearer picture of which party voters regarded as the closest to their original choice. For example, Elliott and Smith note that 75.3 percent of DUP terminal transfers went to the OUP and 81.7 percent from OUP to DUP; terminal transfers from the APNI to unionist and nationalist parties were divided, with 35.9 percent going to the OUP and 43 percent going to the SDLP.

The picture that emerges from Elliott and Smith's analysis of the transfers between the SDLP and Sinn Fein is an interesting one that reveals important distinctions between the preference relationship of the two electorates. While 34 percent of SDLP terminal transfers went to Sinn Fein, a much larger portion, 51.4 percent, went to Alliance. Sinn Fein terminal transfers, on the other hand, were clearly far more favorable to the SDLP at 50.5 percent. I should note, however, that the party's percentage of nontransferable votes was higher. Given the struggle between the two main nationalist parties, the patterns of transfers from smaller nationalist groups to the SDLP and Sinn Fein was especially interesting. IIP terminal transfers broke 41 percent to 33 percent for Sinn Fein, while transfers from the "other nationalist" parties (IRSP, Independents, People's Democracy) favored the SDLP more heavily, with 56.8 percent going to Sinn Fein. Hence, "despite signs of more communal voting among nationalists in 1985, the respective party voters regard the two main parties as competing rather than complementary nationalist parties."[32]

Not Many Floating Voters Here

Both the ideological and socioeconomic differences between Sinn Fein and the SDLP reflected two largely distinct electorates—only to a limited extent were they competing for "floating" voters. Looking at table 4.1, we see that the two parties were supported by different, but overlapping, sections of the Catholic minority. Sinn Fein voters tended to be younger: about half were under thirty-four, whereas this was true for only a third of SDLP voters.[33]

Sinn Fein voters were also heavily concentrated among manual and semiskilled labor groups, and were twice as likely as SDLP voters to be unemployed. Also, while almost 60 percent of Sinn Fein voters lived in public housing, almost 50 percent of SDLP voters owned their homes. These two factors may help to explain the different remedies for the conflict that the

Table 4.1. Social Background of Sinn Fein and SDLP Voters

Party	Sinn Fein (N=131)	SDLP (N=304)
Gender		
Female	46%	53%
Male	54	47
Age		
18–24	33	18
25–34	24	21
35–44	18	19
45–54	15	19
55–64	11	23
65+	0	0
Socioeconomic Status		
ABC1	24	38
C2DE	76	62
Work Status		
Full/Part-Time	42	50
Unemployed	30	15
Not Working	28	35
Housing Tenure		
Owner Occupier	36	52
Public Housing	58	44
Private Tenant	06	04

Notes: ABC1 = Professional, white-collar, students, skilled workers, independent farmers; C2DE = Retired workers, pensioners, blue-collar, service employees, unskilled workers, casual laborers.
Source: MORI, June 24–28, 1984.

two parties offered. Most SDLP voters had a much larger investment in the "British" economy than did Sinn Fein supporters. For the SDLP, therefore, nationalism was tempered by a willingness to compromise and use the existing political and legal framework to secure advantages.

For Sinn Fein, however, nationalism was fired by a resolve to challenge the system as inherently loaded against the Catholic working class. Interestingly, however, the Sinn Fein analysis stopped short of perceiving the political impasses as economically determined. Rather, the economic inequalities were perceived as by-products of a fundamentally inequitable political system. In a way, the SDLP analysis is reversed: the economic system was seen as clearly inequitable, and unionist hegemony in the economy constrained the prospects for political change.

At the heart of these differences lie contrasting views of the causes of the conflict. Table 4.2 reveals that the majority of Sinn Fein voters perceived the conflict as essentially one of opposed nationalisms, but none of the four possible causes of the conflict mentioned in the survey commanded overwhelming support among SDLP voters. These contrasting views of the conflict are reflected in the preferred solution to the conflict. While the most acceptable political solution for Sinn Fein voters was a united Ireland, the most popular option for SDLP supporters was power-sharing within the United Kingdom. What divided the two parties was, essentially, the SDLP's belief that some recognition had to be given to the British in Ireland.

Table 4.2. Perceived Causes of the Northern Ireland Conflict among Sinn Fein and SDLP Voters

Party (Percent Attributing Significance)	Sinn Fein (N=131)	SDLP (N=304)
To Be British or Irish	56%	32%
Unemployment	17	21
Religion	14	15
Terrorism	04	24
Don't Know/ No Opinion	04	08

Source: MORI, June 24–28, 1984.

These differences were also evident in the electorate's image of its own party and its competitor. Data from the same survey revealed that the overwhelming majority of Sinn Fein voters perceived their party as able to make the British government take note of nationalist demands.[34] Most also characterized their party as having good policies, as responsive to its electorate, and as offering the most hope of a solution to the conflict. Like Sinn Fein voters, most SDLP voters characterized their party as representing people like themselves. Perhaps reflecting the party's willingness to negotiate and compromise, SDLP voters perceived the party as having good policies, good leaders, and offering the most hope of a resolution of the conflict. In keeping with Sinn Fein's opposition to an internal political solution and its characterization of the SDLP as the linchpin in a "British" power-sharing solution, the majority of the party's supporters perceived the SDLP as being "too cooperative with the British." Another one-third characterized the SDLP as "moderate" and "out of touch."

SDLP voters presented almost a mirror image of Sinn Fein. The majority of SDLP voters perceived Sinn Fein as being "extreme," one-third viewed it as "tough," and one-fourth characterized it as "evil." These perceptions revealed the great distance between Sinn Fein and SDLP voters on the acceptability of violence as a means of achieving political goals. The survey data also revealed that while over 70 percent of SDLP voters rejected political violence, almost the same proportion of Sinn Fein voters supported it; however, while four out of five SDLP voters thought Sinn Fein should renounce the armed struggle of the IRA, approximately one-third of the Sinn Fein supporters held the same view. These findings challenge the notion that a vote for Sinn Fein was merely a vote for the IRA and illustrate why competition between the nationalist parties focused primarily on winning the hearts and minds of the "Green Rump" of the SDLP and of those within Sinn Fein who were uneasy with the armed struggle of the IRA. In the next section of this chapter, we see that competition between Herri Batasuna and the PNV created a similar dynamic.

ETA in Transition

In 1978, ETA killed more people than it had in all of the preceding years combined. Table 4.3 illustrates that as the level of violence in Northern Ireland was beginning to fall, it was rising dramatically in the Basque provinces. In 1979 and 1980, the Basque Country acquired the unwanted distinction of being the site of more politically motivated violence than any other comparably sized territory in Europe. In 1980, for example, of the 126 political killings recorded in Spain, 110 of these took place in the Basque provinces. Of these, 93 were committed by ETA. The relationship of ETA actions to important political events clearly illustrates that ETA was aware of its position as the primary obstacle to the consolidation of Spanish democracy and sought to affect political outcomes through the strategic use of violence.[35] Table 4.3 shows that the rate of assassinations peaked during the most important events of the transition: the referendums to approve the Spanish Constitution in 1978 and the Basque Autonomy Statute in 1979, and the first regional election in the Basque Country in 1980.

The Basque Party System in Post-Franco Spain

As Clark (1984, 95) has noted, the Basque political system of the 1970s inherited three sets of parties from the 1930s: a Spanish Left, consisting primarily of the Spanish Socialist Workers' Party (Partido Socialista Obrero Español, PSOE) and the Spanish Communist Party (Partido Comunista Español, PCE); a Spanish coalition of center-right parties; and the Basque

Table 4.3. Deaths from Political Violence in Northern Ireland and the Southern Basque Provinces, 1971–1981

Year	By the IRA	By ETA
1971	174	0
1972	468	1
1973	250	7
1974	216	19
1975	247	16
1976	297	15
1977	112	12
1978	81	64
1979	113	78
1980	75	93
1981	101	30

Sources: Sutton (1994); *EGIN 1977–1982.*

center, occupied by the Basque Nationalist Party (Partido Nacionalista Vasca, PNV). These three sets would be joined by a new phenomenon, the Basque Left. As all Basque parties entered into discussions regarding their potential participation in the Spanish parliamentary process, four issues emerged that clearly set the Basque Left apart from the PNV.

The first issue concerned the extent to which Basque parties should co-operate with Spanish parties. All ethnic Basque parties, including the PNV, took for themselves the title of *abertzale,* a Basque word meaning "patriotic." The PNV was willing to cooperate, on occasion, with Spanish parties, but the Basque Left was more intransigent: it explicitly rejected all cooperation with Spanish political organizations.

The second issue concerned the territorial base for the Basque ethno-nation, Euskadi. The Basque Left demanded that the province of Nafarroa be automatically included in any Basque autonomous region and that all Basque parties establish as a long-range goal their reunification with the three Basque provinces in the French State.[36] The PNV, perhaps because of its historical weakness in Nafarroa,[37] was less intransigent on that score and more willing to consider a Basque autonomous region without Nafarroa's inclusion. The call for reunification with the Basque provinces in the French State was viewed as a symbolic, rather than a realistic, goal by the PNV.

The third issue was the exact nature of the ties between an autonomous Basque region and the rest of Spain. The PNV seemed generally inclined to accept a form of federal status, while the Basque Left argued strongly for a greater degree of separation and called for the almost immediate expulsion of all Spanish civil and military officials.

The fourth issue concerned the need for radical social and economic change. The PNV reaffirmed its faith in the free market and private property, although it recognized the importance of meeting the social needs of a growing urban, working-class population. The Basque Left, on the other hand, advocated substantial social changes, among them the nationalization of the major industries in Euskadi, greater democratization of industries, including the use of workers' committees to run the firms, and a greater redistribution of income.

Given these sharp differences between the Basque Left and the PNV, it was unrealistic to expect that the parties could agree on a set of common demands that had to be met before they would participate in the Spanish electoral process. Still, the Basque parties were keenly aware of their powerful bargaining position during the transition period, and several attempts were made to form a common Basque nationalist front in the hope of pressuring Madrid into granting amnesty to all Basque political prisoners and legalizing all political parties, including those that explicitly advocated separation from Spain.

As the following excerpt reveals, the Basque Left was also quite aware of the political strength of the PNV and recognized that without its participation, the pressure on Madrid would be greatly reduced. Thus considerable attention was given to the historic role that the PNV had played in Basque resistance to Spanish rule, and the Basque Left urged the PNV not to "betray" the political prisoners.

> The time approaches. The question of the elections places a powerful weapon in the hands of the Basque people, a weapon that in the present circumstances could play a decisive role in breaking the power that today keeps Basque political prisoners in jail. In effect, the holding of these elections plays a critical role in the plans that the government intends to use to deal with the so-called Basque problem. Without these elections, the Basque problem will continue to be seen, from the viewpoint of the regime, as something "inaccessible." . . . [I]f the electoral process fails in Euskadi, one could consider that the electoral process has failed for the regime. In this case, the regime would find itself in a corner with nowhere to go. . . . Therefore, it appears clear that a preelectoral pact between certain Basque parties could assure an effective boycott of elections in Euskadi, and herein resides our weapon, because the parties in Euskadi could set minimum conditions for their

participation, and it is evident that among those minimum conditions must be included amnesty. An effective boycott will not be easy to achieve in the current circumstances without a pact between the principal political forces in Euskadi. Besides, if the Right decides to participate in the elections and the Left abstains *en bloque,* it could, perhaps, increase the advantages of the Right within the regime. This is, at least, the belief and the fear of more than one party of the Basque Left. This fear could affect these parties at the hour when they must decide. Day by day the pact increasingly appears as the only way by which to guarantee a boycott, if the government doesn't accept our minimum conditions. Having said this, we must consider our historical responsibility and the consequences of our failure to adopt a united position. It is the moment to give unconditional freedom to our prisoners and exiles.[38]

Despite its support for a general amnesty for Basque political prisoners, the PNV was clearly in favor of participating in the coming elections. Once the PNV had declared its intention to participate in the Spanish parliamentary process, the leaders of the emerging Basque Left worked to form a unified and coherent political manifesto that would reflect the interests of the Basque working class. This work and the broadly felt need to mobilize the population to achieve the aims of Basque nationalism were centered in the Patriotic Socialist Coordinating Council (KAS) composed of ETA(m), ETA(pm), LAIA (the Patriotic Revolutionary Workers Party), LAB (the Patriotic Workers' Council), LAK (Patriotic Workers Committee), HAS (the Popular Socialist Party), EAS (the Basque Socialist Party), and ASK (the Patriotic Socialist Committees).

As the following excerpt from an interview with Patxi Zabaleta illustrates,[39] the council clearly recognized that a united radical Basque front was necessary if the interests of the Basque working class were to be advanced in the new political system:

I believe that the national liberation of Euskadi requires as a necessary condition the strengthening of a coherent, efficient, and ample structure, of a political formation that includes all the Basque Left. The Basque Left is the section that responds most coherently to the double oppression, since it has submitted neither to the oligarchy nor to its state. Class oppression is the oppression of the people of Euskadi and provides us with the necessary political panorama and international solidarity to be at once respectful [of] but not simply imitators of the revolutionary processes of other nations. Also in this camp of the Basque Left, the KAS, in my opinion, must carry forward the initiative and indicate the political guidelines for Euskal Herria and open roads toward a national revolution, that is to say, make possible an independent Euskadi.[40]

As the member organizations sought to construct a political program that they could all support, it soon became clear that the differences regarding strategy, tactics, and organizational structure that had split ETA in 1974 were reemerging. The disagreements and divisions between ETA(pm) and ETA(m) closely resembled those that had resulted in the 1970 split of the IRA and Sinn Fein into the Officials and Provisionals. Moreover, the arguments of ETA(pm) resembled those of the Official IRA and Sinn Fein. Both placed class above ethnicity, viewed participation in electoral politics as a necessary and effective means of political struggle, and argued for the subordination of the armed struggle to the needs of the political struggle.

Those most closely linked to ETA(pm) believed that KAS should adopt a strategy focused on uniting all the national and social forces active in the Basque Country that had participated in the anti-Francoist movement. The short-term objective of this faction was the creation of a political party that would mobilize and actively represent the Basque working class. They maintained that the role of the KAS was to serve as a debating and coordinating body for the divergent interests and approaches expressed by the distinct political organizations.

Those allied to ETA(m) wanted KAS to adopt a strategy that centered on uniting and mobilizing all the *abertzale* forces, that is, all those groups that had Basque autonomy or independence as their primary objective. The KAS was to serve as the mechanism for the resolution of disagreements among its various member organizations and would enforce its own decisions. The role of ETA as the principal force within the Basque Movement of National Liberation (MLVN) was also made quite clear:

> The Movement for National and Social Liberation, which has been unfolding in recent years because of the objective realities of national and class oppression and in the subjective conditions of revolutionary will and consciousness, has always had in ETA its crux and fundamental support.[41]

> KAS has a definite political project, which is directed toward the alternative tactic of a complete democratic break with the current regime and which includes the goal of a Basque-speaking, independent, and socialist Euskadi. It maintains that armed struggle coordinated with the mass and institutional struggle, the latter at the service of the former, represents the key to our advance and revolutionary triumph.[42]

These differences regarding strategy and organization arose, in part, from the opposing views that each faction held regarding the new political environment. For ETA(pm) and its allied organizations, the new political environment represented a real democratization of the current regime. Like the Official IRA and Sinn Fein, ETA (pm) believed that the Spanish regime was reformable and that real political power for Basques could be achieved through the parliamentary process. For EIA and ETA(pm), the opportunity to contest elections represented an important victory for the anti-Francoist forces and could not be ignored without the risk of marginalization. Activists in both organizations were convinced that the people would participate in the parliamentary process and that if they did not, the interests of the Basque people and the revolution would be relegated to the sidelines. Due to its willingness to work through the system, Euskadiko Ezkerra (Basque Left, EE), like the PNV, was derided for its *reformista* tendencies by those closer to ETA(m), for whom the parliamentary process represented little more than a necessary act by the oligarchy to change the appearance of the Francoist state without changing the substance of the former regime. For this group, the *poderes facticos* (real powers) remained the military and the oligarchy. As the Provisional IRA and Sinn Fein had argued, ETA(m) also maintained that these powers would agree to their demands only at gunpoint and declared the need for *ruptura,* that is, a complete break with the Spanish regime.

In an attempt to negotiate a Basque Left strategy that all the member organizations could accept, KAS called a meeting to establish a set of minimal conditions that Madrid had to meet if they were to participate in the elections. Following extensive debates among representatives of ETA(pm), Eusko Herriko Alderdi Sozialista (Basque Popular Socialist Party, EHAS), LAIA, LAB, LAK, and ETA(m), KAS formulated a political program, known as the Alternativa KAS, which specified the terms for the Basque Left's participation in elections and the preconditions for a cease-fire by ETA. The five points of the KAS Alternative were

1. amnesty for all Basque political prisoners;
2. legalization of all political parties;
3. withdrawal from the Basque provinces of all Spanish law-enforcement authorities, especially the Guardia Civil;
4. incorporation of Nafarroa into the Basque regional community, without a referendum; and
5. the right of self-determination.[43]

As the Spanish parliamentary elections scheduled for June 1977 approached, frequent disagreements arose between the member organizations of KAS as to what actions by Madrid met the conditions set out in the KAS Alternative. Although Suarez had not agreed to the conditions by the set date, he did issue an additional amnesty decree in March 1977 that freed all but those accused of the most violent acts. This action had the desired effect of heightening the tensions within KAS and resulting in a decisive split within the Patriotic Left (Izquierda Abertzale), with EIA and ETA(pm) in one faction and ETA(m), EHAS, and LAIA in the other.

The principal disagreement between KAS and EIA focused on whether Basque socialist parties and coalitions should participate in the Spanish parliamentary process. These differences of opinion were also evident within ETA(pm). In the spring of 1977, while the "Pertur" faction of ETA(pm) was attempting to work within the legal political structures through EIA,[44] another faction (Berezi Commandos) under the leadership of Miguel Angel Apalategui Ayerbe ("Apala") launched a new offensive of armed attacks. The renewed offensive was an attempt by the Berezi Commandos to force the "Pertur" faction out of ETA(pm) or at least force them to abandon their plans to form a legal political party.

Despite the renewed military action, however, EIA was officially launched in April 1977 with a mass rally in a working district of Bilbao. In choosing to begin its search for votes in this locale, EIA sent a clear message that it would rely primarily on working-class support and only secondarily on the votes of Basques from the middle class. Although many of the leaders of EIA had been members of ETA(pm), the exact nature of the links between EIA and ETA(pm) remained unclear. This ambiguity not only maximized the ability of the EIA leadership to act publicly, but it allowed the two organizations to pursue apparently contradictory strategies simultaneously.

The Decision to Contest Elections

In June 1977, for example, EIA took advantage of this ambiguity to participate in the Spanish parliamentary elections as part of the electoral coalition Euskadiko Ezkerra (Basque Left, EE), which had been created to contest the election. Thus, although the members of KAS, including ETA(pm), had decided to boycott because the terms they had set for participation, the Alternativa KAS, had not been met, EIA could participate because it was not officially a member of KAS. ETA(pm), therefore, officially boycotted the elections, while its political wing, EIA, officially participated. EE's electoral performance was unanticipated. It won approximately 5 percent of the total vote and elected one member to the Spanish Congress of Deputies. The results of the elections were cited by both EIA and ETA(pm) as a clear affirmation of the correctness of their position:

There are two fundamental lessons to be gleaned from this election. The first is that disunity brings with it confusion. In an election such as this, with a very low level of politicization and a people confronted with the massive propaganda which the transition regime offers, . . . the only possibility of securing anything for the Basque working class was in presenting a single option, one option which should have been presented throughout Euskadi prior to the elections in order to re-cuperate as much as possible the disadvantages born of a real lack of understanding at the mass level regarding the political alternatives of the distinct groups. Instead, the groups of the Basque Left were the last in speaking and in addition offered a bewildering array of acronyms from which to choose, an act which only benefitted the large political formations and especially the PNV. The second is, without doubt, the triumph in this election, from this perspective of vacillations and dis-unity, for EE and its equivalent in Nafarroa, UNAI. What is important is our consolidation as the third force, behind the PNV and PSOE, among those groups which outlined an autonomous political regime for Euskadi. If in a certain way these elections have served as a type of primary between all the groups of the Left and the PNV, the greatest triumph has been that of EE. For us the weapon of abstention as a show of force could and should have been used to wrest conces-sions from the government of Suarez, which did not allow the entire range of political opinion to be expressed in the elections in Euskadi.[45] However, this proof of support was only practical if it was based on a wide consensus among the political parties, at least among those who call themselves *abertzale*. This consensus did not exist, and for this reason the attempt to enforce a strategy of abstention, defended only by KAS as a demonstration of force against Suarez, represented a total utopia. Abstention was reduced to a mere symbolic gesture, demonstrating the refusal by certain forces to participate in the elec-toral game, but apparently without offering an alternative solution to the people.[46]

As EE became actively engaged in the parliamentary process, it soon realized that access to power did not necessarily translate into the ability to exercise power and could create as well as resolve a number of difficult prob-lems. First, although its seat in the Cortes entitled the party to a seat on the Basque General Council (Consejo General Vasco), the pre-autonomy gov-ernment created by the Spanish Ministry of Interior in 1977 to manage the transition of the region to autonomous status, the party was too small to accomplish anything without entering into coalitions with similar parties. Participation in such coalitions, however, left the party vulnerable to charges of selling out to the opposition. Further, as a coalition member with much more moderate parties, like the PNV, EE discovered that it had to modify its position on policy issues or run the risk of being left out of important discussions when key decisions were being made. Consequently, a number of activists in the smaller parties and unions, both inside and outside the EE coalition, began to criticize the EE leadership for moving toward the right to pacify the PNV and Madrid. The failure of EE and its principal party, EIA, to either win a massive share of the vote or to pressure Madrid into complete amnesty was proof to many Basques that the abertzale socialist movement had to shift further to the left and become more intransigent in its demands. Thus, following the June elections, a more intransigent alternative to EE began to attract considerable support from workers, students, and professionals, many of whom had been actively involved in the protests against the executions of the ETA activists Otagei and Manot in September 1975.

On 3 July 1977, EHAS and a group of independent Basque nationalists merged to form the party HASI (Herriko Alderdi Sozialista Iraultzalea, Popular Revolutionary Socialist Party). HASI clearly represented those most closely allied to ETA(m). EHAS had emerged from the combination of the Popular Socialist Party (HAS) active in Spparalde, the French Basque country, and the Basque Socialist Party (EAS). Its role within KAS would be to unite and mobilize the groups that shared ETA's objectives:

> The work of this organization [ETA] is to create in the working class the necessary subjective conditions, in the sense of making them aware, of organizing and directing them toward the achievement of their irreversible objective. Therefore, ETA plays the role of the vanguard. The direction and intervention of the military vanguard can be appreciated in the unfolding of its struggle and its organization, that is to say, in the content and form which it adopts as a consequence of the contradictions which appear in society, and which defines the armed organization as the organization which continues making possible the success of the revolutionary army of the people. The party HASI's role within the organized collective, its role within KAS, is that of participating in all the organizations, in all political activities, of coordinating all the sectoral struggles which are in the realm of the masses or institutions, and in resolving the contradictions in the circumstances of the various struggles and organizations which prevent the realization of the goals of the rest of the bloc.[47]

In October 1977, a coalition of *abertzale* parties and notable independent nationalists was formed to provide an opportunity for discontented Basque socialists to discuss their grievances with EIA and EE. This coalition, which became known as the Mesa de Alsasua, was composed of HASI, LAIA, the new Basque Socialist Assembly (Euskal Sozialista Bilzarrea, ESB), and one older party, Basque National Action (Acción Nacional Vasca, ANV). Its immediate objective was to formulate an alternative position to that of EE and the PNV and to construct a united strategy for the most radical nationalist parties, which promised "to develop with all their energy a politics free of the influence of the bourgeois forces [that] does not depend on strategies foreign to Euskadi for the construction of socialism in a free, independent, reunified, and Basque-speaking Euskadi."[48]

By February 1978, the failure of EE to effect any substantial changes within the proposed constitution led Francisco Letamendia, one of the founders of EIA and its representative to the Cortes, to declare that EE was no longer a potential base for the construction of a unified Basque Left. He urged the creation of a new party from the union of the Mesa de Alsasua members.

On 27 April 1978, the four parties, ANV, ESB, LAIA, and HASI, officially joined together to create an entirely new electoral coalition, Herri Batasuna, which espoused an ideology that combined a radical Basque ethnic ideology with a revolutionary socialism and that clearly supported the armed struggle of ETA. Herri Batasuna was now the most intransigent party in the Basque political system. Also, with the formation of the Herri Batasuna coalition, the split between ETA(m) and ETA(pm) was now reflected in the Basque party system. While the *poli-milis* backed EIA and EE for their commitment to political organization, the *milis* supported Herri Batasuna for its intransigence. Herri Batasuna's role was defined as one of mobilizing and uniting all the progressive forces whose goal was Basque independence, from traditional culturalists to radical trade unionists. Its name, meaning Popular Unity, exemplified the role it was to play within the broader Basque Movement for National Liberation (Movimiento Liberación Vasco Nacional, MLVN), which included all the social and political organizations that shared ETA's objectives.

> [T]he only possible alternative by which to obtain the national and social reconstruction of Euskal Herria is the KAS Alternative, included in the program of Herri Batasuna. Consequently no political groups, neither the PNV nor any other political formation, can say that Herri Batasuna does not have clear and progressive, economic, political, and

cultural alternatives for our people. From its birth, Herri Batasuna has, on the contrary, been a home for everyone from the folk culturalist to the orthodox Marxist.[49]

By explicitly defining itself as an electoral coalition rather than as a political party, Herri Batasuna was also clearly asserting its rejection of the legitimacy of the existing electoral process as well as its rejection of "bourgeois parliamentary democracy."

Although the inability of the Basque parties in parliament to secure any meaningful concessions from Madrid regarding Basque autonomy had convinced ETA(m) that its characterization of the parliamentary process was accurate, the massive participation by Basques in the elections had persuaded ETA(m) to reconsider its position on participating in elections and to adjust its strategy and tactics to respond to the changes in the political environment. ETA(m) concluded that its optimal strategy was to demonstrate that the new political regime was not really new but only a disguised and embellished version of Franco's regime. To the extent that it could succeed at this task, ETA(m) recognized that its justifications for continuing the armed struggle would be more readily accepted. Further, ETA(m) recognized that it would be necessary for Basques not only to hear that they still lived in a dictatorship but also to feel as if they did.

In support of that strategy, ETA(m)'s military struggle would be directed against targets in such a manner and at such a level that the state would be forced into responding to ETA violence with its own repressive force, thus reaffirming that little had changed. Thus ETA(m) dramatically increased its military operations, and the violence produced the desired effect. In July 1978, the Spanish government passed a new antiterrorist law that suspended a number of constitutional guarantees and allowed the police to intrude sharply into the lives of Basques suspected of aiding ETA. Special counterinsurgent units were trained and quickly dispatched to the Basque region. The new antiterrorist measures, however, did little to curb ETA's violence and may well have served only to remind many Basques of the worst features of Francoism. Another important factor in the radicalization of the Basque Left was "the slowness with which Madrid moved in 1977 and 1978 to accommodate Basque demands for regional autonomy" (Clark 1984, 98). Although the proposed constitution offered some advantages to the country's regional minorities, the fact that the regional governments would depend solely on powers granted to them by Madrid led the regional parties to complain that the constitution did not assure autonomy so much as a decentralization of state authority. In May 1978, even the moderate PNV withdrew its representatives from the Cortes as a result of its inability to secure any improvements in the proposed constitution for the country's regional minorities. The weakness of the Basque parties can be seen in the fact that out of the over one hundred amendments they made to the proposed constitution regarding the devolution of power to regional governments, not one was accepted.

Recognizing that the defeat of the constitution was critical to the success of the MLVN's dual strategy of armed struggle and mass mobilization, Herri Batasuna was clearly opposed to the constitution. Nevertheless, the leaders of both Herri Batasuna and ETA were sensitive to the political strength of the PNV and to the PNV's investment in the construction of the constitution. Herri Batasuna accepted, therefore, that abstention rather than rejection was a more practical alternative.

> In a referendum such as the one that is going to be presented to us, there are the following possible responses: Yes, No, Abstention, and Blank votes. If we do not agree with the 1978 Spanish constitution because it does not recognize our rights and character as Basques, we must weigh the choices we can use to make those in Spain see this from our unified actions. The worst that we could do in this case would be to have each party choose its method. This would only serve as an additional element of discord among the nationalist forces. In order to avoid any break over irreconcilable positions, it is necessary that each party analyze our mutual conditions and finally adopt whatever posture guarantees our demonstration of our opinion. This is the only way by which we can have an appreciable political impact during the negotiation of the Statute as well as place in question the validity of the constitution. . . .
>
> Regarding all the *abertzale* forces, we all know that the PNV holds the key to the situation because of its power to call together and discipline its supporters. The PNV, therefore, is faced with a year of very serious dilemmas full of historical responsibility, not only in regard to the Basque Country, but also to Spain. If the constitution was only going to apply to Euskadi, the PNV would have no problems in rejecting it; however, besides the fact that it has invested a great deal of time and effort in an attempt to improve the constitution in parliamentary meetings, there is threat of constant denigration and hatred that . . . a total rejection . . . supposes on the part of the Spanish parties and the Spanish media, since its parliamentarians would be considered responsible for not only the rejection of the constitution in Euskadi but also

in Spain, a posture that could only strengthen the position of the Francoists and those most nostalgic for the dictatorship. These are the conditions in which the PNV must make its decision. Although "No" is the response that EIA and Herri Batasuna support, it is clear that, for the reasons given before, such a position would be difficult for the PNV to adopt. Abstention, therefore, is the best option for the Basque nationalist forces.[50]

As Herri Batasuna had predicted, the PNV, during an extraordinary national assembly, voted to join with the parties of the Basque Left and advocate a boycott of the referendum on the new Spanish constitution. Consequently, whereas the constitution received wide support throughout the rest of Spain, voters in the Basque Country overwhelmingly abstained from voting for it. For ETA, the high abstention rate (45 percent) in the referendum on the constitution appeared to vindicate its interpretation of the Basque political environment.[51] Most important, it appeared to mandate its continued reliance on military as well as political struggle to secure Basque independence. ETA now believed that it could justly claim that it was fighting a political war. Euskadi had not accepted the new Spain any more than it had accepted Francoist Spain. Nothing, ETA claimed, had really changed, except perhaps for the color of the uniforms of the Guardia Civil. Spanish forces were still occupying an Euskadi that had once again asserted its desire for autonomy. ETA would henceforth justify its activities in the post-Franco period by the people's democratic "rejection" of the Spanish constitution.

Despite their rejection of the constitution, representatives of EE and the PNV accepted that they would have to work through the constitution to secure any form of autonomy. On 29 December, the day following the promulgation of the new Spanish constitution by King Juan Carlos, their representatives met in the historic city of Gernika to approve a draft autonomy statute, which was then sent to Madrid to begin the long process of consideration by parliament. Two elections would intervene, however, before the Basque people would have the opportunity to vote on the proposed autonomy statute.

Herri Batasuna : Militant Nationalism at the Polls

New elections were scheduled for 1 March 1979 to produce a national legislative assembly with a mandate under the terms of the new constitution. Herri Batasuna was confronted with the question of whether or not to participate in the elections. Although the rejection of the constitution appeared to confirm their analysis of the political sentiments of the Basque electorate, both Herri Batasuna and ETA were aware of the risk of being marginalized and isolated if they did not participate. The issue for Herri Batasuna was no longer participation, but rather how to participate: "ETA(m), even if it has been reaffirmed in its analysis and in the correctness of the positions advocated by KAS, recognizes that it cannot remain inactive faced with the new possibilities of the electoral game. Therefore, we will look for an alternative form of participation."[52] The logic that Herri Batasuna followed in its decision to contest elections but not to take their seats is strikingly similar to that used by those within the IRA and Sinn Fein who were opposed to Sinn Fein's elected representatives taking their seats:

> If the majority of the Basque people did not share the PNV's vision of the institutional integration of Euskadi into the Spanish state, why should we have limited ourselves simply to abstaining from politics rather than unmasking and discrediting the institutions from within with the very mechanisms of this feigned democracy? . . . Was it not more effective to demonstrate that we had the votes necessary to be elected but, because those who supported us did not wish us to participate in the anti-Basque, antidemocratic institutions of the Spanish parliament, that our seats would remain vacant as a signal of protest and our profound dissatisfaction with its means of conducting politics?[53]

Although Herri Batasuna had not yet been legalized as a political coalition, the KAS officially supported the participation in the elections of Herri Batasuna candidates who had adopted the KAS Alternative as their political manifesto. ETA(m), as the IRA had done for Sinn Fein, would publicly support Herri Batasuna's participation in the election and encourage all Basque nationalists to vote for Herri Batasuna. ETA(m)'s justification for its support of Herri Batasuna closely mirrors that of the IRA for Sinn Fein:

> Without doubt, practice, master of all theory, teaches us that on certain occasions astuteness serves us better than force, and that an even better strategy for defeating the enemy is one in which both are united in a common cause. We believe that the decision of KAS and Herri Batasuna to contest the general elections serves perfectly the objective of blocking the reform process foreseen by the Spanish government and does not imply any renunciation of the tactical objectives and strategies of revolutionary Basques who are determined to continue in the revolution for an independent and socialist Euskadi. . . . We believe that this program (KAS Alternative) meets the conditions necessary to bring to light the real injustices that our people experience. Their

manifesto is the real democratic alternative. In any case, the candidates, if elected, will not take the seats that they are assigned in parliament. Rather their work will be the denunciation and condemnation of the constitution while supporting those methods of struggle that have always characterized our people, leading us to the complete liberation of Euskadi. . . . We are not, therefore, about to participate in antidemocratic and anti-Basque institutions. We seek rather to bring about the defeat of the bourgeoisie in the opposition. When all is said and done, this participation provides a tactical replacement of the abstentionist position supported since the beginning by the patriotic Basque Left. From this perspective, we consider that the election of Herri Batasuna is correct and at one with the Basque people. ETA expresses its total support for Herri Batasuna and calls on the people to vote for the Herri Batasuna candidates for the Congress and Senate.[54]

The Basque Ballot Bomb

It would be an understatement to say that the election results shocked both moderate Basque nationalists and Madrid.[55] Although the share of the vote given to the PNV declined from its 1977 level (from 24.4 percent to 22.2 percent of the vote in all four provinces), the vote awarded to all the Basque Left parties rose dramatically (from 11.2 percent in 1977 to 21 percent in 1979). The EE coalition won 6.8 percent of the vote and retained its single seat in the Congress of Deputies, but Herri Batasuna won 13 percent of the vote and elected three members to the Cortes's lower chamber. One week later, following a national debate among its members, Herri Batasuna announced that its delegates would refuse to occupy their seats in the Spanish parliament. It was now certain that Herri Batasuna would use the electoral process primarily as a mechanism for demonstrating a high level of voter discontent in the Basque provinces and to denounce the existing political system:

> Our decision not to take our seats in the Congress and the Senate is unequivocal. First, by conviction, because we are convinced that these bodies are not the bodies of a democratic state. The fundamental reason, however, is that 172,000 voters have voted for us precisely because we will not go to Madrid and in order to express their protest against the genocidal attitude to Basques that the PSOE and PCE are fomenting. . . . Fundamentally, Herri Batasuna will not participate in the Spanish parliament because it is the legislative body of a nondemocratic State and because this state will not accept our political demands. We will not participate in plenary sessions or in committees. In

our decision not to participate we do not wish to oppose the Spanish people, only the state, which is undemocratic. Spain is something that is not Catalonia, not Euskadi, not Galicia, nor the Canaries.[56]

Thus, following the same logic used by those who advocated the abstentionist position in Sinn Fein, Herri Batasuna argued that "to the extent that we participate in them, that is the degree to which we grant them democratic credibility, precisely what the radical struggle of ETA is contesting."[57]

In April 1979, provincial assembly and municipal elections were held for the first time since the end of the civil war. Again, Herri Batasuna officially declared that its delegates to the various provincial assemblies, if elected, would not take their seats. This time, however, representatives of the various Herri Batasuna coalition partners, especially those from ESB, chose to participate and took their seats on municipal councils. Although Herri Batasuna could not prevent those members from taking their seats as representatives of their own party, their actions led to considerable tensions within the coalition that would splinter the party the following year.

The PNV, demonstrating its long-standing strength at the local level, won slightly less than 30 percent of the popular vote but elected nearly half (1,054 of 2,309) of the candidates chosen. Once again, Herri Batasuna's share of the vote increased, and the overall share of the vote given to the Basque Left rose to 25.4 percent. Euskadiko Ezkerra (EE) won 5 percent of the total Basque vote and 85 seats, and Herri Batasuna won 15.1 percent and 304 seats. Herri Batasuna thus became the second strongest party in the Basque provinces, running about 1 percent behind the PSOE in the popular vote, but beating the PSOE by nearly 100 seats. When the votes cast for all Basque parties were combined, they accounted for over one-half of all votes cast (55.3 percent) for the first time in history.[58] In June and July, the level of ETA violence increased dramatically when ETA(pm) broke an eighteen-month cease-fire that had been in effect since EIA was founded. Although the principal reason given by ETA(pm) for its resumption of armed struggle was the attempted assassination of one of its former leaders, Jon Etxabe, it was evident that ETA(pm) was attempting to regain its influence within the Basque Left, which had declined with the electoral fortunes of EE. Arguing that it had not anticipated that the new Spanish state would not only retain the same repressive apparatus that had existed under Franco but would also use that apparatus to deny Basques their democratic rights, ETA(pm) reasserted the necessity for armed struggle. It launched a well-orchestrated campaign against the Spanish tourist industry.[59] This campaign introduced the new tactic of exploding bombs in public places.

ETA(pm)'s choice of tactics in its antitourism campaign resulted in a large number of innocent civilian victims. As both branches of ETA continued their military operations, the differences in their respective conceptions of the armed struggle became more and more marked. For ETA(m), the armed struggle was the driving force in a war of national liberation.

> ETA openly declares its war against the repressive military apparatus of the Spanish state, which has invaded the Basque territory. Exposing the enemy, the imperialist Spanish oligarchy, the monarchical-bourgeois state and the military, the guardian of the Francoist dictatorship, we seek to intensify the offensive armed campaign in order to force a truce in the short term as the first necessary step toward a socialist revolution in Euskadi.[60]

Once the KAS Alternative had been accepted by Madrid, ETA(m) would be ready to declare a cease-fire. For ETA(pm), however, the armed struggle was viewed as a weapon of workers as well as Basques; ETA(pm) asserted that it was waging a class war as well as a war of national liberation and that it would not abandon violence until Basque social as well as national needs were met.

> To ask ETA(pm) to abandon armed struggle is to ask it to renounce its identity as a revolutionary political party of the Basque working class. It is like asking for the dissolution of the Spanish army. Those who would think of convincing us to definitively renounce armed struggle are wasting their time. The situation is this: there is occurring an intense confrontation between Basque workers and the national bourgeoisie. The statute represents an occasion and a vehicle by which to bring about a rupture. . . . We must build the basis of a popular nationalist and socialist rebellion, revolution. We would be stupid to think about renouncing armed struggle.[61]

As its political wing (EE) became more deeply committed to parliamentary politics, ETA(pm) would find it increasingly difficult to reconcile the social and national struggles, as had Official Sinn Fein. Similarly, ETA(pm), like the official IRA, would be outflanked both politically and militarily by its more intransigent and single-minded competitors, Herri Batasuna and ETA(m). The differences between the two groups were clearly seen in their respective attitudes to the proposed Basque autonomy statute, which was submitted for referendum on 25 October 1979. While KAS, Herri Batasuna, and ETA(m) urged Basque voters once again to abstain, EE and the PNV asked voters to support the proposed statute. Herri Batasuna's and ETA(m)'s opposition to the statute centered on their claim that a statute derived from a Spanish constitution that had not been approved by Basques could not serve as the basis for an independent Euskadi.

Meanwhile, both the PNV and EE supported the statute on the grounds that it provided the best opportunity for Basques to achieve some measure of autonomy from Madrid. As in most abstentionist campaigns, the outcome of the vote was ambiguous and enabled both sides to interpret it as they wished.[62] Once the autonomy statute was in place, the parties in the Autonomous Basque Community (CAV), which included the provinces of Araba, Gipuzkoa, and Bizkaia (Nafarroa having been excluded from the autonomy agreement), began preparing for the first Basque parliamentary elections.

The Basque Parliament: Sovereignty or Sellout?

As voters went to the polls, they could choose between a wide selection of parties, which were divided into two major blocs: one centralist and predominantly Spanish, the other regionalist and predominantly Basque. The Spanish bloc was primarily divided between the Spanish Left (PSOE and PCE) and the Spanish center-right (primarily the UCD of Adolfo Suarez). The Basque bloc was similarly divided between a moderate center occupied by PNV, and a left divided between the *reformista* EE and the *rupturista* Herri Batasuna. Data from a 1979 survey,[63] in which each party indicated its preferred structure for a future Basque country, illustrates not only the distance between the Spanish and Basque blocs, but also significant differences within the ethnic Basque electorate.

Although less than 25 percent of the voters of all parties within the Spanish *(estatalista)* bloc preferred a political arrangement that included either a federal state or an independent Basque country, over 30 percent of voters for all Basque parties supported such an arrangement. Within the Basque Left, over 60 percent of the voters supported the most separatist options, that is, a federal Spanish state or an independent Euskadi. Within the Basque bloc, however, significant differences existed regarding the preferred political solution. While over 60 percent of PNV voters supported an arrangement that maintained the connection with Spain, an equal proportion of Herri Batasuna voters preferred the creation of an independent Euskadi. EE voters were somewhat more divided in their preferences, although over 60 percent supported the two most separatist options. It is interesting to note that the percentage of those in each party who hold positive images of ETA corresponded closely to the percentage of those in each party whose preferred option was independence. The differences between the Basque parties regarding the preferred relations between Spain and Euskadi are also better understood if we consider the relationship between national self-identification and partisanship. According to the same public opinion poll, while the overwhelming majority of Herri Batasuna and EE voters were likely to identify themselves as purely Basque, almost 50 percent of PNV voters claimed some identification with Spain.

Data from Linz (1986, 590–95) reveals that these differences were clearly reflected in the voters' images of their own party and its competitors. The overwhelming majority of all Basque party voters perceived their own party as being in favor of Basque independence, but Herri Batasuna and EE voters were far less likely to view the PNV as supportive of an independent Euskadi.

In terms of economic issues, public opinion data (Linz 1986, 163) revealed that a majority of each party's voters believed that economic conditions would improve with autonomy. Herri Batasuna voters were the most likely to see an improvement in economic conditions in an independent Basque Country.

The ideological differences between the parties were quite evident to each constituency. Although each constituency viewed its own party as supporting the interests of workers, only a small percentage of Herri Batasuna and EE voters perceived the PNV as supporting workers' rights. This difference was also noticed by PNV voters, and the PNV was the only party in which almost half of its members supported the interests of business. These factors help to explain the differences in the political options supported by the PNV and Herri Batasuna. Since PNV voters had a larger investment in the Spanish economy than did Herri Batasuna voters, their nationalism was tempered by a willingness to compromise and use the existing political institutions. Herri Batasuna and EE appeared as revolutionary and Marxist to both their own and PNV voters, while the PNV was perceived as social-democratic by its own supporters as well as by Herri Batasuna and EE voters. These findings were further supported by each party's self-positioning on the left-right dimension.[64]

Finally, in terms of the issue of social conflict, although a majority of each party's voters characterized their own party as supporting democracy and being capable of avoiding intra-Basque confrontations, less than one-third of PNV voters characterized Herri Batasuna as capable of either.

In addition to the ideological differences between the Basque parties, data from the 1979 FOESSA study cited above revealed a number of socio-economic factors that distinguished the PNV electorate from that of Herri Batasuna and EE. Most noticeably, the PNV was the only party to receive over 50 percent of its support from women. It also had the oldest electorate, with over 80 percent of its support coming from those over thirty-five, while 55 percent of the Herri Batasuna and EE vote came from those under thirty-five. Thus it appears that the electoral battle between the parties will continue to be fought among the youngest Basque voters. The PNV also had the highest percentage of voters who identified themselves as upper middle class and having nonmanual jobs. In contrast, Herri Batasuna and EE voters were heavily concentrated in manual and semiskilled employment, and were more likely to identify themselves as working class. As in the Northern Irish case, therefore, only to a limited extent were the radical Basque nationalist parties competing for votes from the same section of the nationalist community that supported the more moderate PNV; rather, competition for floating voters appeared to occur largely between Herri Batasuna and EE.

The analysis of the social background of the voters of the most militant nationalist parties, Sinn Fein and Herri Batasuna, and those of their more moderate opponents, the PNV and the SDLP, has revealed that the two electorates are divided along rather similar lines, with Sinn Fein and Herri Batasuna voters being predominantly under forty-five, male, and working class (see table 4.4).

Table 4.4. Social Background of Irish and Basque Nationalist Voters

Political Party Characteristics	SF (N=131)	HB (N=197)	SDLP (N=304)	PNV (N=455)
Gender				
Female	46%	41%	53%	60%
Male	54	59	47	40
Age				
18–24	33	28	18	5
25–34	24	27	21	14
35–44	18	17	19	23
45–54	15	14	19	23
55+	11	14	23	35
Socioeconomic Status				
ABC1	24	44	38	61
C2DE	76	56	62	40

Notes: ABC1 = Professional, white-collar, students, skilled workers, independent farmers; C2DE = Retired workers, pensioners, blue-collar, service employees, unskilled workers, casual laborers.

Sources: MORI, June 24–28, 1984; FOESSA (1981); Linz (1986), 575–76.

A review of the data also reveals that in both cases, competition between the two sets of parties occurs principally along the political (independence/ autonomy), rather than the ideological (left/right) dimension. Dramatic positive or negative shifts in economic conditions could heighten competition around class issues in both cases. However, to the extent that both Sinn Fein and Herri Batasuna portray economic inequalities as the by-products of fundamentally illegitimate and inequitable political systems, the metadiscourse of competition remains that of ethnicity and nationalism.

The First Basque Parliamentary Election

The results of the 9 March 1980 Basque parliamentary elections confirmed the existence of an extremely fragmented and polarized party system. Although the PNV once again emerged as the single strongest party, with 40.6 percent of the vote and 25 of 60 seats, the success of Herri Batasuna, which again emerged as the second strongest party in the Basque provinces, winning 11 seats and 17.6 percent of the popular vote, prevented the PNV from securing an outright majority. EE won 10.4 percent of the popular vote and 6 seats. The Basque Left together had won about 28 percent of the vote and 17 seats,[65] but Herri Batasuna's decision not to occupy its seats enabled the PNV to constitute an absolute majority by the slim margin of one vote. The PNV was thus able to organize the Basque parliament as a single dominant party. Following the election of Carlos Garaikoetxea, the PNV leader from Nafarroa, as its first president, the parliament began its work on 31 March. Despite this historic political achievement, the nationalist aspirations of many within the Basque Country remained unmet. As Clark (1984, 119) has noted, although "peace may have been what most Basques wanted at the end of 1980," it did not seem likely they would get it as ETA violence rose to an all-time high.[66]

Summary

In this chapter, I examined the effect of the IRA hunger strikes on the nationalist community in Northern Ireland and the effect of the political reforms of the post-Franco transition to democracy on the Basque minority in Spain. Variations in the strength and influence of Sinn Fein and the SDLP in the Northern Irish party system and changes in the strategy of Sinn Fein and the IRA were related to the mobilization of a broad spectrum of Irish society during the H-Block and hunger strike campaigns. A detailed examination of the Sinn Fein and SDLP electorates revealed that only to a limited extent did these parties draw from the same segments of the Catholic community in Northern Ireland. The SDLP vote came largely from the Catholic middle class, while the overwhelming majority of Sinn Fein supporters are from the working class. What most clearly distinguished the two parties, however, their respective attitudes toward the use of violence to secure the reunification of Ireland. While four out of every five Sinn Fein supporters approved the use of violence to secure political goals, an equal proportion of SDLP supporters rejected violence as a mechanism of political change.

Similarly, variations in support for the many different factions of ETA, its political offshoots, and the PNV were related to shifts in the structure of political institutions in post-Franco Spain. An analysis of the Basque party system revealed an electorate divided along both class and ethnic lines. The ethnically Basque parties showed stark differences in the social bases of their support and preferred political arrangements with Madrid.

Shifts in the level of regime repression, organizational support, and the strength of competing organizations were related to the decisions by the IRA and ETA to encourage the participation of their respective political wings, Sinn Fein and Herri Batasuna, in the parliamentary process and to adopt a dual strategy of armed struggle and electoral mobilization. The precise mechanisms of strategic change are discussed in the following chapter, which focuses on the social and political biographies of Sinn Fein and Herri Batasuna activists in an attempt to understand better how their support for the armed struggle of their military wings, the IRA and ETA, as well as the responses of the state to that struggle affects their choice of strategy.

5

Republicans and *Abertzales:* Pathways to Activism

Activists and Motivations

Although determining what motivates people to participate in an organization is (as students of both social movements and party activism have noted) a process fraught with many difficulties, the theoretical aim of this chapter is to assess the microdynamics of individual decisions to participate in Sinn Fein and Herri Batasuna. Using findings from the set of interviews I conducted with Sinn Fein and Herri Batasuna activists and from the survey of the Herri Batasuna activists, I first analyze the activists' social backgrounds and pathways to activism. Second, I examine their ideological, organizational, and strategic preferences. Finally, I attempt to distinguish the ideologues, radicals, and politicos in each party.

Prior to Sinn Fein's and Herri Batasuna's participation in elections, support for the IRA and ETA was publicly asserted by the British, Irish, and Spanish governments to be extremely marginal.[1] What support these organizations did receive, according to government sources, was limited only to the most "fanatical" individuals. Further, as the following excerpts illustrate, no distinctions were made between members of Sinn Fein and the IRA, or between members of Herri Batasuna and ETA:

> While this type of criminal organization [Herri Batasuna] has access to parliamentary institutions, while it can influence the life of citizens through infiltrating all types of businesses, while it can continue publishing a newspaper, while it can continue dispensing public subventions, at the same time that it is taking to the street wearing balaclavas

and assassinating citizens, we cannot assume a peaceful coexistence with them.[2]

There is little difference between the Provisional IRA and Provisional Sinn Fein. They comprise one and the same organization. As I have said in the past, they are like rats scurrying around in the sewers of Irish mythology. The sooner the poison is set to eradicate these pests from our society forever, the sooner we will get peace in our land.[3]

Despite the success of the IRA hunger strike candidates, both the British and Irish governments continued to view support for Sinn Fein and the IRA as insignificant and ephemeral. Even as Sinn Fein prepared to launch its first direct challenge to the SDLP in the 1982 Northern Ireland Assembly elections, no less astute an observer of Irish politics than Conor Cruise O'Brien argued that the support Sinn Fein had received during the hunger strike was based largely on emotion and had died with the passing of the H-Block campaign:

> On the Catholic side, Provisional Sinn Fein doesn't seem to present as formidable a threat to the SDLP as once seemed possible. At the time of the hunger strike, the Provos could appear in their most acceptable role: that of martyrs. But at the end of the hunger strike, the Provo leaders denounced a Catholic priest, a fervent republican sympathizer, for helping relatives of hunger strikers to get the prisoners to end their fast, and live. That made a sour end to the H-Block campaign. Memories of that period are now likely to do Provo candidates more harm than good.[4]

It was not surprising therefore that Sinn Fein's electoral performance stunned not only the Northern Irish electorate but the British and Irish governments as well. As Guelke (1983, 7) has noted, "[T]he shock to mainland British opinion was enormous. . . . [B]oth BBC and ITN announcers appeared visibly shaken as they read out the news of Sinn Fein's electoral success." Sinn Fein's electoral success clearly undermined the British government's public stereotyping of Sinn Fein and IRA supporters as a "tiny, evil, extremist minority."

For at least one unionist politician, however, the only adjustment necessary to bring the stereotype back in line with reality was to characterize Sinn Fein supporters as a large, evil, extremist minority:

> Perhaps I had not made myself clear . . . when I suggested that 103,000 ordinary, decent Roman Catholics had voted for Sinn Fein. Earlier I said

that the phrase "ordinary, decent Roman Catholics" would need to be in inverted commas. I do not believe that anyone who goes out and gives his first preference vote to Sinn Fein . . . is ordinary and decent. A person could not be ordinary and decent and go out and vote for murder. . . . Those who vote for Sinn Fein know exactly what they are doing. . . . Of course, some Roman Catholics who vote for Sinn Fein try to justify their reprehensible actions by saying that they vote for Sinn Fein only because of its great community work. If the Yorkshire Ripper were a social worker, the same people would probably argue that he was worthy of our support.[5]

Sinn Fein's success also provided the public in Britain with the first indications of the political costs of Thatcher's partial victory on the H-Block issue. Further, the vote appeared to indicate a substantial level of support for the armed struggle of the IRA, including the bombing in Hyde Park in July that had killed eleven soldiers. It also appeared as a serious challenge to the SDLP's position within the nationalist community. Finally, and perhaps most worrisome to both the British and Irish governments, was the possibility that the vote for Sinn Fein would result in greater international support for the IRA and its goal of a united Ireland. Facing these bleak prospects, both the Irish and British governments recognized the need to examine in detail the motivations that led "ordinary, decent, Roman Catholics" to support Sinn Fein.

The most significant of the immediate post-assembly analyses of the conflict in Northern Ireland, the *New Ireland Forum Report,* was published in 1984. Generally acknowledged to have been conceived, supported, and introduced by the SDLP and the Dublin government as an attempt to strengthen the moderate center and limit the electoral advance of Sinn Fein, the report ascribed the impasses in Northern Ireland to the alienation of nationalists in Northern Ireland from political and civil institutions, from the security forces, and from the manner of application of the law. Although the recommendations for a political solution contained in the report were dismissed by Prime Minister Thatcher in her now famous "Out, out, out" remark, the recognition that 35 percent of the Northern Irish nationalist population was sufficiently alienated to vote for Sinn Fein would lead to further discussions between the two governments that would culminate in the signing of the Anglo-Irish Agreement in November 1985. Thus, although "criminal" and "terrorist" remain popular epithets for the IRA, Sinn Fein supporters, excluding party activists, are now generally described as "alienated," "marginalized," or "misguided idealists." A similar transformation in the image of Herri Batasuna has accompanied its electoral advances. In March 1979, the unanticipated success of Herri Batasuna, which secured 13 percent of the Basque vote, elicited the following qualification by the editor of *El País,* Javier Pradera, to his preelection editorial, in which he had declared that "the terrorism of ETA receives each day less and less popular support":

> Unfortunately, my predictions were proven to be quite erroneous. This obliges all of us to reconsider the significance of a movement with populist elements and of the conditions which have not only engendered terrorism but also the social support which it receives.[6]

In 1982, the explanation of Herri Batasuna's support shifted. Now the other parties focused on discrediting its image as the defender of the interests of Basque youth. For example, Joseba Elósegui of the PNV stated,

> Herri Batasuna has no solutions to offer this generation of young people. Indeed, they should remind them of those whom they have forced to suffer in prisons . . . . Today's youth are in the hands of those without scruples who take advantage of them to carry out their protests and propaganda activities.[7]

Prior to the June 1986 Spanish general elections, representatives of all the major parties once again directed attacks against Herri Batasuna, whose vote, according to public opinion polls, was expected to increase. In this election a clear distinction existed between Spanish and Basque explanations of the Herri Batasuna support. While Spanish parties focused on the Herri Batasuna-ETA relationship, within the Basque community the potential Herri Batasuna vote was more frequently described in terms of the social rather than the psychological characteristics of its supporters. Herri Batasuna voters weren't necessarily pro-ETA accomplices; rather, they were Basque workers and young people who had been severely affected by the restructuring of Basque industries and were voting for Herri Batasuna to protest the policies of the PSOE:

> The votes for Herri Batasuna are used by ETA to continue killing. . . . HB receives instructions directly from ETA. If the HB vote rises, it is clear that the State has not succeeded in delegitimizing the political wing of ETA-M.[8]

> ETA-Militar is the number one enemy of Spain. It is no libel or defamation to say the only objective of Herri Batasuna is to provide popular support for and justify the actions of the ETA terrorists. . . . There is no difference between those who support and justify terrorism and the terrorists who commit the acts of terrorism.[9]

Not everyone who votes for HB agrees with the tactics of ETA. . . .
This contradiction can be explained by the fact that often in Euskadi
those who vote for HB are those who are angry because they are unemployed, those who are dissatisfied with the lack of serious discussion
about the grave economic crisis affecting our society. They vote for HB
because they see no other way to express their anger.[10]

On 7 June 1987, Herri Batasuna delivered its second "ballot bomb" by
winning a seat in Spain's first European parliament elections and displacing
the PNV as the most voted Basque party. The fact that Herri Batasuna had
received over fifty thousand votes from outside the Basque provinces, as well
as a high percentage of the immigrant vote within the Basque provinces, was
equally shocking to parties of the Left and the Right. The first of the explanations for Herri Batasuna's support to fall victim to these results was that
which had envisioned some visceral hatred of all things Spanish among the
party's supporters. The argument was reworked, and the immigrant vote in
the Basque provinces was explained as an attempt by immigrants to assert
their "Basqueness."

In the immigrant barrios in Bilbao there was a surprisingly high degree
of support for HB. This support is interpreted as representing a means
by which first- or second-generation immigrants who spoke no Basque,
who were not integrated into Basque society, could earn a type of certificate confirming their "Basqueness."[11]

Similarly, the explanation that a "vote for Herri Batasuna is a vote for ETA"
was somewhat damaged, although many within the PSOE and PNV privately feared that a quarter of a million people did, in fact, support ETA.
The PNV, fearful lest the electoral results prompt Madrid to increase its security presence and operations within the Basque provinces and actually
stimulate further ETA activity, publicly stated,

The danger now is that there is a group of individuals in the Interior
Ministry who wish to try to physically eliminate ETA. ETA, however,
is not just ETA, but represents something much more, something
much closer to the people, something symbolic that is shared by thousands of people. One cannot speak simply of ETA and the Herri
Batasuna supporters; support for ETA is something that transcends the
vote for HB.[12]

Once again, however, the most popular explanation for Herri Batasuna's
success, among both Basque and Spanish parties, focused on the "desperation"

and "marginalization" of those sectors most affected by the PSOE's labor policies: "The Herri Batasuna vote in Spain is the vote of those who feel marginalized by the current system. Their vote is a protest against the PSOE."[13]

As in the Irish case, Herri Batasuna's 1987 "ballot bomb" would provoke a concerted effort by both the Spanish and the Basque governments to stabilize the political situation and devise a strategy to thwart further electoral advances by the party. By the end of January 1988, the PNV and PSOE working together passed an "anti-violence, anti-ETA" document, which was signed by all the parties except Herri Batasuna. Those who signed the document agreed not to work with any elected representative who had not signed the document. Consequently, Herri Batasuna representatives were excluded from all committees, commissions, and so forth within the municipal governments. They were technically excluded from such positions at all levels of government. However, as Herri Batasuna representatives only took their seats on local councils, those councils were the principal sites of real confrontation.

In both the Basque and Irish cases, then, we see first an attempt by the governments in power and opposition parties to dismiss the supporters of the radical nationalist options represented by Sinn Fein and Herri Batasuna as insignificant, evil minorities. Individual participation in these organizations was presumably explained by the pathology of the militants. But when the repeated electoral successes of both parties undermined the sociopathic stereotype of Sinn Fein and Herri Batasuna supporters, new explanations that used terms like *deprivation, marginalization,* and *alienation* were introduced into the political discourse. Although these revised explanations of radical nationalist activism still centered on the psychological attributes of the individual participants, they evinced a more explicitly political foundation for the perceived grievances of the minority community.

In Northern Ireland, *alienation* became the explanatory term of choice. This nationalist alienation was generally explained as the result of fifty years of exclusion from meaningful participation in the political institutions of Northern Ireland, persistent patterns of social and economic discrimination and deprivation, and on occasion as a consequence of the exercise of coercive force by the state against nationalists. In the Basque case, particularly after Herri Batasuna's success in the 1987 and 1989 European Parliament elections, *frustration* was the term most frequently used by those seeking to explain the persistence of the radical nationalist vote. The Basque nationalist frustration was explained as a consequence both of the rising unemployment rates in the Basque provinces due to the restructuring of the numerous heavy industries located there,[14] and of Madrid's failure to facilitate the transfer of powers to the Basque government that had been negotiated in the Basque autonomy statute. The support that Herri Batasuna received in the rest of Spain was largely viewed as a sign of the "frustration" and "disenchantment" of the more radical sectors of Spanish society with the "pseudo-socialist" politics of the PSOE, especially its labor policies.

The most widely accepted explanations of the continuing support for ETA focused on the "subculture" of violence in Basque society that had evolved as a response to Francoist repression and the counterviolence of ETA during the 1970s.

In the literature on social movements, each of the explanatory variables mentioned above—sociopathology, marginalization, alienation, frustration, and deprivation—has informed a particular model of rebellious collective action. Likewise, numerous models of nationalism have relied to some extent on many of these variables to explain the (re)emergence of regionalism and nationalism as sources of political organization and to understand its appeal. The following section examines the extent to which the actual social, economic, and political characteristics of Sinn Fein and Herri Batasuna activists correspond with those portrayed in government documents and the media.

Social Background

Although a considerable amount of information regarding the Sinn Fein and Herri Batasuna electorate exists, comparable information on party activists is not available. Indeed, to the best of my knowledge, this study contains the first empirical analysis of Herri Batasuna activists. We might reasonably expect, however, that activists would be recruited from the same spectrum of the Irish and Basque electorate that exhibits the strongest support for the radical nationalist options: young, working-class males with a middle/secondary school education. Tables 5.1 and 5.2, which compare the socioeconomic characteristics of the Sinn Fein and Herri Batasuna activists interviewed with a sample of Sinn Fein and Herri Batasuna voters, as well as elected representatives, show that, in fact, Sinn Fein and Herri Batasuna activists are remarkably similar to their electorates.

In both Sinn Fein and Herri Batasuna, over 50 percent of activists were male and under the age of 35. The average age was between 31 and 35 years across all subgroups, including candidates for elected office. Among those under 30, a much larger percentage of those in Herri Batasuna were university students. Given the scarcity of material incentives these parties can offer and the considerable social sanctions attached to membership, the proportion of those under 34 is not inconsistent with findings that more free time

Table 5.1. Age and Gender Profile of Sinn Fein and Herri Batasuna Activists and Voters

	Under 25	25–34	35–44	45–54	55+	Median	Female	Male
SF Activists (N=60)	14%	39%	26%	14%	7%	34 100%	30%	70%
SF Candidates, Northern Ireland, 1985 (N=91)	9	41	34	14	2	33.8 100%	14	86
SF Candidates, Eire, 1985 (N=82)	5	46	30	15	4	32.4 100%	10	90
SF Voters (N=131)	33	24	18	15	11	100%	46	54
HB Activists (Interviews; N=40)	15	40	30	10	5	33.7 100%	25	75
HB Activists (Survey; N=108)	26	49	17	7	3	31.6 100%	34	66
HB Candidates, Oct. 1989 (N=36)	86	40	33	18	3	100%	19	81
HB Voters (N=197)	28	27	17	14	14	100%	41	59

Sources: Interviews with author (rows 1, 5, 7); own survey (row 6); MORI, June 24–28, 1984 (row 4); FOESSA 1981(row 8); An Phoblacht/Republican News (rows 2, 3); calculations by the author.

and a reduced risk of social sanctions are associated with participation in radical social movement organizations and parties (della Porta 1988; della Porta and Tarrow 1986; Keniston 1970; Braungart and Braungart 1987).

In both parties, the majority of activists held blue-collar jobs, although candidates in Herri Batasuna were almost twice as likely to hold professional positions than were ordinary party activists. Also, the percentage of Herri Batasuna activists in the survey who reported being unemployed (21.1 percent) was almost equal to the 1988 average Basque unemployment rate of 21.4 percent. Sinn Fein activists who did not hold full-time party positions were twice as likely as Herri Batasuna activists to be unemployed,[15] and

**Table 5.2. Socioeconomic Profiles of Sinn Fein and
Herri Batasuna Activists and Voters**

	ABC1	C2DE
SF Activists (*N*= 60)	25%	75%
SF Candidates, Northern Ireland, 1985 (*N*= 91)	27	73
SF Candidates, Eire, 1985 (*N*= 82)	26	74
SF Voters (*N*=131)	24	76
HB Activists (Interviews; *N*= 40)	52	48
HB Activists (Survey; *N*=108)	28	72
HB Candidates, Oct. 1989 (*N*= 36)	66	34
HB Voters (*N*=197)	26	74

Notes: ABC1 = Professional, white-collar, students, skilled workers, independent farmers;
C2DE = Retired workers, pensioners, blue-collar, service employees, unskilled workers,
casual laborers.
Sources: Interviews with author (rows 1, 5, 7); own survey (row 6); MORI, June 24–28,
1984 (row 4); FOESSA 1981 (row 8), An Phoblact/Republican News (rows 2, 3); calculations by the author.

twice as many Sinn Fein activists stated that they had experienced job discrimination as a result of their party membership. Also, Sinn Fein members active in the Republic of Ireland were equally as likely to report that they had been denied or lost a job as a result of their party activism. Over half of both Sinn Fein and Herri Batasuna activists were equally likely to state that they had been discriminated against because of their ethnic origins. Among those Sinn Fein activists interviewed, the majority of complaints related to job discrimination and the allocation of resources for community development, including the siting of new industries. Among Basque interviewees, complaints focused primarily on discrimination against them as Basque speakers. In particular, they criticized the failure of the state to provide funding for Basque language education and its unwillingness to expand the number of public schools with a stream for Basque language speakers. For example, as one Herri Batasuna activist noted,

> It's terrible that I was fluent in Basque until I was four years old when I went to school and they took away my language. It's ridiculous that when I was eighteen, I had to relearn my native language. And now the Spanish government has the gall to call us imperialists because we want to speak our own language in our country and because we want those who live in Euskadi to learn Euskara. It's a completely schizophrenic situation.[16]

They also complained of the restrictions placed on the Basque television station, ETB, and its comparatively low level of state subvention. Herri Batasuna activists were also critical of the Basque government for its failure to publish all documents in both Euskara and Spanish, and for their failure to use Basque as the primary language of government. Similar complaints were raised by several Sinn Fein activists.

Data from the interviews with Sinn Fein and Herri Batasuna activists indicated that there were more Herri Batasuna activists (40 percent) who could speak Basque than Sinn Fein activists (28 percent) who could speak Gaelic *prior* to becoming active in the parties. More Herri Batasuna activists also reported using Basque in daily situations than Sinn Fein activists did Gaelic. Although both parties have an unofficial policy of encouraging activists to learn and use their native languages, Herri Batasuna also requires that members of the national executive and candidates for public office be proficient or acquire proficiency. Indeed, data from the interviews and survey revealed that the total proportion of Herri Batasuna activists who could speak Basque well or very well (58 percent) was much higher than that of Sinn Fein activists who could speak Gaelic well (35 percent). This finding suggests that ethnicity, as indicated by the ability to speak one's native language, plays a more significant role in Herri Batasuna party ideology and strategy than it does in Sinn Fein's. Given the role of IRA and ETA activists and supporters in establishing the growing numbers of schools in which Irish and Basque are spoken, an interesting avenue for future research would be a study of the political partisanship of the graduates of these schools. Sinn Fein activists apparently experienced discrimination based on their overlapping memberships in the minority community in Northern Ireland and in the party, while Herri Batasuna activists experienced discrimination largely on the grounds of their ethnic identity, particularly in terms of their ability to use Euskara.

With regard to educational background, data from the interviews and survey of Herri Batasuna activists revealed that two-thirds of activists in both parties had a middle or secondary school education, with a somewhat larger share of Sinn Fein activists having received only an elementary or middle school education. Herri Batasuna activists were moderately more likely than those in Sinn Fein to hold university or professional degrees. They were also almost twice as likely as the party's voters to hold advanced degrees but were no more likely to do so than the Basque population in general. However, as Linz (1985, 114) has noted, Herri Batasuna activists, on average, were better educated than those in the PNV and equally as well educated as those in EE.

Similarly, the educational profile of Sinn Fein activists did not vary greatly from that of the nationalist population in general. Although no hard data is available on the educational profiles of SDLP and Sinn Fein voters, based on the percentage of those in the SDLP holding professional/white-collar jobs, it would be reasonable to assume that, on average, SDLP supporters were much more likely to have at least a secondary education, and most probably some higher academic qualifications.

On the whole, then, the age, occupational, and educational distribution of Sinn Fein and Herri Batasuna activists is at variance with the expectation that nationalist parties are composed of an upwardly mobile but insecure intelligentsia with few alternative options for advancement. Rather, it is more in keeping with explanations that focus on the experience of deprivation and discrimination (economic and/or cultural) on the basis of ethnic identity and, certainly in the Irish case, on generational shifts in expectations as a result of increased educational opportunities.

Northern Ireland: Education, Unemployment, and Militant Nationalism

Although there is relatively little published information on the religious composition of the university student population in Northern Ireland, it seems clear that Catholics were generally underrepresented among university students until relatively recently. Figures produced by the Catholic Chaplaincy at Queen's University Belfast suggested that the proportion of Catholics in 1953–54 was 19.1 percent, and this steadily rose to 27.4 percent by 1968–69. Osborne and Cormack (1983) suggest that this steady increase in the proportion of Catholics was enhanced in the 1970s. They calculate that between 1973 and 1979, overall student numbers increased by 45 percent and that the number of Protestant students increased by 39 percent, while the number of Catholic students grew by about 71 percent. This increase in academic qualifications did not, however, translate into increased employment rates for Catholics. Studies by Cormack, Osborne, and Thompson (1980), and Murray and Darby (1978), which examined the differential experiences of pupils leaving Protestant and Catholic secondary schools in Belfast, Strabane, and Derry, found not only that a much higher proportion of the pupils leaving Protestant schools had employment, but also that Protestants were more likely than Catholics to be employed regardless of education qualifications. A further common finding of both studies was the disillusionment of those from Catholic schools with education. Before entering the labor market, many had been convinced that the possession of some qualifications would enhance their employment opportunities. Unfortunately, for most that hope was not realized. While the studies noted that fewer Catholics than Protestants had above-average educational qualifications, these Catholics were still less likely to have full-time employment than Protestants with below-average educational qualifications.

Data from two analyses of inequality of opportunity in Northern Ireland by the London-based Policy Studies Institute reveal that between 1971 and 1985, Catholics were, on average, more than twice as likely as Protestants to be unemployed, even when academic qualifications were held constant.[17] Not surprisingly, the discrepancies in objective conditions were mirrored in the subjective perceptions of Catholics and Protestants. While two-thirds of Protestants thought that members of both communities had the same chance of securing a job, two-thirds of the Catholic respondents thought they did not. However, in response to questions regarding changes most needed to end the current conflict, only 2 percent of Protestants and 13 percent of Catholics mentioned discrimination. Equality of rights and opportunities was chosen by approximately 19 percent of both Catholics and Protestants. These findings suggest that Sinn Fein's argument that the economic disadvantages experienced by the Catholic community are a consequence rather than a cause of the political divisions in Northern Ireland is widely accepted by that community.

This discrepancy between expanding educational opportunities and existing political and economic conditions would mobilize a generation of Catholic students to challenge the authority of the Northern Irish and British governments. For example, students from Queen's University (perhaps the best known of whom is Bernadette Devlin McAliskey) who were active in the political organization Peoples' Democracy played a key role in the 1968–72 Northern Irish Civil Rights Campaign as organizers, strategists, and participants.

Greatly influenced by the civil rights and anti-Vietnam protests in the United States and the events in Paris and Prague, these students, many of whom were the first in their families to enjoy access to a university education, rejected the conservative, accommodative politics of the existing Irish Nationalist and Northern Irish Labor parties. As one Queen's University graduate and Sinn Fein activist told me,

> In the States, I suppose knowing exactly where you were on November 22, 1963, the day of Kennedy's assassination, identifies you as a member of the "baby-boom" generation. Similarly, here, knowing where you were on Saturday, October 5, 1968, marks you as a member of the civil rights generation. . . . We were all very much influenced by the civil rights campaign in the U.S. We even sang "We Shall Overcome" on our marches. It was an exciting time to be at university, although

Queen's was certainly duller than most university campuses at the
time, until, that is, the RUC made the mistake of trying to baton us off
the streets. Our generation simply wasn't going to accept second-class
status, as many of our parents had. Nor were we going to accept the
"do-nothing" politics of the existing nationalist parties. We were at
odds not only with the Northern Irish and British governments but
also with the middle-class constitutional nationalists, especially those
in the SDLP who were content to carve out a place for themselves
within the existing state. . . . After Bloody Sunday, it was clear that the
Northern Irish state was irreformable, and after the heady days of the
fall of Stormont, republicans surely, if slowly, came to recognize that
the war against the British would be a long war. Further, as more and
more young IRA members were imprisoned for long stretches at a
time, primarily as a result of the increase in activity in the 1970s, the
cages of Long Kesh increasingly became the campus of the "University
of Freedom." As Gerry Adams and others have noted, during the
1970s the internees and prisoners had the chance to read and study
the writings of a variety of revolutionary leaders. As they became more
widely read, these prisoners would significantly influence the IRA and
Sinn Fein's politicization. . . . In turn, the hunger strike campaign
would mobilize this generation's youth in much the same way as the
civil rights campaign had mine.[18]

Basque Country: Language, Culture, and Militant Nationalism

Basque students would also play a critical role in the resurgence of a militant
nationalism. As in the Irish case, this militancy would be spurred on by
the passivity of the existing nationalist political parties. However, whereas
the impetus for much of the activism by Irish students had been blatant
economic and political discrimination, for Basques, as the quotation below
from a long-time Basque activist reveals, it was the sociocultural threat posed
to the Basque language, Euskara, and to Basque culture in general by the
influx of immigrants into the Basque Country during the 1950s as well as
Franco's harsh repression of all things Basque:

> Under Franco, the repression was so severe that we became strangers
> in our own homes. We had gone so far as to no longer know our own
> language. There were people who because they did not know Basque
> were unsure if they were French or Spanish or Basque. The crisis
> which unfolded before the young people who came of age in the
> decade of the fifties was a crisis of identity and signaled, in a certain

sense, the independent entry of young people into politics. The crisis which had erupted as a result of an immobilist situation seemed almost impossible to resolve. The loss of Euskadi's historic rights to fascism and the Allies' abandonment of the cause of Basque independence after the war—all of these issues raised questions in the minds of the young people and widened the gulf which would forever separate the new generation from that which had lived through the war. Our generation saw our world disappearing around us every day, while the Basque government in exile did nothing to halt the disappearance of our language, which is the fundamental basis of our identity as Basques. While they waited on support to come from America, we were watching our culture being eroded more and more each day. We realized we had to do something, anything, to mobilize the people if we wished to save our language, our identity, and our country.[19]

In sum, in both the Irish and Basque cases, the experience of discrimination based on ethnic identity was cited as a factor motivating the participation of the party activists. In each case, there was also an explicit generational rejection of both the existing regime and nationalist political organizations. But the most striking similarity between the Basque and Irish that the data revealed was their personal experience of state repression *prior* to their participation in Sinn Fein or Herri Batasuna.

Data drawn from my interviews with the Sinn Fein and Herri Batasuna activists (see table 5.3) shows that approximately half of both sets of activists indicated personal experience of state repression in some way prior to joining their respective parties. Among Sinn Fein activists, one in four had already been imprisoned or forced to live in the Republic of Ireland as a result of their participation in the nationalist movement. Although a smaller percentage of Herri Batasuna activists had been imprisoned, one in five had been detained by the security forces. Activists in both organizations were also equally likely to have had a family member or close friend arrested. Sinn Fein activists, however, were more than twice as likely to have had a family member or close friend killed by either a member of the security forces or a Protestant paramilitary organization. The difference between the Sinn Fein and Herri Batasuna figures corresponds with a much higher level of sectarian conflict in Northern Ireland.

Thus, the profile of Sinn Fein and Herri Batasuna activists suggests that youth and its correlate, a reduced fear of social sanction, along with personal experience of discrimination based on ethnic identification and prior

Table 5.3. Sinn Fein and Herri Batasuna Activists' Experience of Coercive Force Prior to Membership

	Percent Responding Affirmatively (Interviewees)	
	SF (N=60)	*HB* (N=40)
Were you ever harassed (physically or verbally) by a member of the Irish/British, Basque/Spanish/French security forces?	60%	45%
Were you ever held in custody by any branch of the Irish/British, Basque/Spanish/French security forces?	60	25
Were you ever arrested by a member of the Irish/British or Basque/Spanish security forces?	40	20
Were you ever interned/imprisoned/exiled in Britain/Ireland, Euskadi/Spain, or any other country?	30	18
Was any member of your family/close friend(s) arrested by a member of the Irish/British, Basque/Spanish security forces?	25	25
Was any member of your family/close friend(s) interned/imprisoned/exiled in Ireland/Britain, Euskadi/Spain, or any other country?	37	18
Was any member of your family/close friend(s) wounded or killed by a member of the Irish/British, Basque/Spanish security forces, or other paramilitary groups?	60	25

Source: Author's interviews with Sinn Fein and Herri Batasuna activists.

experience of state repression are significant factors in motivating an individual's participation in militant nationalist organizations. The following excerpt from an interview with a Herri Batasuna activist, who had previously been active in ETA, illustrates how these factors combined to encourage his decision to join ETA:

Our generation was the first of parents who had lost the war. We were very much influenced by the history of our families. In our homes, things had gone very poorly because our fathers had fought against Franco and were nationalists as well. Our fathers had all been imprisoned and knew what resistance was. We all were aware of what they had fought for. We were very political because of our families' experiences. The family is very important in Basque society. However, many of us never learned Basque because our parents were afraid to use it in the house and afraid we would be punished if we learned it. Without a doubt, our lives were very much influenced by the repressive conditions that existed during the dictatorship.

When I became active in ETA, I was seventeen years old, and although I wasn't sure what I could do, I knew I wanted to do something, anything. It was overwhelming to see how much needed to be done. There were so many things we needed, wanted to respond to. In the final years of Franco we began to participate more actively, more directly, in the popular struggle.[20]

An interesting avenue for future research would be to compare the experience of discrimination and violence across nationalist parties. For example, are Sinn Fein members more likely to have experienced discrimination and state repression than those in the SDLP? Basque survey data does indicate that Herri Batasuna members were more than twice as likely to fear that they or a family member would be unjustly arrested.[21] Not knowing whether this fear preceded or followed party activism leaves us with the problem of causation or correlation, although the following statement by a Herri Batasuna activist suggests that such fear existed prior to participation in the party:

The police are nothing more than torturers, and they torture with the state's permission. They are not here to protect us. They are here to control us because we are opposed to them and the state they represent. One reason for the massive demonstrations against the Lemóniz nuclear power plant was our belief that more police would be sent here to protect the plant. . . . Real democracy will exist when the Spanish police have been withdrawn from the Basque Country. Until they go, you cannot talk about any real changes in political conditions in Euskadi. One reason the people here have so little confidence in political institutions is their [the institutions'] support for the police, for those who continue to unjustly imprison and torture Basques because we desire our independence. How can we believe in leaders who commend the little dirty wars the police engage in against Basques?[22]

Pathways to Activism

Although the profiles of the activists suggest a type of individual who may be more inclined to participate in a revolutionary nationalist organization, we have yet to determine how those activists became involved in Sinn Fein or Herri Batasuna.

Table 5.4 shows that among the Sinn Fein activists interviewed, an almost equal number (40 percent and 38 percent) referred to themselves as "cradle" republicans or had been active in the IRA prior to becoming active in the party. For those who did not have a nationalist family background, participation in the Civil Rights or H-Block Campaigns was the most frequently mentioned path to activism in Sinn Fein. In contrast to the Herri Batasuna sample, only 12 percent of Sinn Fein activists mentioned trade union activism as influencing their participation in Sinn Fein. It is interesting that only one in five Sinn Fein activists mentioned participation in Irish language/cultural/sport groups as influencing their decision to become active in Sinn Fein.

Table 5.4. Pathways to Activism for Sinn Fein Activists

Pathway	SF Activists (N=60)
Nationalist Family	40%
IRA	38
Trade Union	12
Civil Rights/H-Block	65
Language/Culture/Sports	20
Feminist	20
No Prior Activism	10
Other Party	7

Source: Author's interviews with Sinn Fein activists. Percents sum to more than 100 due to responses in multiple categories.

Although 40 percent of female activists had been involved in feminist organizations, only 5 percent of male activists had participated in feminist protests, including protests against the strip-searching of women prisoners or in International Women's Day activities. Less than 8 percent mentioned prior participation in another party (primarily the SDLP and PD), and 10 percent mentioned no prior activism. Most of those in this group had come into contact with Sinn Fein as a result of receiving assistance at one of the party's advice centers.

In sum, the great majority of Sinn Fein members became active in Sinn Fein as a result either of their family background, or their involvement in organizations explicitly opposed to the existing regime or supportive of those engaged in the armed struggle against the state.

Looking at Table 5.5, we see that the political experiences of activists in Herri Batasuna are significantly more varied than those in Sinn Fein. Given the origins of Herri Batasuna, it is not surprising that among the Herri Batasuna interviewees, the most frequently mentioned prior activism involved participation in protests in support of amnesty for ETA prisoners (55 percent) and in Basque language/cultural organizations (45 percent). Only one in five, however, indicated they had been previously involved with ETA, and only 30 percent stated they had a nationalist family background.

Table 5.5. Pathways to Activism for Herri Batasuna Activists

Pathway	HB Activists (N = 40)
Anti-Repression/ Prisoner Support Groups	55%
Language/Culture/Sports	58
Nationalist Family	40
Trade Union	35
Environmental	85
ETA	20
HB Precursor	60
Youth Organizations	20
Feminist	20
No Prior Activism	15
Other Party	7

Source: Author's interviews with Herri Batasuna activists. Percents sum to more than 100 due to responses in multiple categories.

In contrast to the Sinn Fein sample, a much larger percentage (35 percent) of Herri Batasuna activists stated they had participated in trade union activities. Within the survey sample, the number reporting participation in a trade union was slightly larger at 39 percent. Sixty percent also reported activism in one of Herri Batasuna's precursors: EHAS, HAS, ESB, LAIA, or in the KAS youth affiliate Revolutionary Patriotic Youth (JARRAI).

In considerable contrast to the Sinn Fein sample, 85 percent of those interviewed reported that they had been active in the antinuclear campaign and had participated in protests against the construction of the Lemóniz nuclear power plant. Among the activists surveyed, this proportion was 80.3 percent. Twenty percent of all activists and 70 percent of female activists had participated in feminist protests, particularly in International Women's Day activities and pro-choice marches. Only 7 percent stated that they had left another party to join Herri Batasuna. Finally, 15 percent of those interviewed reported no significant political activism prior to becoming involved with Herri Batasuna. Six of the nine activists in this group indicated that they joined Herri Batasuna because of the worsening economic crisis and believed that they would be better off in an independent socialist Euskadi. This suggests that Herri Batasuna had been somewhat successful in securing party loyalty on the basis of its social and economic as well as political activism.

In sum, the political biographies of Herri Batasuna activists illustrate a considerably more diverse pattern of political participation as well as a higher level of overall protest activity than do those of Sinn Fein activists. In particular, whereas trade union activism was rather limited in the Sinn Fein sample, it was a significant pathway to activism for Herri Batasuna militants. Herri Batasuna appears, therefore, to continue to benefit from the high levels of militant labor activism that have historically characterized the Basque provinces. Zirakzadeh (1991, 67), for example, notes that although less than 11 percent of all industrial workers in Spain lived in the Basque provinces during the 1960s, these provinces accounted for 37 percent of all officially recorded strikes between 1967 and 1974, 30 percent of all workers who went on strike during that period, and 36 percent of all working hours lost as a result of strikes between 1968 and 1974.

Conversely, given Sinn Fein's increasing emphasis on social and economic issues, the relatively low number of members active in trade unions suggests that the party has been unable to persuade trade unionists in Ireland that they offer a credible alternative economic program. Without trade union support, Sinn Fein's ability to capture votes from either the Workers' Party or Labor in the South appears to be extremely limited.

Finally, while fewer than 10 percent of Sinn Fein activists interviewed mentioned participation in an environmental protest, almost all of the Herri Batasuna activists interviewed had participated in antinuclear demonstrations. What appears to have occurred in both the Basque Country and Catalonia, where a number of antinuclear protests also took place, is that Franco's decision to build the plants on the Cantabrian and Mediterranean coasts was viewed both as an attempt to improve the Spanish economy while placing the Catalans and Basques at risk, and as an affront to national sovereignty. In regard to the plant scheduled for construction in the Basque

Country, the choice of the proposed site, Lemóniz, located in the heart of the Vizcayan coast, was hardly a propitious one. The area around Lemóniz is populated by small fishing villages in which a majority of people still speak Basque and felt under threat not only from the Spanish fishing fleets but from those of the other European countries. Thus environmentalism, far from representing a cross-cutting cleavage within Basque society, actually reinforced the identification of Franco with the degradation of the Basque provinces.

These findings suggest that Herri Batasuna and ETA have been able to benefit from a higher level of general social mobilization than has Sinn Fein. They also suggest that contrary to pluralist expectations, class, ethnicity, and environmentalism, rather than reducing conflict by creating cross-cutting cleavages, reinforced anti-Madrid sentiment among a wide sector of society, including non-Basques. This particular confluence of anti-Francoism and Basque ethnicity partly explains the presence within ETA of social-democratic professors of Euskara and militant Spanish trade unionists.

For both Herri Batasuna and Sinn Fein activists, however, participation in protests against the existing regime or in support of those engaged in the armed struggle remained the most frequent precursors to party activism. This finding suggests that antiterrorist strategies that seek to weaken these organizations by reducing the number of potential recruits through intensifying the repression of prisoners are likely to be counterproductive. Although prisoners represent the most vulnerable link in the paramilitary chain, they also represent the most visible victims of government repression. Any attempt, therefore, to manipulate these movements through the coercion of prisoners can, as the H-Block protests proved, serve to increase rather than diminish the flow of recruits into the armed wing of a paramilitary organization. As one Sinn Fein activist told me,

> As far back as you can look in our struggle, the one thing the Brits have never succeeded in doing is criminalizing the IRA. No matter what strategy they have tried, no matter how much repression they have thrown at us, they have never succeeded in convincing the Irish people that the volunteers of Oglaigh na h'Eireann (IRA) are ordinary criminals and that's because as long as this country is divided and there are Brits on the streets, people, even if they disapprove of the IRA activities, understand that the men and women who join the IRA do so not for personal gain but because they wish to see an end to this conflict and division. I think the Brits learned a valuable lesson from the hunger strikes and that is that the prisoners are the heart not only of

the movement but of the communities they come from. Attack the prisoners and you attack their families and communities.[23]

The following section examines the ideological goals of the activists and their preferences for particular strategies, tactics, and organizational form. Based on the activists' positions on these four dimensions, we can reconstruct the purposive motivations of Sinn Fein and Herri Batasuna activists and provide initial insights into internal party divisions.

Ideological Goals: Long and Short-Term Objectives

The stated, long-term objectives of Sinn Fein and Herri Batasuna are, respectively, a united, independent, and socialist Ireland, and a united, independent, and socialist Basque Country, Euskal Herria. Not surprisingly, the overwhelming majority of all activists state that they are active in Sinn Fein and Herri Batasuna because they believe that only their party can achieve their preferred political objective. Within each party, however, various visions exist of what precisely would constitute a "socialist" Ireland or Euskal Herria. Activists also place different values on the class and national components of the long-term goal. While some would be willing to accept an independent, nonsocialist state, others would not view the nationalist struggle as complete until a socialist state had been established.

Sinn Fein: Issues of Class and Nation

The excerpts included below from an internal Sinn Fein education magazine, *Iris Bheag*, illustrate not only the importance of such issues within the party, but also the tensions that such debates can produce. All of the excerpts are from articles that appeared during a series of debates on the relationship between nationalism and socialism.[24]

The initial question in an article by "Tippex," which set the terms of the debate, asked if Sinn Fein would be helping or hindering the advance of its aims by working to bring down Charles Haughey's Fianna Fail government. Noting that Haughey was the most nationalist of the existing government figures, "Tippex" maintained that his downfall would not advance the nationalist struggle; thus it was important for those in Sinn Fein to ask themselves, "[Do] we in Sinn Fein see ourselves as the leading edge of Irish nationalism—republicanism being the more politically advanced form of nationalism, or [do we] see ourselves as a socialist party following the idea of James Connolly that in every oppressed person we see a natural ally, whereas in every capitalist we see an enemy?"[25]

The first two responses that follow are from those who argue that only by becoming an explicitly socialist party will Sinn Fein be able to achieve its stated goals. The third supports the position that nationalism, not socialism, should remain the party's guiding ideology, at least until an independent Ireland is achieved.

> Sinn Fein . . . has a choice. It can decide to be nationalist and not so-cialist, or it can decide to be socialist, which per se requires support for the struggle of national liberation. However, if Sinn Fein opts to be ex-clusively nationalist, it will be identifying with the class interests of the section of the national bourgeoisie or petit bourgeoisie that sees its fu-ture being best advanced by national independence, an expanded share of the domestic trading market, and perhaps economic protectionism. Such a course, if adopted, would take Sinn Fein back into the dark years of Griffith and De Valera. It would mean Sinn Fein support for the exploitation of the futile strategies of the petit-bourgeoisie—militarism and individualist terrorism.[26]

> Sinn Fein is at a decisive phase in its history both in terms of its inter-nal political development and its capacity to shape external political events. The degree to which it succeeds in the former can greatly cur-tail or increase its overall effectiveness. The form and extent of its internal development will therefore determine its external role. . . . Starting from the premise that only a vanguard socialist party, guardian of the interests of the oppressed masses, can be relied upon to remain staunch in the national liberation phase of the freedom struggle, it fol-lows that the transformation of Sinn Fein into a consciously socialist party becomes the primary internal task.[27]

In issue [Iris Bheag] no. 2, "Penfold" warns us of the dangers of being "exclusively" nationalists, as this could lead to a capitalist sellout simi-lar to the 1922 sellout. This would, according to "Penfold," be "in ac-cordance with the dictates of the bourgeois class interests." This idea that Irish nationalism is "bourgeois" is the sort of revisionist nonsense that is actually being pushed today by the Irish "bourgeoisie," who would love us to forget all about being nationalists. If the Irish ruling classes are so keen on Irish freedom, they have been remarkably quiet about it. The truth is of course that the Irish ruling classes are com-posed of both the big native capitalists . . . and the hirelings of multi-nationals and their political spokespersons. . . . Far better to keep Ireland divided and weak in the interests of these vultures. Anyone who is against this conspiracy is a comrade. It doesn't matter whether they are "exclusively" nationalist or not. . . . In issue [Iris Bheag] no. 5, the same theme crops up again. "Aron" states that "nationalism commands the more limited base of support because it works only in the class interests of a few—the native Irish capitalists who stand to gain from breaking out of the British Empire.". . . Aron, apart from the fact that your grasp of present-day economics is about two centuries out of date, your arguments are a scurrilous attack on the primary aim of our movement and an insult to all those who have died for freedom. The primary aim of our movement is national independence and to be free from the political control of British imperialism. At this stage we cannot lay down any conditions about what sort of republic it will be. Anyone who demands that the fight should be for a socialist republic only are actually laying down conditions upon which they will fight imperialism, and are shying away from the struggle. The article by Aron is an attempt to trivialize the whole issue of national freedom. . . . So when you attack Irish Nationalism, you are really doing the Irish bourgeoisie a big favor. They would dearly love that Irish workers should share their hatred for Irish Nationalism. If they cannot achieve this aim by using right-wing slogans, they will attempt it by using slogans and arguments that appear to be left-wing and which "sound" revolutionary. Beware.[28]

Within Sinn Fein, a clear majority perceived nationalism and socialism to be mutually desirable. Only 30 percent of the activists indicated that they would be content with an independent but capitalist Ireland, and none were willing to accept less than a united and independent Ireland, although activists varied considerably regarding support for interim political arrangements necessary to secure a united Ireland. Given the socioeconomic characteristics of Sinn Fein, this finding supports the argument that Sinn Fein competes with the SDLP as much, if not more, along class lines as it does on the issue of Irish independence. Also, the fact that activists with no prior activism who entered the party in the South stated that they did so not because of Sinn Fein's position on the national question but because of its position on social and economic issues suggests that the party has shifted increasingly to the left since 1983, when Gerry Adams succeeded Ó Brádaigh as president. The fact that no activists said they would be content with a divided, if socialist, Republic of Ireland, although several had said that their purpose in joining Sinn Fein had little to do with the national question, suggests that activists begin to associate the goal of social transformation with that of national liberation as a result of their socialization into the party.

The primary cleavage within Sinn Fein is thus between those who perceive the primary objective of the party and the IRA as being the establishment of a united and independent Ireland and those who perceive it as the
social as well as national liberation of Ireland. As we will see in the second
part of this chapter, the strategic and tactical preferences of activists are intimately linked to their ultimate objectives.

Herri Batasuna: Issues of Class and Nation

As noted in chapters 4 and 5, debates within ETA regarding the primacy of
the ethnic/cultural/national struggle or class struggle split the organization
throughout the 1960s and early 1970s. Following ETA's Seventh Assembly
in 1976, the ideological, though certainly not the strategic or organizational,
question was resolved by linking the social and national struggles and defining ETA's role as the defender of the rights of the Basque Working People
(Pueblo Trabajador Vasco). The following resolutions adopted by the assembly demonstrated ETA's commitment to securing an independent and
socialist Basque state:

1. ETA declares itself to be a nationalist Basque organization
   dedicated to the establishment of an independent Basque
   state as the only solution to national oppression.

2. ETA declares itself to be a revolutionary organization at
   the service of the working class, that is, which fights for
   the conquest of power by the popular classes under the
   direction of the workers and supports the establishment
   of a socialist society, which implies the socialization of the
   means of production.

3. ETA proposes, within the limits of bourgeois democracy,
   a strategy of people's power, based on the empowerment
   of the organizations of the Basque popular classes with
   priority on the development of the means of participating
   in the electoral process.[29]

Within Herri Batasuna, the overwhelming majority (70 percent) of activists declared that they were committed to both an independent and socialist Euskal Herria. Only four activists (10 percent) interviewed indicated
they would be satisfied with an independent but capitalist Basque state. The
majority of Herri Batasuna and Sinn Fein activists appear, therefore, to be in
general agreement on both the national and the social and economic goals of
the organization. However, while no Sinn Fein activists indicated that they

would be satisfied with less than a united and independent Ireland, a small percentage of Herri Batasuna activists (5 percent) appeared willing to accept a political arrangement short of independence and to believe that their class interests could be met as a result of social and economic reforms. These activists were asked why they were active in Herri Batasuna rather than in one of the radical Spanish parties, Spanish Communist Movement (Movimiento Comunista de España, MCE) or Revolutionary Organization of Workers (Organización Revoluncionaria de Trabajadores, ORT). Each stated that they believed that Herri Batasuna was the most credible of the three alternatives and the only organization with the potential of implementing any real political changes.

Given the historical ideological incompatibility of nationalism and socialism, both Sinn Fein and Herri Batasuna are interesting examples of organizations that "by redefining ethnic interests in terms used to characterize class positions" (Horowitz 1985, 337) have succeeded in making the class struggle synonymous with the national struggle.

While there is little doubt that a significant proportion of the members of both organizations have, historically, been drawn from and identified with the interests of the working class, the following excerpts from Herri Batasuna and Sinn Fein documents indicate that the decision to ally with workers was also a strategic one made in order to compensate for the lack of sufficient support among members of their ethnic group for the national struggle, particularly when it involved armed resistance to the central state:

> ETA at first attempted to court both the intransigent nationalists who, unfamiliar with the class struggle, maintained a middle-class ideology. However, as repression fell upon us, the reality of the armed struggle taught us that only the workers could respond to this violence. Only the solidarity of the workers could protect us. We realized that only the workers, the small farmers, and other oppressed social groups who also felt the repression of the state had sufficient interests that would lead them to support an armed struggle against the existing system. In Euskadi, where national oppression serves as the catalyst of the armed struggle, the history of ETA had always been a continual and difficult dialogue between nationalists of middle-class origins, but supportive of the armed struggle, and the workers, who represented the only social group capable of giving us refuge and continual support. Finally, after the Fifth Assembly, when ETA declared itself to be a revolutionary organization at the service of the working class and the socialist revolution, the break with our middle-class origins was made. The

origin of this break was our realization that only the workers had sufficient solidarity and interests to continue the armed struggle against the
system.[30]

The Republican Movement has clung to its nationalist ideals, and as
a result contains within its ranks strong influences of the Catholic
church, capitalism, and chauvinism in all senses of the word. This tendency has been diminished in latter years through the purifying effect
of the war in the North, where those engaged in Republican struggle
stood to lose not only their property but their lives. Increasingly, the
"people of no property" are those who identify with the movement.
The movement owes it to those people to ensure that the "new
Ireland" they are fighting for is not the "Nation Once Again," where
the farmers, the property owners, the Church, and the chauvinist interests will simply be substituted for the politicians at Westminster, . . .
but rather the New Ireland will be a social, economic, and political system where the class interests that are served are those of the working
class, women, the old and the sick, and where cultural and other minorities can be recognized. If the aim of the movement is to enlarge
and strengthen the pressure and agitation for a New Ireland, then it
must build a strong working-class movement. This implies . . . that
priority be given to building political strength in the 26 counties and
that much of the political resources of the Republican movement
be devoted to this. . . . We cannot afford to ally ourselves with anti-
working-class interests such as the church or the bourgeoisie. In recent
years there has been a mutual distancing between the bourgeoisie and
the movement, but the movement remains confused and hand-cuffed
by its inability to handle the church. . . . The main argument of this
paper is that what is needed is an all-Ireland political organization which
identifies with the majority North and South and represents their interests. That majority are those people who are gaining least under the
present regime, the working class, male and female, . . . the poor, the
low-paid, the old, the unemployed. In so doing, the Republican movement will pose a greater-than-ever challenge to the State, North and
South.[31]

In many ways, due to their minority position within their ethnonational
group, the leadership of each party faces a dilemma that is somewhat analo-
gous to that of explicitly class-based parties. As Przeworski and Sprague
(1986) have demonstrated, communist and socialist parties are faced with
the perpetual dilemma of choosing strategies that focus on the particular

interests of workers and thus alienate potential allies among the middle class, or strategies that diminish the saliency of class and thereby attract nonworker allies but erode their support among workers. The leadership of Sinn Fein and Herri Batasuna must choose between strategies that stress the ethno-national dimension and thus may alienate potential allies among the radical left, or strategies that stress the class dimension and thus may erode the fundamental sources of their strength among the ethnonational group. The following excerpt from a Sinn Fein discussion document addressing the issue of how Sinn Fein might win some of the SDLP vote illustrates this dilemma:

> Sinn Fein's share of the vote, it must be said, has not dramatically dug into the SDLP votes and does not look like it will succeed in doing so. The question of priorities now must arise. SF must decide on whether they want to be seen as concentrating their energies on the anti-SDLP fight or on the anti-British imperialism fight. Sinn Fein does have the majority of the younger vote and seems set to hold on to this section of the vote. However, there is a danger of alienating older republicans, many of whom, like it or not, dislike the talk of socialism and see the war as the be-all and end-all.[32]

Given that the optimal political environment for both parties would be one in which class and ethnonational interests are perceived as complementary rather than competing, it is not surprising that the political program and strategies of each organization have been designed to foster the image and effect the formation of such an environment. Nor is it surprising that the attempt to reconcile these interests has produced numerous fissures in both organizations.

The examination of the Sinn Fein and Herri Batasuna activists' pathways to participation in the parties provides some important insights into the divergent motivations for participation and illustrates significant differences between those drawn to the organization because of its national/ethnic goals and those who support its class as well as national objectives. The data indicate that 100 percent of the Sinn Fein and Herri Batasuna activists espousing specifically *nationalist* goals had a nationalist family background. A review of each of their biographies revealed that family members active in the 1918–22 Anglo-Irish war or the Irish and Spanish Civil Wars were either still living or had died within the past decade. For those in Sinn Fein, the current campaign for Irish independence clearly represents unfinished business. Although several of these activists mentioned the need for reunification and independence as a means to improve the Irish economy and their own economic circumstances, the overwhelming majority explained the continuation of the conflict in terms of group legitimacy. The two most frequently mentioned justifications for Irish independence were (1) the Irish were in Ireland first; and (2) the Irish were a distinct people with a Gaelic culture with quite different values than those of their Anglo-Saxon oppressors. For these activists, the struggle for Irish independence is not a struggle for material rewards but a contest for worth and place.

In an analysis of young elites in French Canada, Hargrove (1970) found a similar set of sentiments expressed by the most separatist of the elites interviewed. For these activists, the desire for Quebec's independence was the expression of the desire to have a "*société globale*," a distinct and complete social system in which members participate in all aspects from top to bottom. Reaction against the colonial situation has historically thwarted the full development of the colonized culture. Likewise, for those in Herri Batasuna, the threat of being swamped culturally, if not eradication as a distinct people, remains so long as the Basque people lack control of the political mechanisms to ensure their survival, particularly as gauged by the survival of the Basque language. For many of the "culturalists" within Herri Batasuna and ETA, the survival of the Basque language is crucial because it is viewed as being the depository of a unique set of cultural values that differentiate Basques from the other peoples of Spain. As the following excerpts illustrate, the most separatist of the Quebec elites interviewed by Hargrove (1970) shared this perception of the relationship between language, identity, and worth:

> If you reject this [French] background that you have within yourself, you become rootless. You are no longer the same kind of individual. That is what I'm afraid of. I want to learn English, to be able to speak it very well. But I feel as strongly that I must maintain the quality of my French. I've seen French people learn English very well but they no longer know French. It's a pity. They are like a shell with nothing in it. You want to maintain your own values. (481)

Also prominent in the narratives of Sinn Fein and Herri Batasuna activists were references to the sacrifices of family members and friends who had died in prior phases of the conflict. Participation in the current phase is viewed, therefore, as a moral obligation to those who have died in the cause of Irish and Basque independence. This finding provides strong support for the role of collective memory in the intergenerational transfer of ethnic antagonisms and nationalist sentiments and helps to explain the extraordinary persistence of ethnic antipathies. The history of past injustices and, particularly in the Irish and Basque cases, of defeat and domination by those from another ethnic group remains a source of conflict and passion that far exceeds what might be expected to flow from "any fair reckoning" of a conflict of material interests.[33]

The murals of King "Billy" of Orange on the walls in the loyalist ghetto on one side of the "peace" wall, and the murals of Bobby Sands on the walls in the nationalist ghetto on the other side of the "peace" wall are testaments to the influence of the past on the future in Northern Ireland. Similarly, the murals of Gernika and of Santi Brouard, the Herri Batasuna leader assassinated on the day of Franco's death, symbolize the connection between past and present repression of Basques. Indeed, history's control of the present may be the greatest obstacle to the cessation of violence in Northern Ireland and the Basque Country. As Bell (1993) has so eloquently written,

> Ireland has always found hope in history not in the future. . . . Those who control the past determine any future. . . . History is . . . written backwards, a chronicle of winners as losers and losers as just. . . . The future is only prologue to the faith triumphant, triumphant over grievance, triumphant at the end of a long dialectic, the clash of opposites that this last time will let justice win and history end. And if there can be no victory, there can yet be revenge. History in Ireland has yet no end, no tomorrow, no date with hope, no final author. (833)

The most ethnically nationalist of activists were also speakers of their native languages and active in cultural associations.[34] They also came mostly from small, rural communities (less than twenty thousand inhabitants). This finding makes sense, given that in both Ireland and Euskadi, Basque tends to be used more frequently in small, rural communities. A slightly larger number (eleven versus seven) of those within Sinn Fein with a specifically nationalist focus lived in the Republic of Ireland. These activists were somewhat more likely to hold skilled jobs or to be self-employed, and over 80 percent were over the age of forty-five. In sum, the age, academic, and occupational profile of these activists is inconsistent with the argument advanced earlier that linked militant nationalism to youth, the experience of economic deprivation, and the lack of upward mobility. In particular, it is at odds with the view prevalent among "modernization" theorists of ethnic conflict that "it is the competitor within the modern sphere who feels the insecurities of change most strongly and who seeks the communal shelter of tribalism" (Melson and Wolpe 1970, 115).[35]

Yet the profile is consistent with explanations that focus on nationalism as a response to sociocultural threats. The following comments by one of the explicitly avowed Irish "nationalists" I interviewed typify this type of activist:

Lots of people say we need to focus more on the social and economic issues affecting people. They say that the national question isn't an issue for people here in the twenty-six counties. I disagree. I agree that people worry about being able to feed their families, about being forced to emigrate to get work, but the struggle isn't about workers fighting capitalists. The assertion of Ireland's separate national identity is what this struggle is all about. Our very identity as human beings is being attacked. . . . This is why the restoration of the Irish language and every other expression of Irish culture is of such importance to republicanism. National identity is bound up with an individual's identity. If you deny your nationality, you deny your individuality. This is what the Free-staters want. If we lose our national identity but gain higher wages could we say we had won the struggle? Our main task must be to achieve an independent and democratic Ireland. If the Irish people decide that they want a socialist government of our own making, fine. If they don't, I will be content to live with that decision.[36]

Interestingly, these Sinn Fein activists were only slightly more likely (50 percent versus 43 percent) to have been active in the IRA than those claiming to support the goal of both political and social transformation. In Herri Batasuna only one of the four activists in this group had been active in ETA. One possible conclusion is that the propensity to adopt violence as a strategy for securing political goals is not inextricably linked to parochialism or the persistence of nationalist aspirations. Rather, on occasion, it reflects the intensity with which certain goals are held (the fear of extinction, physical or cultural, being one of the most intense) and complex evaluation of the costs and benefits associated with violent and nonviolent strategies for political change.

For the Sinn Fein activists, politics had been tried and found wanting in 1918 when the only all-Irish parliamentary elections were declared null and void. Politics failed again in 1922 and again in 1929 when De Valera, "abandoned the faithful," entered the Irish Parliament, and then turned on his former colleagues in the IRA. Politics had been found wanting again in 1968–69 when the politicals, Goulding and McGiolla, again betrayed the faithful by failing to protect the northern Catholics, and by entering the illegitimate Dail Eireann. Politics, finally, had failed to save the hunger strikers. Conversely, physical force had driven the British to the negotiating table, and bombs, not ballots, had brought down Stormont.

For the Basques, Gernika is a potent symbol of the futility of politics. A bomb under the seat of Admiral Carerro, not ballots, had prevented a fascist from assuming control of Spain after Franco. For the Irish and Basque "faithful," therefore, the most important lessons of history are that only force has weakened the control of the "colonizers." It is for these activists that the words of O'Donnovan Rossa, one of the most famous of the Irish martyrs who died on hunger strike during the Fenian uprising of 1848, ring most true: "It is *not* those who inflict the most suffering, but those who can endure the most who will endure." For these activists, to persist in the struggle is to remain true to the faithful. It is to endure and by enduring win.

In contrast to those with specific national interests, the interview data shows that the majority of those activists who viewed both social and national liberation as their primary objectives were under the age of thirty-five. These activists were also more likely to come from urban than rural areas. Those who did come from rural towns lived, primarily, in areas characterized by a high level of confrontations between IRA and British security forces. Almost 60 percent of these activists also reported personal experiences of physical abuse or detention by state security forces. Forty percent of this group also reported having been a victim or knowing someone who had been a victim of an attack by sectarian or pro-state paramilitary organizations. However, these activists were less likely to have had a nationalist family background (36 percent SF; 50 percent HB). This finding suggests that a commitment to militant nationalism is not limited to those whose families have long been involved in resistance to the state and who continue to express a quasi-religious adherence to past ideals, but is often the response of previously quiescent, apolitical individuals to indiscriminate repression and inadequate policy responses by a central government to the grievances of the minority community. But the willingness of such activists to engage in political struggle indicates a belief in the potential success of resolving issues through mediation and compromise that is not present in those more committed to the ideal republics formulated in 1916 or 1936.

Although this group contained the largest percentage of activists with a university degree, the majority had a middle- or secondary-school education. Also, despite the self-characterization of many of these activists as "urban revolutionaries with no need for Irish," more than one-third of these activists indicated that they knew or were studying Gaelic. Among those studying Gaelic, many stated that they had begun their study of the language because their children attended, or they wished them to attend, the Gaelic medium schools, which have rapidly increased in both size and number during the decade. Many of these activists said that the primary reasons for the dramatic increase in the interest in Gaelic were the identification of the language with the hunger strikers, especially Bobby Sands, and the realization that Gaelic was a weapon that anyone could pick up and use in the fight against the British presence in Ireland. As one activist put it,

> Since partition, the Brits, but especially the unionists, have tried to portray this place as being, to borrow a phrase, "as British as Finchley." They have tried to eliminate everything Irish. Just look how many people have been injured at the funerals of dead [IRA] volunteers because they won't let us drape a tri-color [Irish flag] over the coffins. Our language is something uniquely ours. It's an affirmation that there exists a distinct culture and nation on this island. Every time someone uses an Irish word instead of an English word, he or she is exposing the contradictions in the claim that Ulster is British and as far as I am concerned is putting perhaps a very small, but nonetheless permanent nail in the coffin of British imperialism.[37]

Finally, although the number of activists holding skilled or unskilled jobs was almost equal within the group, a much larger percentage of these activists held unskilled jobs or were unemployed than those in the "pure nationalist" group. On the whole, then, the profile of these activists is consistent with explanations of ethnic violence that focus on cultural as well as economic discrimination by the state against an ethnic minority as factors contributing to the emergence of militant nationalist organizations. In particular, the profiles of both groups underscore the role of state repression in mobilizing support for violent strategies of political protest.

In regard to the small set of activists (four) in Herri Batasuna who indicated they would be willing to accept less than a fully autonomous or independent Basque state, closer review of their biographies revealed that they were first- or second-generation immigrants to the Basque Country. Three, however, had one Basque parent. These activists also had minimal academic qualifications and held manual jobs or were unemployed. None spoke Euskara. However, one activist was sending his child to an *ikastola*,[38] and another was encouraging his children to study Euskara at school. When asked why they were encouraging their children to learn Euskara, both said that they thought it would help their children get a job. At least among second-generation immigrants, therefore, Euskara appears as a key to economic advance as well as a symbol of "Basqueness." In sum, the social background and political experiences of these activists are consistent with the expectation that nonethnic support for radical nationalist parties would be drawn from the sector of the population that was most disadvantaged by the policies of the central government. An unanticipated finding that is consistent with the general profile of Herri Batasuna and Sinn Fein activists is that each activist in this group also indicated that he had been involved in confrontations with the police during strikes or other labor disputes.

Strategies and Structures

The key demand of the Republican Movement is an end to British imperialist influence in Ireland. For "nationalists," this is a demand in itself; for socialists of the "stagist" variety, this is the first step to social-ism; for socialists of the "permanent revolution" variety, this is the weak link in the joint forces of capitalism and imperialism and will be the key to immediate and ongoing revolution.[39]

A second dimension along which activists vary is their support for armed struggle and their attitude toward electoral interventions and participation in the institutions of government. Each organization includes, roughly speak-ing, three groups. The first group, which I refer to as "militarists," believes that armed struggle and mass mobilization are the keys to the success of the nationalist movement and that the needs of the military wing take prece-dence over those of the political wing. They view electoral contests only as means of publicly counting the support for the armed struggle. Electoral politics, in and of themselves, are seen as being incapable of providing any meaningful political change and, more dangerously, as potentially leading to a demobilization of the organization. Consequently, these activists are op-posed to any regularized participation by their elected representatives in po-litical institutions above the level of local government. As one Herri Batasuna activist stated,

> Peoples' victories, the real victories, are won in the streets not in the po-litical institutions. The Basque Parliament has yet to legislate anything of real value to the Basque people, and the problems are just growing larger and larger. Besides, in Euskadi, real politics takes place in the streets. Whatever victories the Basque people, the workers, have won have been won as a result of popular demonstrations. The real political confrontations don't take place in Parliament. They take place between those demanding their rights on the streets and those who would deny them their rights sitting comfortably in Gasteiz or Madrid.[40]

In the Irish case, activists in this group would be opposed on principle to participation by Sinn Fein in either a new Northern Ireland government or in Westminster. Many within this group also disagreed with the 1986 de-cision to participate in the Irish Parliament but remained within the party. In the Basque case, these activists would be opposed to Herri Batasuna's participation in either the Spanish, Basque, or Foral Parliament of Navarra. A Sinn Fein discussion document on electoralism provides another apt characterization of the "militarist" position:

> A revolutionary movement either succeeds or fails badly. There is hardly an in-between position. So many things are put at risk that often failure or the possibility of failure can inveigle some participants into reformism in order to "save something from the collapse," as it is put. Constitutional nationalists, repealers, homerulers, etc., of so many hues, of course do so and in all cases, without exception, were sucked into and became part of the colonial or neocolonial system. That is what the parliamentary system is designed for and well it does their work. The Sinn Fein attitude has been that taking part in local councils is as near to that system—which we seek to replace—as we dare go. Even at that time we have trouble from some of our councilors from time to time. Strict discipline and control of our councilors is very necessary at all stages. Abstention from taking part in enemy parliaments has a definite role in maintaining Sinn Fein's nonconformism with regard to such institutions and the system they bolster and perpetuate. The lesson which Sinn Fein seeks to drive home is that switching the personnel operating such institutions or even replacing them with well-meaning and politically educated Republican personnel may ameliorate conditions from time to time, but will not and cannot, because of the nature of those institutions, bring about the fundamental changes needed to put the Irish people in control of their own affairs. A big and successful heave to topple and replace is what is needed rather than tinkering with the existing system. . . . Slow growth is not possible through parliamentary elections. Electoral defeat or sidetracking into fragmentation and reformism will be the price to be paid for attempting this. Electoral interventions can be partially successful in the short term but highly dangerous for the movement engaging in them. In a revolutionary movement, elections are not the dynamic.[41]

The second group, which I refer to as "paramilitarists," is also committed to the armed struggle but views mass mobilization and electoral politics as being equally important to the success of the nationalist movement. For these activists, participation or nonparticipation in existing political institutions is a matter of tactics rather than an issue of principle: "Elections do have a part to play in our strategy, but only if we ensure that we use them properly. That requires that we develop a disciplined movement guided by well-defined and coherent revolutionary ideology."[42]

The attitudes of "paramilitarists" were remarkably similar in both Sinn Fein and Herri Batasuna. The first pair of responses that follow describes how these activists viewed the role of electoral politics in capitalist democracies. The second pair addresses their fear regarding the dangers that becoming too involved in electoral politics could pose for a militant organization:

> SF: In capitalist societies elections are used to create the impression that the people have a say in who governs them. That's actually a false impression. The ruling classes who exploit the minority have absolutely no intention of ever giving up their position regardless of the outcome of any election. I mean, if there was ever any danger of the system coming under threat through elections you can be sure they would be done away with. . . . For example, I think it was Kissinger who said regarding Chile under Allende, "I don't see why we have to stand by and watch a country go communist due to the irresponsibility of its own people." In other words, elections are a great democratic achievement, so long as the right results occur. Elections are really a way of maintaining control over society without having to visibly coerce people. If you can make people believe that by voting one out of every four or five years they are good citizens, well then the real powers that be can go quietly about their business of exploiting the wealth of the people. I read a joke somewhere that pretty much sums up my attitude towards elections: "If voting could change things, it would be banned."[43]

> HB: The other parties accuse HB of being "antidemocracy" because we do not participate in parliament. The other parties are afraid of us because we have succeeded in revealing just what a sham our so-called democracy is. We show people that elections in capitalist democracies don't really give people a voice in the decision-making process. Our so-called representative democracy doesn't represent the people. It represents the real powers in this state: the army, the industrialists, the financial oligarchs. Look at what "representative" politics really does to people. It doesn't give them more power. If anything, it makes them feel powerless to do anything on their own. It makes people believe that political problems can only be solved through elected representatives. This makes people believe that politicians are there to deal with their problems, and they the people are powerless to do anything without them. Thus, parliamentary politics makes the people feel dependent on their elected representatives to solve their problems, and this is exactly what capitalist democracies want to achieve: to assure that the people never, never become aware of their own power, because, if they

did they might realize the revolutionary potential that might really change things.[44]

SF: Our participation in elections has not only enabled us to quantify our support but also to force the SDLP to adopt a more nationalist position, which will sooner or later expose the contradictions within that party. However, we have to be aware that electoralism also poses a number of potential problems, probably the most dangerous of which is that winning elections becomes an end in itself rather than a means to a much more important end. As a revolutionary party, we must be very careful that we do not perpetuate a system in which the people are kept powerless. If we do, then we are really just undermining our own struggle.[45]

HB: As a revolutionary party, we must be different from the other parties. We must use elections as a means for mobilizing people, for making them aware of their own power, for exposing the existing system for the pseudo-democracy it is. We must make sure that we are not perpetuating the view that the people are powerless to deal with their own problems. We have to make sure that winning votes never dictates our actions. Elections for a revolutionary movement should only be about increasing people's awareness of their own power. That's what poses the greatest threat to Gasteiz and Madrid.[46]

The third group, or "electoralists," is composed of those who view the popular and electoral struggle of Sinn Fein and Herri Batasuna as the key to political victory. For these activists, the armed struggle of the IRA or ETA, although never repudiated (particularly for internal political reasons), represents a serious impediment to the political advance of the organization and its ability to negotiate resolution to the current conflicts. The following suggestion, presented by a Sinn Fein activist in *Iris Bheag,* for the formation of a new party to be allied with Sinn Fein indicates the difficulties these activists associated with the party's support for the armed struggle:

A gap has opened in the political spectrum to the Left and Green of Fianna Fail and to the constitutional right of Sinn Fein. It sits there unoccupied. The gap was created by the yuppification and de-republicanizing of Fianna Fail. Voters will not, in practice, cross that gap in one stride to vote for us—they need a stepping stone. There is, in my view, an urgent need to fill that gap with a new political party, a political party which neither condemns nor condones militant republican activity in the six counties but which cannot be held directly responsible for it. Such a party could make very rapid progress, and its success would be clearly advantageous to us.[47]

The following excerpt from an interview with a long-time Herri Batasuna activist reveals similar sentiments:

> I think that we in HB underestimated the impact of the anti-ETA pact on our support. It has fixed in the public's mind the identification of HB with ETA, which is of course what the Spanish government wants, that is, to shift the image of the struggle from one of a Basque-Spanish confrontation to one of a radical "antidemocratic" Basque versus democratic Basque confrontation. While our militants see very well what the government is up to, it is more difficult for some of our supporters to join in our marches or to vote for us, and that's where our real power lies. That's where we get our power to pressure the Basque and Spanish governments to negotiate a political solution to the current conflict. I mean, when the government eventually negotiates, it will be because of popular demonstrations in favor of negotiation, not because of some new ETA operation. The government can handle ETA. What it can't ignore is 200,000 votes and 100,000 people on the streets demanding some sort of negotiated settlement. Our strength, but also our dilemma, is that many [people] turn out for our marches because they support ETA. So ETA needs us, and we need ETA. But we need an ETA that is very, very careful in its operations.[48]

Table 5.6 indicates the percentage of each type of activist among the Sinn Fein and Herri Batasuna interview samples and among the Herri Batasuna survey sample.[49]

Looking first at the distribution of all activists, we note that as one might anticipate, the overwhelming majority supported the armed struggle of the

Table 5.6. Distribution of Sinn Fein and Herri Batasuna Activists by Strategic Preference

Type	SF (N=60)	HB (N=40)	HB (N=117)	Total (N=217)
Militarists	33%	52%	50%	45%
Paramilitarists	57	30	33	40
Electoralists	10	18	17	15

Source: Author's interviews with Sinn Fein and Herri Batasuna activists (columns 1–2); HB survey (column 3).

IRA and ETA. What appears most clearly to divide militant nationalists is their perception of the role of electoral struggle and their positions on participation in existing political institutions.

Looking individually at Sinn Fein and Herri Batasuna, we see that each had a distinct distribution of each type of activist. In Sinn Fein, for example, paramilitarists were in a hegemonic position. But militarists, who represented one-third of the activists, retained considerable power because their exit could potentially have crippled the organization. In terms of Sinn Fein's strategy of electoral mobilization, this finding suggests that any further moves on the part of the current leadership to involve Sinn Fein in institutional politics would have required persuading a majority of the militarists that fundamental organizational principles were not being compromised and that any decrease in the level of armed struggle would be offset by significant tangible political gains.

In contrast to Sinn Fein, militarists outnumbered paramilitarists in Herri Batasuna. Nevertheless, the party contained a larger percentage of activists who were opposed, either on principle or strategically, to the use of violence to secure political goals and who would support more extensive involvement in institutional politics than did the Sinn Fein sample. This mix of activists illustrates the greater complexity of the internal politics of Herri Batasuna and why it has been considerably more susceptible to rapid changes in its political environment than has Sinn Fein.

Table 5.7 indicates that the choice of strategy is, indeed, linked to an activist's pathway to activism. Militarists, as hypothesized, were the most likely to have had a nationalist family background and to be the most "ethnic" in the sense of being speakers of their native languages. This finding underscores the significance of the apprehension of cultural submergence with its concomitant loss of self-worth and self-identity as an explanation for the intensity of the violence directed against the majority by the minority, despite the enormous costs to the minority.

Horowitz (1985, 180), for example, notes that "so much hostility can only be justified if there is a large threat emanating from the target of aggression." In regard to the distribution of activists with IRA experience, a closer examination of their biographies revealed that, although there was some overlap in their period of service in the IRA, there were two distinct generations of activists, with paramilitarists being most representative of those who joined the IRA as young men and women in the 1970s. Since the 1970s was a period of massive mobilization by the nationalist community and intense IRA activity, this finding is consistent with the hypothesis that repressive force, if it is applied indiscriminately and without sufficient magnitude,

Table 5.7. Pathways to Activism by Strategic Preference

Pathway	Militarists			Paramilitarists			Electoralists		
	SF (N=20)	HB (N=21)	All (N=41)	SF (N=34)	HB (N=12)	All (N=46)	SF (N=6)	HB (N=7)	All (N=13)
Nationalist Family	78%	50%	56%	50%	29%	46%	10%	21%	21%
IRA/ETA	45	36	16	55	17	41	0	0	0
Fluency in Irish/Euskara Cultural SMO	65	65	63	35	45	43	10	0	7
Trade Union	6	64	31	25	56	31	0	25	29
Other SMO	33	65	47	55	80	69	50	40	50
Other Party	0	0	0	6	8	7	33	25	29
No Prior Activism	0	0	0	8	8	8	50	50	50

Note: SMO = Social Movement Organization.
Source: Author's interviews with Sinn Fein and Herri Batasuna activists.

serves to radicalize and mobilize rather than demoralize and demobilize opposition to the state.

The 1970s also witnessed the shift of the center of conflict from the rural areas of Northern Ireland to the nationalist "ghettoes" in Belfast and Derry. Consequently, the generation of nationalists joining the IRA from those areas was as aware of the economic injustices of the Northern Irish state as they were of the political injustice and physical repression that maintained the desperate inequalities in employment and housing conditions for nationalists. Also, the early success of the Diplock courts and "supergrass" trials in securing convictions of IRA activists had the perhaps unanticipated result of providing this generation of activists with the opportunity while imprisoned to study the works of other revolutionaries and to analyze the development of other anticolonial and nationalist movements. The works of Marx, Lenin, Mao, Marighella, Guevera, Fanon, Cabral, and others, as well as the writings of the Irish socialists James Connolly and Peadar O'Donnell, were brought back into the mainstream of republican politics. Connolly's statement that the "cause of Ireland is the cause of Labor and the cause of Labor is the cause of Ireland" slowly began to be heard along with the omnipresent chant of "Brits Out." Nationalist mobilization on social and economic issues as well as the national question helped to bring republicans out of their militarist isolation, with the result that the movement was infused with new perspectives and new members from nonrepublican backgrounds who, as one activist stated, "did not share the traditional republican's disdain and/or fear of politics." Not surprisingly, then, data from the interviews with Sinn Fein activists indicated that paramilitarists in Sinn Fein were more than twice as likely as other activists to have been active in other social movement protests or involved in trade unions.

Even this group of activists, however, was somewhat less likely than their Herri Batasuna counterparts to have been active in other social movement organizations or trade unions. Perhaps the most striking difference between the two sets of activists is the generally higher level of participation in social movement protests among the Herri Batasuna interview sample.

An analysis of the Herri Batasuna survey data indicates a similar level of participation in other social movement organizations and acts of political protest among the broader population of activists.[50] Thus one possible explanation for the fact that Herri Batasuna, despite the dominance of militarists within the organization, has not been isolationist is that its activists are extensively interconnected with other social movement organizations.

Tactics

Although conditioned by strategy, tactics are not identical with strategy and therefore represent a third dimension by which to distinguish activists. The first group, which I have labeled "opportunists," supports the formation of broad-front alliances that focus primarily on the issue of self-determination. They believe that only a movement that mobilizes a broad cross-section of society will be sufficiently powerful to extract political concessions from the central governments.

> I think the key to our success is that the Basque Movement for National Liberation has as its central demand the right to national self-determination. Such a demand allows the broadest possible involvement by Basques. It appeals to all those who have a common interest in getting rid of imperialism, Spanish, European, or otherwise. It is something that workers, small farmers, fishermen, and small business people understand and are willing to fight for. National self-determination is a principle that can be supported by nationalists, patriots, socialists and nonsocialists.[51]

The second group, which I refer to as "pragmatists," supports alliances with both class and nationalist allies but prefers to ally with those who share the organization's class interests. These activists, in general, fear that too heterogeneous an organization will be both less efficient and more prone to factionalization. Thus they choose to ally with the more radical sectors in society:

> The desired social composition of the republican movement must surely consist of as broad a section of the oppressed people as possible, that is, working class, small farmers, petite bourgeoisie, and substrata. There is no advantage, only disadvantage, to be gained by having capitalists in the movement. Moreover the dominant voice and ideology within the movement should be that of the revolutionary socialist working class. . . . There can be no cessation in the ideological conflict between the socialist party and the parties of capitalism, Fianna Fail, Fine Gael, the Progressive democrats, or the bourgeois social reformist Workers' Party and Labor. A socialist party that ceases to engage the parties of capitalist or social reformist ideologically ceases to be socialist. That does not preclude, however, tactical alliances or agreements of a temporary nature, provided such alliances or agreements [further] the strategic objective of the revolutionary movement, are fully in accordance with and do not compromise any part of the revolutionary program or organization of the working class.[52]

The analysis of the interview and survey data shows that the distribution of the two groups among the Sinn Fein and Herri Batasuna activists interviewed was somewhat different.[53] On the whole, Sinn Fein activists were more willing to support pan-nationalist, broad-front campaigns than the Herri Batasuna activists. This finding is consistent with the fact, noted above, that a larger percentage of activists within Sinn Fein supported purely nationalist objectives. It is also consistent with the expectation that paramilitarists seek to expand the organization's base of support. Given the small size of the interview sample, the slight variation in the proportion of pragmatists and opportunists could be due to chance, but it could also suggest that party elites are somewhat more committed to the party's political goals.

Further analysis of the data revealed that tactical preferences are, indeed, linked to specific strategic choices. In both Sinn Fein and Herri Batasuna, militarists were more likely to be pragmatists (70 percent), while paramilitarists were more frequently opportunists (85 percent). From the distribution of activists in Sinn Fein, it is reasonable to assume that Sinn Fein's preferred strategy would include moral support for the armed struggle, active participation in electoral politics, and participation in pan-nationalist political fronts. Conversely, the distribution of activists in Herri Batasuna suggests that Herri Batasuna would pursue a strategy of limited institutional participation and participation in popular campaigns with other radical organizations that expressed strong commitment to the armed struggle of ETA. The Sinn Fein and Herri Batasuna strategy documents and actual strategic choices examined in the next chapter enable us to assess how well our analysis of activist preferences is reflected in official doctrine and actual party actions.

Organization

Both Sinn Fein and Herri Batasuna explicitly reject the image of the traditional bureaucratic party. Herri Batasuna, for example, defines itself not as a political party but as a "historical alliance between the workers and the populist groups." Their entry into electoral politics, however, has fostered divisions within each organization between activists who prefer a more open, movement-style organization that encourages the participation of members with divergent beliefs and the participation of grassroots members in policy formation and decision-making processes. As one Herri Batasuna member stated, "Some of us believe strongly that Herri Batasuna should not function as a formal or bureaucratic organization but as a social movement, and others might prefer a more professional, internally cohesive, highly disciplined, 'efficient' party." The following statement by another activist clearly illustrates this view:

> We all know that winning elections is more a consequence of what goes on in the party between elections, rather than during the campaign. One of our greatest internal needs is the development of a more permanent and professionalized head office staff, a middle leadership, and a more formalized and efficient set of party structures.[54]

Thus, a final way to distinguish activists concerns their view of how the party should be organized. For those favoring the more participatory organization, a key concern was the lack of communication between the various levels of the organization. "The organizational form of Herri Batasuna is somewhat idiosyncratic. It is more complicated than that of a regular political party. Here, there is more interaction, a different dialectic between the leadership and the different levels of the party. This form is certainly richer, but it is also more complicated and sometimes inhibiting."[55]

For many within this group in both parties, communication was inadequate in both directions. However, in both parties only a small minority of activists viewed the communications problems as the result of a deliberate attempt by the national leadership to exert its control over the organization or the inability or unwillingness of local activists to deal with issues of national importance. Rather, the majority of activists viewed the national office's need to make quick decisions as the principal impediment to greater grassroots involvement in the decision-making process. Also, as the excerpts below (the first from Sinn Fein and the second from Herri Batasuna) reveal, activists and national leaders in both organizations shared the view that the party relied too much on a few national political leaders and that stronger and more active leadership had to be developed at the local and middle levels of the organization:

> Although Sinn Fein is a 32-county organization, it has been as subject to the uneven development of the two statelets as any other aspect of life on the island, and one way in which this unevenness expresses itself is in terms of a problem of public leadership. The organization in the 26 counties is in a relatively retarded position and lacks its own identifiable leadership. There are very many able people in the membership and in local leadership positions who are not publicly identifiable outside of their own areas. There are members with plenty of ability, talent, and commitment who nevertheless might not even be known by most other Sinn Fein members. And this is a problem which has special importance in terms of our ability to field and develop candidates for local elections.[56]

> One of the reasons for our restructuring in 1988 was the realization that we needed to be better prepared for the institutional struggle which would . . . accompany and follow the negotiation of the KAS Alternative by Madrid and ETA. For many years the leadership of Herri Batasuna had depended on a number of notable figures, which gave the movement a readily identifiable face. What we realized, though, was that in addition to these people, we needed to prepare a staff of people who would be prepared to deal with social, environmental, economic, as well as political issues once political resolution [was] negotiated.[57]

Among the principal concerns of those preferring a more ideologically homogeneous, disciplined, and centralized party organization was the need to project a coherent party platform at all levels of the organization. As one Sinn Fein activist noted, "Given the lack of coordination between cummains (local party units) and head office and even between Sinn Fein officers in different areas of the country, we have often found ourselves in the situation where people are putting out entirely contradictory statements on the same issue. Now, clearly, that doesn't make us look very organized or credible in the eyes of potential supporters."[58] Similarly, one of the stated goals of Herri Batasuna's reorganization in 1988 was "to carry out an extensive debate with the aim of taking all the different political views and opinions into consideration and deciding on the specific direction in which we wish to move."[59]

Of the four dimensions analyzed, this dimension was clearly the most divisive in both Sinn Fein (53 percent participatory, 47 percent efficient) and Herri Batasuna (41 percent participatory, 59 percent efficient). In both Sinn Fein and Herri Batasuna, militarists were most likely to prefer an ideologically homogeneous organization that functions as the vanguard of the popular struggle. Given the dependence of the military organization on the support of the people, militarists are committed to building an organization that can effectively mobilize activists for demonstrations in support of the military organization and its goals. Paramilitarists, on the other hand, are committed not only to providing political support for the armed struggle but also to building a party that will be successful in elections and is prepared to assume a role in government once its key political demands have been met. In order to attract supporters and involve large numbers of people in the political struggle, paramilitarists seek to involve the membership as much as possible in the construction of the party. From this perspective, the more "efficient" outlook of Herri Batasuna and the more "participatory" outlook of Sinn Fein are consistent with the distribution of militarists and paramilitarists within the two organizations.

Despite the difference of opinion among activists regarding the ideal degree of internal democracy and efficiency, all activists agreed that the ability of the organization to recruit and keep members was seriously affected by the level of state repression its members experienced. Without exception, the activists interviewed recounted examples of attacks on their members and attempts by the police to intimidate the families or employers of prospective members.

> HB: The only organizational problem we have is the terrorism of the State. People are afraid to attend local party meetings. They are constantly watched, and many are detained and abused in jail. Fear and repression [are things that] every HB activist must learn to deal with no matter at what level they are active.[60]

> SF: It is essential that Sinn Fein in the 26 counties take on and defeat intimidation of new members, and so on by the *Gardai*. This is much more important than the possible loss of new members. It is a matter of accepting or rejecting semicriminal status in the minds of ourselves, the *Gardai*, and the general public. Likewise, any moves against Sinn Fein members in their employment must be fought.[61]

Activists in both organizations noted that the "criminalization" of their organizations by the state and other political parties had often restricted their participation in popular protest on a partisan basis. As one Sinn Fein activist stated, "Our participation could conceivably be used by the government as a reason to dismiss the aims of those protesting as yet another IRA plot."[62] Many activists in both Sinn Fein and Herri Batasuna felt that the question of whether, or when, to participate in a movement with or without explicit partisan identification was one of the most important issues that needed to be more fully discussed by the membership. Those in favor of participating with an explicit partisan identification argued that even if they were the only political "party" participating in a popular protest, they should identify themselves, since not to do so might allow other parties to take credit for any political changes resulting from the protest. In particular, these activists felt that too often members who had provided much of the support for protests did not receive any credit for their participation. The following comment from a Sinn Fein activist critical of the party's tendency not to call attention to itself within broad-front campaigns clearly illustrates this position:

> In reference to the Single European Act campaign in 1987, the policy of not having a distinct Sinn Fein position in the campaign was defended at the time on the grounds that it would be opportunist to project Sinn Fein at the expense of working towards the greatest possible no vote. This is bad political reasoning. It presupposes that once SF identifies with a cause, we automatically weaken support for that cause. On this reasoning we should go home. . . . What did we lose by not having a Sinn Fein campaign, as well as participating in the broad campaign[?] [W]e left the way open to the Workers' Party to become the uncontested . . . political leadership of the opposition to the establishment parties.[63]

Ideologues, Radicals, and Politicos

Having reviewed the strategic, tactical, and organizational outlooks of Sinn Fein and Herri Batasuna activists, we can now determine the relative strength of ideologues, radicals, and politicos in each organization by combining these three dimensions. If most of the activists can be described by these types, then the types are useful for an analysis of intraparty dynamics. Table 5.8 is designed to test this claim.

In militant nationalist organizations, ideologues are those who are committed to the strategies of armed struggle and popular mobilization. They support participation in elections but reject participation in institutions and prefer an ideologically homogeneous organization and efficient organization. Among the activists, 29 percent fit into this category. The largest percentage of this group are Herri Batasuna activists. A second group of "near-ideologues," all Herri Batasuna activists, accounts for an additional 3 percent of the sample. These activists also prefer a more militant and homogeneous organization, but are strongly committed to internal party democracy.

Radicals value the armed struggle as well, but are equally committed to the strategies of popular mobilization and electoral politics. They support a more active participation in political institutions, although they reject participation in the institutions of the central government. They also prefer an inclusive and democratic organization that involves as much of the membership as possible in the decision-making process. This group of activists, together with "near-radicals," who prefer a more efficient organization to a more participatory one, account for 40 percent of the sample. Sinn Fein activists, who make up the majority of this group, are almost twice as likely to be radicals as Herri Batasuna activists.

Finally, politicos are opposed, for moral or tactical reasons, to the use of violence to secure political goals. They prefer strategies that focus on popular mobilization and electoral struggle. They are most concerned with securing tangible political gains and thus prefer a more professional and efficient party organization. They also prefer an inclusive organization, but if ideological homogeneity is necessary for the success of the organization, they are willing to accept restrictions on membership. These activists, including "near-politicos," represent 10 percent of the total sample and are equally distributed in Sinn Fein and Herri Batasuna. If we consider only their strategic preferences, it is interesting to note that Herri Batasuna activists are twice as likely (20 percent) as Sinn Fein activists (10 percent) to view political violence as an ineffective strategy for securing organizational goals.

In sum, ideologues, radicals, and politicos represent six of the twelve cells in Table 5.8 but 82 percent of the activists, leaving only 18 percent distributed among the remaining six cells, none of which contains more than 5 percent of the activists. Ideologues, radicals, and politicos thus appear to be empirically significant types of militant nationalist activists.[64]

An examination of the distribution of the three types of activists according to their political objectives provides us with an additional insight into the strategic choices of militant nationalist parties (see table 5.9). Given the reality that ethnic and national conflicts are more often fought over "either/or" rather than "more or less" issues, the dominance of militarists among those with primarily nationalist objectives is consistent with our expectations.

Table 5.8. Distribution of Ideologues, Radicals, and Politicos in Sinn Fein and Herri Batasuna

	Participatory		Efficient	
	Opportunists	Pragmatists	Opportunists	Pragmatists
Militarists	SF 6% (N=4) HB 2% (N=1) All 5% (N=5)	SF — HB 7% (N=3) All 3% (N=3) **Near-ideologues**	SF 3% (N=2) HB 5% (N=2) All 4% (N=4)	SF 23% (N=14) HB 38% (N=15) All 29% (N=29) **Ideologues**
Paramilitarists	SF 40% (N=24) HB 23% (N=9) All 33% (N=33) **Radicals**	SF 5% (N=3) HB 2% (N=1) All 4% (N=4)	SF 8% (N=5) HB 5% (N=2) All 7% (N=7) **Near-radicals**	SF 3% (N=2) HB — All 2% (N=2)
Electoralists	SF — HB — All —	SF 1% (N=1) HB 5% (N=2) All 3% (N=3)	SF 7% (N=4) HB 10% (N=4) All 8% (N=8) **Politicos**	SF 1% (N=1) HB 2% (N=1) All 2% (N=2) **Near-politicos**

Source: Author's interviews with Sinn Fein and Herri Batasuna activists.

Table 5.9. Distribution of Subgroup Types by Political Objectives

Subgroup Types	Political Objectives		
	Independence SF (N=18) HB (N=4)	National and Social Liberation SF (N=42) HB (N=32)	Socialism and Autonomy HB (N=4)
Ideologues and Near-Ideologues	SF 44% HB 50 All 45	SF 14% HB 40 All 26	SF — HB — All —
Radicals and Near-Radicals	SF 22 HB 25 All 23	SF 48 HB 25 All 37	SF — HB 25% All 25
Politicos and Near-Politicos	SF 5 HB — All 4	SF 12 HB 13 All 12	SF — HB 50 All 50

Source: Author's interviews with Sinn Fein and Herri Batasuna activists. Percents do not sum to 100 since some activists do not fit into one of these types.

These activists can make no compromise with the state from which they are trying to separate. The only issues amenable to negotiation and compromise concern the terms and timing of the withdrawal of the occupying forces and the establishment of a new, sovereign government. For these activists, there is nothing to be gained from participation in the institutions of "foreign" government, and because they represent a minority within the "foreign" state, parliamentary politics and the prospect of being a small, permanent opposition offer few incentives for adopting an electoralist strategy. In this situation, where insurgent nationalists must choose between armed struggle and mass mobilization, the state's actions can have a significant effect on the organization's choice of strategy. Attempts to suppress the demands of the minority through the use of extreme repressive force are likely to enhance the influence of the militarists and lead them to adopt a strategy of armed struggle and terrorism. At this point, the state must either erode its own civil liberties to exert the repressive force sufficient to crush the nationalist movement, or accept a situation, such as that in Northern Ireland, where the political violence is reduced to levels "acceptable" to all parties in the conflict. Conversely, if a state chooses not to repress a militant nationalist movement, it may or may not be contributing to its eventual division. As Zariski (1989, 264) has noted, "[T]he nature of the long-term relationship between central government intransigence and repression, central concessions to ethnoterritorial demands following periods of repression, and the degree of ethnic extremism" has not been sufficiently explored. The fact that the overwhelming majority of activists in both Sinn Fein and Herri Batasuna reported the experience of state repression as a factor motivating their commitment to an independent Ireland or Euskal Herria and their participation in Sinn Fein and Herri Batasuna suggests at least that state repression serves only to drive challengers underground and sustain a period of uneasy peace. Also, the fact that most activists in both Sinn Fein and Herri Batasuna cited the experience of discrimination on the basis of cultural markers, particularly in terms of educational and economic opportunities, as well as the inability to resolve any of these issues through legitimate political means as reasons for their commitment to armed struggle suggests that by negotiating some devolution of power to minority groups and implementing policies designed to address specific cultural and economic concerns of the minority group central governments could at least enhance the influence of the paramilitarist and politicos within nationalist movements and thus perhaps reduce the level of separatist violence and encourage the participation of the militant nationalists in the political process.

Summary

The analysis of the ideological, strategic, tactical, and organizational preferences of activists in militant nationalist organizations has demonstrated the utility of disaggregating the activists into subgroups. This allows us to interpret variations in party organization and strategy in a more meaningful way. It suggests that Herri Batasuna is likely to continue to implement a strategy designed to mobilize a mass movement in support of ETA and of the demand for Basque independence, and to participate only on a limited basis in either Basque or Spanish political institutions. With regard to Sinn Fein, this analysis suggests that the party will have difficulty abandoning its support for a mixed strategy of armed struggle and electoral mobilization while attempting to increase its participation in the parliamentary process. In sum, it appears that Sinn Fein is becoming increasingly committed to a strategy of demilitarization, political mobilization, and negotiation, while Herri Batasuna remains divided regarding the relative merit of institutional politics as a means of securing movement goals and remains dependent upon the armed struggle of ETA and the state's response to that struggle to mobilize support for radical Basque nationalist goals. This analysis also illustrates an association between activists' social and political backgrounds and their strategic orientations and suggests linkages between external conditions (regime responsiveness, the existence and strength of competing nationalist organizations) and the relative strength of the interparty groups. Chapter 6 aims to establish more precisely the relationship between macro-political factors and the relative strength of intraparty groups in Sinn Fein and Herri Batasuna.

6

Regime Responsiveness, Recruitment, and Movement Strategies

Chapter 5 empirically identified three types of movement activists with distinct political, strategic, tactical, and organizational preferences. Each type was also shown to be associated with a particular social background and pattern of prior political experience. But merely identifying different types of activists does not explain or predict the size and influence of a particular group in a specific situation. Nor does it provide us with much analytical understanding of why specific intraorganizational coalitions emerge, dominate, or decline.

Although the skills and choices of individual activists are important in the formation of internal coalitions, strategic situations clearly influence not only the relative strength of each subgroup of movement activists, but also their propensity to form coalitions and to shape the movement leadership. The main hypothesis of this study is that the relative strength of ideologues, radicals, and politicos is influenced by the degree of regime responsiveness, organizational resources, and the absence or presence and relative strength of competing organizations. Each of these variables is, of course, partly endogenous, influenced by the organization's past strategic and policy choices, which define the boundaries of its constituency and contribute, if not to the creation, at least to the exploitation of shifts in the structure of political opportunities. The aim of this chapter is to assess the relationship between shifts in these macropolitical factors, the distribution of ideologues, radicals, and politicos in Sinn Fein and Herri Batasuna, and the strategies adopted by each organization.

In chapter 2, I argued that in periods characterized by high levels of state repression, revolutionary nationalist organizations are most likely to attract ideologues and radicals, who will prefer a strategy focused primarily on an armed confrontation with the state, while politicos are most likely to enter during periods of greater regime openness. Examining the activists' social background and political experiences prior to becoming active in Sinn Fein or Herri Batasuna provided considerable evidence of a link between the personal experience of state repression and participation in militant nationalist organizations.

In what follows, I relate the level of state repression, as measured by the number of politically motivated deaths, arrests, and the use of special, emergency-powers laws, to the entry of each subgroup of activists into the political organization. In the process I also analyze the geographic distribution of IRA and ETA prisoners and the relationship between the level of support for the IRA and ETA as measured by the vote for Sinn Fein and Herri Batasuna, and the geographic distribution of IRA and ETA attacks.

Northern Ireland

Table 6.1 provides a brief overview of the major stages in the Northern Ireland conflict for the period 1969–89. Although the longitudinal division of a conflict is somewhat arbitrary, each of the phases outlined below was characterized by a particular set of political demands, strategies, and tactics adopted by nationalists and a specific set of political and security responses by the Northern Ireland and British governments.

Stage 1: Asserting Civil Rights

During stage 1, the IRA, which was still recovering from the effects of the disastrous 1956–62 border campaign, remained quiescent. Until 1968, Northern Ireland experienced a relative calm punctuated by rumblings of nationalist discontent. These rumblings would ultimately take form as the demands for one person, one vote; the remapping of gerrymandered electoral boundaries; the enactment of antidiscrimination laws; the establishment of government machinery to address citizens' complaints; a point system, based on need, for the allocation of housing; the repeal of the Special Powers Act; and the abolition of the B-Specials, the all-Protestant reserve security. The end to partition was deliberately excluded from the list of demands in order to demonstrate that the protestors were seeking to democratize, not overthrow, the existing state. The Civil Rights Campaign resulted in a massive mobilization of the nationalist community.

Despite the fact that the Civil Rights Campaign had not included the national issue in its agenda and, like its American counterpart, had adopted

Table 6.1. Overview of British and Irish Security Policy, 1969–1989

Dates	Period	Official Policy	Legal Basis	Abuses
1968–70	Civil Rights Campaign	Policing by RUC and B-Specials Joint control by army and RUC UDR replaces B-Specials	Special Powers Act Public Order Acts Reports: Cameron Report, 1969; Scarman Inquiry, 1969–72	Loyalist pogroms in nationalist Belfast Massive evacuations Loyalist attacks on Civil Rights activists
1971–75	Internment Mass civil disorder Diplock Courts Normalization	Elimination of IRA Arrest and internment of all SF/IRA leaders and activists. All IRA members tried as ordinary criminals in Diplock courts. Eire /Reenactment of Offenses Against the State Act, which allows for detentions and trials outside of the normal legal & judicial procedures	Detention Order, 1972 Emergency Provisions Act, 1973 and 1975 Prevention of Terrorism Act/Reports 1971: Compton 1972: Parker, Widgery, Diplock	Indiscriminate arrest and detention British Army attacks on Civil Rights activists "Bloody Sunday" Widespread use of curfews, CS-gas "Rape of the Falls" Torture
1976–79	Criminalization Ulsterization	End of special category status Transfer of primary control of violence to the RUC from the British army Use of SAS in undercover operations	Prevention of Terrorism Act, 1976; Emergency Provisions Act, 1978 Reports 1975: Gardiner 1978: Shackelton 1979: Bennett	Mass screening and house searches in Catholic areas Beatings during interrogation "Blanket" and "No Wash" protests

Table 6.1. Continued

Dates	Period	Official Policy	Legal Basis	Abuses
1980–81	Hunger strikes	No concessions to political prisoners RUC assumes principal responsibility for security Increased use of plastic bullets for riot control	No change	Numerous questionable plastic-bullet killings
1982–84	Shoot-to-kill "Supergrass" trials	Use of "informers" and "converted terrorists" to secure arrests of IRA leadership Transfer of undercover operations to RUC	No change Reports 1983: Jellicoe Review	Disputed killings of both IRA members and civilians by security forces Suspects mistreated to secure cooperation as informers
1985–89	Inter-governmental talks	Abandonment of use of "supergrasses" Broadcast media ban on Sinn Fein Increased cooperation by Eire with UK on extradition of IRA members	PTA re-enacted, 1989 Extradition Amendment Act, 1987; European Convention Act on Terrorism, 1987; Amendment to British Broadcast Act, Oct. 1988; Stalker/Sampson Report, 1988/89; Colville, 1990	Disputed killings of IRA members and civilians by security forces

Sources: Hadden, Boyle, and Campbell (1987); Irish Information Partnership: *Agenda, 1990.*

a strategy of nonviolent resistance, the Northern Irish government responded with ferocious force. Civil rights marches were banned, and protestors
were viciously attacked by the RUC, the B-Specials, and loyalist gangs oper-
ating with the tacit permission of the security forces.

Despite the increasing attacks on nationalists, the IRA, under the
Goulding leadership, remained inactive. Both Goulding and Tomas McGiolla,
the president of Sinn Fein, remained committed to the "stages" strategy, in
which the democratization of the Northern Irish state was stage one.
Following the failure of Goulding to provide weapons to the northern IRA
volunteers during the Belfast pogroms in August 1969, the divisions within
the IRA and Sinn Fein intensified. They culminated in the January 1970
split of the IRA and Sinn Fein.

In an analysis of the events of the period, Gerry Adams (1982) describes
the effect of the civil rights period on the Republican Movement, especially
on the Provisional IRA and Sinn Fein. His comments illuminate the reasons
for the hostility to politics shared by many within the Republican Movement at the time and explain how that hostility influenced the development
of the IRA and Sinn Fein.

> The republican strategy of organizing politically to achieve democracy
> within the state, which had involved a turning away from the physical
> force tradition and a dumping of arms, had run headlong into the reali-
> ty of the irreformably sectarian state. . . .
>
> The republican movement of the 1960s had proved incapable of
> responding adequately to events as they evolved in the 6 counties. . . .
> Failure and inadequacy did not relate solely to the question of defense
> for beleaguered nationalist areas. Indeed, lack of guns was not a pri-
> mary problem, as it was made up quite rapidly. . . . the leadership was
> clearly lacking in political understanding, and this led to their failure
> to prepare properly on all fronts, not least the question of defense.
> Understandable in the circumstances, their failure was seen simply in
> terms of military preparedness, and this view, allied to a suspicion
> amongst the older republicans of the politicization process in which
> the movement was engaged, led to the split in 1970, a major set-back
> for the republican cause. It also ensured that the reinvigorated republi-
> can struggle which emerged then was an inadequate one because the
> only republican organization which arose from the ashes was a military
> one: it had little or no proper educational process, no formal politiciza-
> tion course, and there was scant regard paid by the leadership to such
> needs. (34–35)

With politics on the shelf, the IRA assumed its role as defender of the nationalist communities in the North. As the level of sectarian and security forces' attacks increased, the IRA turned increasingly from defensive to offensive operations. By 1971, the Northern Irish government, in a desperate attempt to eliminate the IRA, implemented the internment of all suspected republican activists and sympathizers. This act, rather than defeating the IRA, swelled its ranks and led Northern Ireland to the brink of all-out civil war.

Stage Two: Repression and Reactions

The decision to introduce internment in August 1971 marked the beginning of the most violent stage of the conflict. At the 1971 Sinn Fein party conference, then president Ruairí Ó Brádaigh said that the most desirable prelude to a thirty-two-county Republic would be to make the North ungovernable and to destroy Stormont. The IRA, he announced, had now gone over to the offensive. By 24 March, the IRA had succeeded in toppling Stormont, and Westminster assumed direct control of the government of Northern Ireland. The level of attacks by all parties escalated throughout the summer, and by December the British government had accepted the recommendations of the jurist Lord Diplock to retain internment and introduce the use of juryless courts:

> The only hope of restoring the efficiency of criminal courts in Northern Ireland to deal with terrorist crimes is by using an extra-judicial process to deprive of their ability to operate in Northern Ireland those terrorists whose activities result in the intimidation of witnesses; . . . the only way of doing this is to put them in detention by an executive act and to keep them confined.[1]

In addition to introducing juryless courts for those suspected of terrorist crimes, the British government accepted Diplock's recommendation that the onus of proof be shifted to the defendant in cases involving alleged weapons possessions, and that confessions made by suspected terrorists be admissible unless it could be proved that they were secured through the use of "torture or inhuman and degrading treatment."

The incorporation of these recommendations into legislation in 1973 marked the beginning of Britain's strategy of "normalizing" the conflict in Northern Ireland. Britain would now define the situation in the province essentially as a problem of law and order, of gangsterism and terrorism. With the Diplock courts in place, the strategy of the British government was to argue that a responsible government did not negotiate with gangsters or look for political solutions to a crime wave. The answer to the Northern Ireland problem would be found instead in a "get-tough" policy of mass arrests, interrogations, and convictions.

"Getting tough" is precisely what the British security forces did, with massive numbers of house searches, peaking at over seventy-four thousand in 1973.[2] Following a loyalist bombing in Dublin that killed two people and injured 127 others, the Lynch government also decided that the time had come to halt the IRA's campaign and reduce the risk of a further escalation of the war. In December 1972, on the day following the Dublin bombing, the Irish Parliament approved an amendment to the existing Offenses Against the State Act that widened police powers for combating terrorism.

Stage 3: The IRA in Disarray

Following the failure of the cease-fire negotiations in 1975, the British government further extended its strategy of criminalization by announcing that special category status would be withdrawn as of 1 March 1976, and IRA and loyalist prisoners would henceforth be treated as ordinary criminals. With the IRA in disarray as a result of the success of the Diplock courts in securing convictions and its inaction during the 1972 truces and the 1974–75 cease-fire, Britain was able to implement part three of its strategy for Northern Ireland, "Ulsterization." This strategy entailed the gradual transfer of responsibility for prosecuting from the British security forces to Ulster's indigenous forces, the Royal Ulster Constabulary (RUC) and the Ulster Defense Regiment (UDR). During this period, a new RUC holding facility and interrogation center was constructed in Castlereagh, Northern Ireland. Castlereagh would quickly become infamous as the site of numerous cases of serious ill-treatment of prisoners that would be investigated by Amnesty International and ultimately referred to the European Court of Human Rights. By 1980, the British strategy had reduced the level of violence to its lowest point in the past ten years. The prisons were full of IRA members from whom confessions had been extracted in Castlereagh and who had been successfully convicted in the Diplock courts.

In those prisons, IRA volunteers, who were facing the prospect of years "on the blanket" and the horrific conditions of the No Wash protest, came to the decision that they had no choice but to use the IRA volunteer's most symbolic and potent weapon, the hunger strike, to secure their demands for a restoration of special category status. The hunger strike, although it failed in its aim, succeeded in mobilizing a new generation of Irish nationalists and putting Northern Ireland back on the political agenda of both the Irish and British governments. It also initiated a shift in power within Sinn Fein to those who advocated increasing involvement in the parliamentary process.

Stage 4: Supergrasses and Shoot-to-Kill

To prevent a renewed offensive by an IRA whose ranks had once again swelled in response to the hunger strike, the British government adopted a policy of relying on evidence from firsthand informers or "converted terrorists" as a means not only of identifying people, but also of securing convictions against other suspected terrorists. The decision to rely on "supergrasses" was almost certainly related to the perceived difficulty of obtaining confessions following the implementation of the Bennett Report recommendations, which addressed the worst of the abuses that had accompanied the interrogations of suspected terrorists in Castlereagh.[3]

By 1982, more than twenty potential supergrasses had been recruited, and a series of mass trials began. Between November 1981 and November 1983, at least seven loyalist and eighteen republican supergrasses were responsible for nearly six hundred people being arrested and charged with offenses connected with paramilitary activities in Northern Ireland. The trials quickly became public dramas, and were widely denounced as "show trials." Although initially effective, the strategy of using supergrasses to secure convictions, like internment, raised doubts in large sections of both the nationalist and loyalist communities as to the legitimacy of the supergrass system, and it was essentially abandoned by the end of 1984.

Linked to the general policy of RUC primacy and army withdrawal taking effect during this period was the emergence of an apparent shoot-to-kill strategy. In 1982, a specially trained RUC undercover squad, similar to those developed by the Special Air Services (SAS) in the late 1970s, was established. According to English barrister Anthony Jennings (1987, 113), this squad was given the go-ahead following Sinn Fein's success in the October 1982 assembly elections. Between 1982 and 1985, the squad was involved in a series of incidents in which twenty-three persons were shot dead in disputed circumstances. The combination of the supergrass and shoot-to-kill strategies contributed to a dramatic increase in the percentage of charges relating to political violence in Northern Ireland and to the reduction of the overall level of violence to its lowest point since 1970.[4] The success of these strategies in reducing the effectiveness of the IRA would also interact with the power struggle taking place within Sinn Fein between those wanting to increase its involvement in the electoral process and those wanting to increase the level of military operations.

The election of Gerry Adams as a member of the British Parliament for the constituency of West Belfast in June 1983 was the prelude to his election as president of Sinn Fein at that year's party conference and to the party's shift to the left and toward an increasing commitment to electoral politics. The nearly successful attempt by the IRA to assassinate Prime Minister Thatcher in 1984 and the spectacular success of Sinn Fein in the May 1985 Northern Ireland local government elections, in which the party secured fifty-nine seats, 11 percent of the overall vote, and almost 40 percent of the nationalist vote, contributed to the reestablishment of talks between the British and Irish governments that culminated in the signing of the Anglo-Irish Agreement in November 1985. The tensions between the ideologues and the radicals were evident in their responses concerning which was the greater influence on Prime Minister Thatcher's policy shift. For the ideologues, it was quite clearly the bombing of the Grand Hotel; for the radicals, it was the specter of Sinn Fein displacing the SDLP, with a push from the Brighton bombing.

The Anglo-Irish Agreement and Aftermath

Among the most important issues to be addressed by the intergovernmental council established by the Anglo-Irish agreement have been those relating to security. Consequently, during this period several security policies faced increasing scrutiny by both domestic and international investigators and observers. The RUC responded with new policies designed to regulate the conduct of its members more effectively. However, the failure of the RUC to cooperate with the investigation of John Stalker, the deputy chief constable of Greater Manchester, who was appointed to investigate the alleged shoot-to-kill policy, as well as the January 1988 decision by British Attorney General Sir Patrick Mayhew not to prosecute eight RUC officers involved in a conspiracy "to pervert the course of justice and responsible for obstructing the Stalker inquiry" on the grounds of national security undermined the confidence of the minority community in the sincerity of the reforms.

As noted previously, there was a slight increase in the level of violence following the signing of the Anglo-Irish Agreement. This was due, in part, to the demonstrations carried out by loyalists opposed to the agreement, an increase in sectarian attacks on nationalists in response to the Anglo-Irish process, and an increase in IRA operations in response to Sinn Fein's decision in November 1986 to drop the policy of abstention from Dail Eireann from its constitution.

Beginning in 1985 and continuing until the capture of the freighter *Eskund* off the coast of France in October 1987, the IRA received huge shipments of arms and cash from Libya.[5] This considerable input of resources into the IRA arsenal provided the Sinn Fein leadership with much-needed maneuvering room regarding the new emphasis to be placed on electoral politics both in the North and the South. With these caches of arms in place, the leadership could legitimately argue that involvement in electoral politics would not lead to a "running down" of the war machine, as had happened when the Goulding leadership had tried to take the movement in a similar direction. As hypothesized by the model, the influx of resources provided support to the militarist activists within Sinn Fein while allowing the radicals to press forward with the politicization process, the main points of which would surface in the 1987 publication of *A Scenario for Peace*.[6]

Special Powers and Political Conflicts

This brief review indicates that the pattern of abuses in Northern Ireland is far from fortuitous and can be directly related to successive phases in security policy, although we cannot conclude that the abuses were deliberately planned. They may have arisen from a lack of control by senior officers over soldiers and policemen acting under enormous stress, both in terms of their personal safety and the pressure to produce results. But such a pattern would still indicate the inability of senior officers to control the actions of their counterparts and the continued existence of a sectarian, "supremacist" mindset among members of the force.

The most significant feature of the successive phases and the failure in security policy has been the apparent belief among many senior commanders that if only the right security policy could be identified and implemented without external interference, "terrorists" on both sides could be defeated. As each policy has been marred and eventually frustrated by the revelation of abuses, the government has been persuaded that some new policy—internment, interrogation in depth, the use of supergrasses, or even shooting to kill—would do the trick. However, the new policies have been implemented with little or no attempt to foresee and control possible abuses, with the invariable result that they have been accompanied by new abuses. This, in turn, has confirmed the conviction among the minority communities in Northern Ireland and the Basque Country that the security forces are incapable of acting fairly and that the administration of justice is inherently corrupt. Ironically, it has also sustained the IRA's claim that the Irish will never receive justice in a British state. A decade later, the events of July 1996, during which, despite the murder of a Catholic taxi-driver in the Portadown area, Chief Constable Hugh Annesley of the RUC reversed his decision to ban a march by the sectarian Protestant Orange Order down the Garvaghy Road in Portadown, tragically confirmed the fears of the minority community. The IRA could now legitimately claim that it had always been and remained justified in its decision not to decommission its arms before a negotiated settlement to the conflict had been secured.[7]

188   REGIME RESPONSIVENESS

Regime Repression and Recruitment: Sinn Fein

Table 6.2, which shows the distribution of ideologues, radicals, and politicos
in Sinn Fein by the period in which they became active, supports the argument that regime repression, unless extremely severe, serves as a stimulus
rather than a brake on the recruitment of activists into revolutionary nationalist organizations. If we compare periods 2 and 3, we see that the proportion of activists entering Sinn Fein doubled following the introduction of internment. Similarly, if we compare period 4, which covers the time of severe
abuses of prisoners during interrogation at Castlereagh and the withdrawal
of special category status and the blanket and no-wash protests, with period
5, that of the hunger strikes, we see that the number of those entering the
party almost doubled. If 1979, the year of the no-wash protest, is included
with period 5 rather than period 4, the difference in the numbers entering
is over 60 percent. Despite the small size of the interview sample, it appears
that the two strategies, internment and criminalization, specifically aimed at
breaking the ability and the will of the nationalist community to continue
the armed struggle against British rule, not only failed but encouraged rather
than diminished participation in Sinn Fein and the IRA.

Table 6.2. Distribution of Sinn Fein Activist Subgroups by Period of Entry

Period of Entry	Ideologues	Radicals	Politicos	All Activists	
1. Pre-1968	4	2	0	6	10%
2. 1968–70	2	3	0	8	13%
3. 1971–75	6	9	0	15	25%
4. 1976–79	1	3	0	7	12%
5. 1980–81	1	7	1	14	23%
6. 1982–84	—	3	1	4	7%
7. 1985–89	—	2	4	6	10%

Source: Author's interviews with Sinn Fein activists ($N = 60$).

Table 6.2 also provides some support for the argument that the level of
repression is related to the type of activist recruited; that is, in periods of
widespread repression, nationalist movements attract primarily ideologues
and radicals, while politicos are more likely to participate when the level of
repression has diminished. It is also interesting to note that after 1981, those
entering Sinn Fein supported the party's social and economic goals as well as
the objective of national independence. This finding supports the proposition raised in chapter 5 that ideologues value armed struggle above institu-

tional struggle and are primarily concerned with the struggle for national, not social, liberation.

Community Support and Political Violence

In chapter 2, I suggested that examining the relationship between a community's experience of violence and its willingness to support those who engage in violence might give us additional insight into the capacity of small radical organizations to survive. An examination of the geographic distribution of conflict-related fatalities by agent (i.e., loyalists, security forces, nationalists) during the period 1969–89 revealed a close association among all types of deaths.

Data on conflict-related deaths shows that Belfast has experienced the greatest number of fatalities at the hands of all groups.[8] In particular, nationalists living in Belfast represent almost three-quarters of all victims of sectarian attacks by loyalists. Clearly, nationalist communities in Belfast have experienced the worst of combined state and sectarian violence. The fact that the largest percentage of IRA prisoners come from Belfast would appear to support the argument that more militant activists are recruited from areas most exposed to state violence.

Table 6.3, which shows the distribution of Northern Ireland conflict fatalities across Westminster constituencies, provides additional information regarding the relationship between the level of fatalities and the size of the nationalist communities. A comparison of the figures on the percentage of nationalists in a constituency with the figures on fatalities shows that constituencies in which over one-third of the population is nationalist are, in general, associated with larger numbers of fatalities. Considering the nature of terrorism, this finding is not surprising. It is clearly much easier for IRA activists to conduct operations and to hide in nationalist communities, where they can blend in with the local population. Finally, table 6.3 reveals a strong association between the level of killings by members of the security forces and electoral support for Sinn Fein. While some of the security force killings involved Protestant paramilitaries, it is reasonable to assume that killings in areas with large nationalist majorities involved primarily nationalists. In sum, both the longitudinal and spatial distribution of political violence and electoral support for Sinn Fein are consistent with the argument presented in chapter 4.

Security Policy and Political Violence: The Basque Case

Table 6.4 outlines the major stages in the development of Spanish security policy relating to the Basque conflict and ETA. As in Northern Ireland, each

Table 6.3. Distribution of All Northern Ireland Fatalities (1969–1989) across Westminster Constituencies

Constituency	1987 Electorate	Percent of Northern Ireland Electorate	1987 Percent Unionist	1987 Percent Nationalist	1987 Percent of SF Vote	All Deaths, 1968–89	Killings by Security Forces	Percent of Northern Ireland Deaths
Antrim East	58,863	5.61%	95.8%	4.2%	0%	24	2	0.87%
Antrim North	63,254	6.03	78.5	21.5	6.4	27	5	0.98
Antrim South	59,321	5.64	85.7	14.3	4.4	53	3	1.92
Belfast East	55,581	5.29	95.4	4.2	2.0	111	10*	4.02
Belfast North	61,128	5.81	69.5	32.5	13.7	544	60	19.69
Belfast South	53,694	5.12	86.1	13.9	3.1	137	8	4.96
Belfast West	59,750	5.68	9.9	89.1	41.2	544	75	19.69
Down North	61,574	5.86	97.4	1.6	0	8	1	0.29
Down South	66,987	6.38	51.1	48.6	4.2	81	12	2.93
Fermanagh/ South Tyrone	67,880	6.46	47.6	52.4	26.4	228	18	8.25
Foyle	67,432	6.42	32.5	67.5	17.9	275	53	9.95
Lagan Valley	60,009	5.71	87.3	13.6	6.4	75	3	2.71
Londonderry East	67,362	6.41	67.7	33.3	11.2	59	4	2.14
Mid Ulster	68,899	6.09	46.3	53.7	23.9	119	20	4.31
Newry and Armagh	62,837	5.98	40.0	60.0	11.8	352	32	12.74
Strangford	60,232	5.73	95.6	4.4	0	23	2	0.83
Upper Bann	60,797	5.78	77.3	22.7	7.4	103	6	3.73
Total	1,055,600	100			Percent of all votes 11.4	2763	314	100

Sources: Irish Information Partnership: *Agenda, 1990*; Sutton (1994).   * An additional thirteen people were killed in the Central Belfast area.

of the phases outlined below was characterized by a particular set of political demands, strategies, and tactics adopted by nationalists and a specific set of political and security responses by the Spanish and Basque governments. Table 6.4 provides a way to interpret the fluctuations in the number of fatalities and the levels of arrests in the Basque Country during the past twenty years, which are shown in Table 6.5.

Stage 1: The Franco Years

During this period, all dissident groups were harshly suppressed. The definition of crimes of "military" rebellion was extended to include the dissemination of information to cause disturbances in public order, international conflict, or a decline in the prestige of the state, its institutions, the government, the army, or the authorities. Terrorism was also broadly defined to include the following acts: attacks against public security; revenge or reprisals of a political or social character; disturbing public order; causing explosions or fires; the possession of arms, munitions, or other lethal devices; the manufacture, transport, or supply of any such items; the placing of any such substances or artifacts, even if they failed to explode or malfunctioned; and the derailment of trains or the sinking of naval vessels.

Under the 1960 Decree Law, persons accused of having violated the law were judged not by a civilian court, but by a military tribunal. The extent to which the law was used to stifle political dissent is illustrated by the fact that in 1969, of the 1,100 cases heard in military courts throughout Spain, 867 (almost 80 percent) involved acts that would not be considered crimes in a democratic political system: membership in a political organization opposed to the state, attending political meetings, participating in demonstrations, distributing literature, and so on. Penalties for acts covered by the 1960 Decree Law were severe. Death penalties were obligatory for any of the punishable offenses if the offense resulted in the death of any person, whether or not that person was the intended victim. Life imprisonment was required for armed attack, kidnapping, and terrorism.

As violence increased during the last year of Franco's rule, provisions for the preventive detention of suspected terrorists were authorized, and Francoist Spain instituted its own version of internment. In addition to the use of military courts in cases of political dissent, the other device used to crush political dissent was the State of Exception, during which the normal constitutional protections available to Spanish citizens were set aside.

Franco imposed twelve states of exception during the period 1956–76, and all but one affected the Basque provinces. During the twenty-year period, at least one Basque province was affected for fifty-six months, or

Table 6.4. Overview of Spanish Security Policies, 1960–1990

Dates	Period	Official Policy	Legal Basis	Abuses
1960–75	Dictatorship	Repression of all public dissent by police, Guardia Civil, and military Substitution of military tribunals for civilian courts	1960 Decree Law on Military Rebellion, Banditry, and Terrorism 1975 Decree Law on the Prevention of Terrorism	Indiscriminate arrest and imprisonment Torture Extralegal violence by parapolicial right-wing groups
1/76–6/78	Transition	Abrogation of Decree Laws on Terrorism; Amnesty/restoration of all civil rights Brief restoration of "special powers" 1/77–3/77	Decree Laws	Assassinations by pro-state right-wing groups Arbitrary arrest Torture
7/78–11/82	Transition/ coup consolidation	Reintroduction of antiterrorist "special powers" legislation Definition of any attack, either verbal or physical, on the "integrity of the Spanish nation" as terrorism	Law 21/1978 Law 56/1978 Decree Law 1/1979 Organic Law 11/1980	Assassinations by parapolicial right-wing groups Arbitrary arrest Torture Extensive censorship

Table 6.4. Continued

Dates	Period	Official Policy	Legal Basis	Abuses
11/82–12/86	First González Government	Strengthening and expansion of antiterrorist policies Introduction of Plan ZEN in 9/83 Introduction of limited internment (two years without trial) of suspected terrorists Increased repression of ETA prisoners and cooperation with France on extradition; increase in arrests for apologia of terrorism, especially among journalists and members of HB	Organic Law 14/1983 Organic Law 6/1984	Extensive media censorship Torture Assassinations of ETA activists/ HB members by parapolicial organization GAL
1/87–1/90	Second González government	Slight relaxation of antiterrorist special powers	Six articles of Organic Law 6/1984 allowed to lapse in January 1987. Right to detain suspects incommunicado reduced from ten days to five. Anti-ETA pact approved by all political parties except HB. Increase in French cooperation in deportation and extradition of *etarras*.	Assassinations of HB activists by parapolicial groups Mistreatment of ETA prisoners

Sources: Clark (1990); *EGIN, 1983.*

**Table 6.5. Euskadi `ta Askatasuna–Related Fatalities
and Antiterrorist Arrests in Euskadi Sur, 1968–1988**

Year	Arrests	Fatalities
1968	434	2
1969	?	1
1970	831	0
1971	?	0
1972	616	1
1973	572	7
1974	1,116	19
1975	4,625	16
1976	?	15
1977	Amnesty	12
1978	287	64
1979	561	78
1980	2,140	93
1981	1,300	30
1982	1,261	31
1983	1,157	34
1984	1,879	24
1985	1,181	31
1986	990	24
1987	601	49
1988	170	19

Sources: *EGIN,* 1982–89

approximately 31 percent of the time. According to Portell,[9] an estimated 8,500 Basques were directly affected through arrest, imprisonment, torture, or exile. A report by Amnesty International regarding the effects of the last two states of exception in 1975 found that massive arrests, totaling over 1,000, had been made in each of the provinces of Bizkaia and Gipuzkoa.[10] The report also mentioned "personal and direct evidence" of the torture of 45 persons and "credible and convincing evidence" that torture was used systematically against a minimum of 350 Basque detainees. The report found that torture had been used for two reasons: to obtain information or confessions, and to intimidate the Basque population into submission and frighten it into abandoning support for the Basque nationalist cause. Franco's approach to internal security was thus primarily military. Spain was divided into military regions whose boundaries were used to determine the jurisdiction of each military court. The four Basque provinces lie in the Sixth

Military Region, whose headquarters are in the city of Burgos, which became famous as a result of trial of the "Burgos Sixteen" in 1970. Table 6.5 shows that the increase in the level of arrests and torture during 1975 failed to affect significantly the number of killings by ETA.

Stage 2: Transitions

On 6 February 1976, less than three months after Franco's death, the 1975 law regarding the prevention of terrorism was abrogated by King Juan Carlos and Premier Carlos Arias Navarro. By December 1976, the two leaders had formally abolished the Tribunals of Public Order, and politically related crimes, including those of a terrorist nature, had been returned to civilian jurisdiction. Thus, in less than a year after Franco's death, virtually all of the former internal security structures had been abolished. Also, between January 1976 and July 1978, Madrid approved a number of policies to improve relations with the Basque people and even with ETA. The most important of these concerned amnesty for Basque political prisoners, of which there were approximately 750 at the time of Franco's death.

Between November 1975 and March 1976, the Spanish government issued three amnesty decrees designed to clear the prisons of most of the Basque prisoners by the June 1977 parliamentary elections. In October 1977, the new parliament approved a general amnesty law for all political prisoners. ETA was still defined as an illegal organization, but the crime that made its members illegal was not its violence but its advocacy of Basque separatism. Thus, by January 1978, the number of Basques in prison for politically related crimes had been reduced to between five and ten, and Spain no longer had any permanent antiterrorist legislation. However, although the number of ETA killings had decreased slightly during 1977, the failure of the government to pardon all Basque prisoners prompted ETA to increase its offensive, and in June 1978, Madrid responded by reintroducing elements of the former Francoist antiterrorist laws. When the draft legislation appeared in May, it was widely condemned by the Basque parties, who accused the government of creating a climate of terror. On 29 June, however, the draft antiterrorist bill was approved as a Decree Law and put into effect without waiting for the parliament to act on it. The state now had at its disposal most of the same powers that Franco had used to suppress political dissent. By October 1980, there would be as many *etarras* in prison as there had been during the Franco years. By 1980, although the Basque provinces accounted for only 3.5 percent of Spain's territory and about 7 percent of its population, approximately 17 percent of the state's security force was committed to the region.

Despite the increase in arrests, the number of ETA killings continued to rise dramatically through 1980. A more detailed examination of the data available on arrests and ETA killings for the five-year period between 1 January 1976 and 31 December 1980 reveals that in the two and one-half years before the reintroduction of antiterrorist legislation, the average number of ETA victims per month was only 3.87, while in the two and one-half years after the implementation of the new antiterrorist policy in July 1978, ETA averaged 15.97 victims per month.[11]

Although it would be simplistic to suggest any direct relationship between the implementation of the legislation and the rise in ETA violence, which is linked to a complex set of factors, it is fair to state that despite the implementation of numerous measures that imposed considerable costs on the Basque civilian population, the new measures did little to halt ETA's operation during this period.

Stage 3: Coup and Consolidation

Following the coup attempt of February 1981, which was viewed as being partly precipitated by the level of ETA killings and the increasing demands by Basques and other autonomous regions for greater powers, the government introduced the Law for the Defense of the Constitution, which defined terrorism as including any attack on the integrity of the Spanish nation or any effort to secure the independence of any part of its territory, even if nonviolent. In essence, any expression of separatism could have been tried under the terms of this law. Activities in support of a terrorist organization were now explicitly included under the terms of the law. The law also greatly increased government censorship of both print and electronic media. Although the level of monthly arrests remained steady at between fifty and one hundred, the stricter detention policies resulted in fewer individuals being released. Thus, when the new González socialist government assumed power in November 1982, almost five hundred Basques were in prison.

Stage 4: The First Socialist Government

In the first two years of the González socialist government, antiterrorist policy grew increasingly more coercive as the socialists sought to prove to their right-wing critics that they were not "soft on terrorism." Perhaps the most immediate consequence of this shift to a tougher antiterrorist policy was the government's crackdown on journalists, especially those who worked for the two publications most closely associated with ETA, the newspaper *Egin* and the Basque magazine *Punto y Hora*.

In January 1982, Javier Sánchez Erauskin, a columnist for *Egin* and a former editor of *Punto y Hora*, was sentenced to eighteen months in prison for publishing articles that insulted the Spanish government and the king. During this period, leaders of Herri Batasuna were also frequently in court defending themselves against charges of "apologia for terrorism" that were leveled in response to their comments during Herri Batasuna press conferences reported in *Egin*.

In June 1983, Interior Minister Barrionuevo introduced his new plan for citizen security, which was officially labeled "Plan ZEN" for Zona Especial del Norte, or "special Northern Zone." The plan included a wide range of actions to establish a coordinated attack on terrorism. But Barrionuevo's plan never received the support of the Basque parties, and in October 1983 the Basque Parliament passed a resolution stating its opposition to Plan ZEN, and it was quietly dropped from Madrid's agenda. The González government, however, was to get something much better: increased cooperation from the French government in extradition hearings. Throughout 1983 and 1984, several meetings between Spanish and French ministers addressed the issue of terrorism and the need for increased cooperation.

By the end of 1984, the Spanish efforts, coupled with the "dirty war" operations of the GAL, a pro-state, paramilitary, "anti-terrorist" organization that carried out attacks on Basques living in France, began to pay dividends. By the end of 1984, the French had deported twenty-three members of ETA, including several top leaders. Following the decision by Belgium in July 1984 to extradite ETA members (the first country to do so), France agreed to return a small number of suspected *etarras* to Spain for trial. Soon, with the assassination of the Herri Batasuna leader, Santi Brouard, in 1984, even many moderate Basque activists admitted that the Spanish antiterrorist policy had become so severe as a result of these new measures that conditions were comparable with the worst years of the Franco dictatorship.

The new law, Organic Law 8/1984, in addition to reaffirming the extraordinary police powers contained in earlier laws, allowed judges to order the detention without trial of suspected terrorists for periods of up to two and a half years. Judges were also authorized to ban political parties and other groups led by convicted terrorists, and to close down newspapers and magazines that supported terrorist aims, and it became a crime for any elected public official to criticize the Spanish nation, its symbols, or its flag. Penalties for terrorist attacks were increased, and people who supported or engaged in apologia for terrorist acts were to be given the same penalties as those who actually committed terrorist acts. A new category of crime for attacks against members of the armed forces was also created. As a result of these tough new laws, the levels of arrests and the numbers of Basques in prison rose once again. The level of ETA killings, however, did not significantly increase or decrease, but remained constant at around thirty per year. Following the reelection of the González government in June 1986 and the election of Jacques Chirac as prime minister of France in March 1986, increasing cooperation between the two states delivered a series of blows to ETA, the first of which was the arrest in April of ETA's top leader, Txomin Iturbe, and a number of other top figures. These arrests effectively dismembered the ETA leadership in France, leaving the organization in the hands of a new and inexperienced generation of leaders.

Stage 5: The Second Socialist Government

On 19 July 1986, the French government began to expel Basque refugees suspected of being involved with ETA to Spain. France also continued its policy of deporting ETA leaders to third countries and by December 1986 it had deported or expelled twenty-nine *etarras*. In November, the French police carried out a massive raid of the SOKOA factory in Hendaye, France, which had long been suspected of being a cover for ETA headquarters. In the factory, the police discovered a huge quantity of documents relating to ETA's organization and operations. Information contained in the documents resulted in subsequent waves of arrests of ETA members. Mobilizations in response to arrests and detentions were massive, and in June 1987, Herri Batasuna achieved its most spectacular electoral success, winning over 250,000 votes, securing a seat in the European parliament, and replacing the Basque Nationalist Party as the voted Basque party receiving the most votes.

Shortly after the elections, ETA bombed the Hipercor shopping center in Barcelona. It was one of ETA's bloodiest attacks, killing fourteen and wounding over one hundred. Outrage at the attack was widespread, and even Herri Batasuna leaders condemned the attack as senseless. It was widely speculated that the attack was carried out by activists within ETA who were opposed to Herri Batasuna's increasing participation in electoral politics and wished to remind them who was in charge.[12]

In September 1987, the French police carried out another series of arrests that included the leader of ETA's armed attack cells, Santiago Arrospide, who had in his possession more than thirty pounds of documents with important information regarding ETA's organizational structure and membership. Together with the documents recovered in the 1986 SOKOA raid, these documents enabled French and Spanish authorities to carry out the most massive series of arrests ETA had ever experienced, which almost succeeded in dismantling the organization.

In December 1987, the Spanish Parliament approved an antiterrorist pact that prohibited any political contact between those who signed the pact and members of any organization that did not condemn ETA.[13] In January 1988, a similar pact, Pacto Ajuria Enea,[14] was approved by the Basque Parliament and signed by representatives of all parties. It seemed possible that ETA had, in fact, been destroyed, and Herri Batasuna had been isolated from the rest of the Basque political parties.

ETA, however, despite the enormous setbacks it had endured, managed to continue its attacks, and in 1988 it was responsible for nineteen deaths and seven injuries. In November, however, ETA offered to call a truce if the Spanish government was willing to enter into negotiations. In December, ETA reiterated its offer in an extensive interview published in the Spanish news magazine *Diario 16*.

In January 1989, contacts were established between ETA and Madrid and a series of "conversations" were held in Algeria. In March, ETA announced that it was willing to extend the truce to June 24 in order to open a second stage of talks. The government responded that it considered the conversations positive. Unfortunately, by the end of March, each side had accused the other of attempting to manipulate the process, and by 6 April the government had reverted to its position of stating that it would agree only to facilitate the reinsertion of *etarras* once the organization had ceased its struggle and turned in its arms to the government. On 8 April, eight bomb attacks signaled ETA's response.

By June 1989, the effect of the anti-ETA pact and the popular revulsion with the 1987 Hipercor bombing was evident in Herri Batasuna's reduced vote.[15] But the anger felt by many Basques at the refusal of Madrid to continue the conversations with ETA helped Herri Batasuna, despite continuous harassment and extensive censorship, to reelect its member to the European Parliament, coming in second to the Basque Nationalist party in votes. Herri Batasuna's electoral performance would also soon reveal the inadequacies of the anti-ETA pact for isolating it from government, as numerous local governments had a majority of Herri Batasuna representatives and continued with business as usual, while those with a near majority of Herri Batasuna representatives were immobilized. As 1990 approached, stalemate seemed the operative word for all parties to the conflict.

Regime Repression and Recruitment: Herri Batasuna
Table 6.6, which shows the distribution of ideologues, radicals, and politicos in Herri Batasuna by the period in which they became active, supports the argument that regime repression, unless extremely severe, as in period 3, serves as a stimulus rather than a brake on the general recruitment of activists

Table 6.6. Distribution of Herri Batasuna Activist Subgroups by Period of Entry

Period of Entry	Ideologues		Radicals		Politicos		
	Interviews (N=18)	*Survey* (N=65)	*Interviews* (N=11)	*Survey* (N=32)	*Interviews* (N=5)	*Survey* (N=20)	*All Activists* (N=157)
1. 1976–78	17%	3%	27%	19%	20%	30%	13%
2. 1978–82	28	40	36	44	0	25	34
3. 1983–86	45	45	18	28	0	5	31
4. 1987–89	11	12	18	9	80	40	22

Source: Author's interviews and survey of Herri Batasuna activists.
Ideologues: Chi^2: p = .007; Cramer's V: .32
Radicals: Chi^2: p = 14; Cramer's V: .21
Politicos: Chi^2: p = .05; Cramer's V: .26

into militant nationalist organizations. The distribution of activists entering Herri Batasuna during the 1983–86 period also supports the hypothesis that paramilitary organizations are most likely to attract ideologues during periods of repression.

Conversely, politicos are most likely to enter in periods of greater regime openness. Although the transition period of 1976–78 was perhaps the least repressive period in the past twenty years, the finding that even the small number of politicos who joined then have remained active in the organization was unanticipated. A review of the information available on these seven activists revealed that two had family members in jail or exile, four were active members of trade unions, all had at least one Basque parent, and four spoke Euskara, one being a professor of Euskara. In the majority of cases, therefore, there was a tie to the Basque culture, ETA, or radical trade unionism, precisely the electorate to which Herri Batasuna directs its appeals.

Community Support and Political Violence: The Basque Case

As mentioned previously, Franco declared twelve states of exception between 1956 and 1975. Only one, in 1958, did not affect the Basque provinces. Of the remaining eleven, five covered all Spanish territory; one covered Asturias, Gipuzkoa, and Bizkaia as a group; one covered only Bizkaia; and three covered Gipuzkoa alone. Thus, during the dictatorship, the Basque provinces endured the longest periods in which constitutional rights were set aside and among the Basque provinces, Gipuzkoa and Bizkaia were affected to a far greater extent than Araba or Nafarroa. Data on the distribution by province of those arrested under antiterrorist legislation in the Basque provinces in 1983 (during the first socialist government) and in 1988 (during the second) reveals that the pattern of resistance and repression has varied little in post-Franco Spain, with Gipuzkoa and Bizkaia still accounting for the largest proportion of political arrests.[16]

The Herri Batasuna survey allows us to compare how activists from the four provinces perceived the effectiveness of ETA's armed struggle and participation in acts of rebellious collective action. If the sample population resembles that of Basque society in general, we would expect more activists from the provinces of Gipuzkoa and Bizkaia to perceive armed struggle as effective and to engage more frequently in political protests, while those in Araba and Nafarroa would be more inclined to support the party's electoral struggle. Tables 6.7, 6.8, and 6.9 confirm these expectations. Activists from Gipuzkoa and Bizkaia are significantly more likely to participate in acts of political protest and to perceive the use of political violence as effective, while those in Araba and Nafarroa are significantly more likely to agree that Herri Batasuna should participate in institutional politics. State violence is, of course, related to acts of political violence, so we would expect some link between the actions and arrests.

Table 6.7. Herri Batasuna Activists' Perception of the Efficacy of Armed Struggle

Area	Percent Perceiving Armed Struggle as Very Effective
Low Repression Araba/Nafarroa (*N* = 58)	46%
High Repression Guipuzcoa/Bizkaia (*N* = 59)	80

Source: Author's survey of Herri Batasuna activists.
Chi^2: $p = .001$; Cramer's $V = .35$

In an analysis of the geographic distribution of 696 ETA victims killed, wounded, or kidnapped prior to 1981, Clark (1984, 186–87) found that more than half the killings and more than one-fourth of the kidnappings had been concentrated in Gipuzkoa, although it included only 25 percent of the Basque population and about 10 percent of the Basque territory. Bizkaia,

Table 6.8. Distribution of Support for Institutional Politics among Herri Batasuna Activists

Area	Agree	Disagree
Low Repression Araba/Nafarroa ($N=58$)	60%	40%
High Repression Gipuzkoa/Bizkaia ($N=59$)	37	63

Source: Author's survey of Herri Batasuna activists.
Chi^2: $p = .01$; Cramer's $V = .24$

which is more densely populated, was found to account for about one-third of all the ETA victims, while relatively few attacks took place in Nafarroa.[17]

Assuming that *etarras* were following the tenets of armed struggle, we might expect that ETA prisoners would be most likely to come from the areas in which its attacks were concentrated. An analysis of *etarras* in prison in 1986–87 by the province of their birth shows that, in fact, the majority of them came from Gipuzkoa and Bizkaia.[18]

If, as hypothesized, support for radical nationalism is related to the experience of state repression, then we would expect support for Herri Batasuna to be greatest in Gipuzkoa and Bizkaia, and, indeed, for every election between 1979 and 1989, the percentage of the Herri Batasuna vote is above average in Gipuzkoa. In Bizkaia, the percentage of support for Herri Batasuna is at least equal to the total average in two-thirds of the elections.

Clark's (1984, 195) indicators of ETA operations related to the percentage of Basque speakers and support for Herri Batasuna provide additional insights into the distribution of support for militant Basque nationalism. In

Table 6.9. Level of Protest Activity among Herri Batasuna Activists

Level of Protest	Araba/Nafarroa ($N=58$)	Guipuzcoa/Bizkaia ($N=59$)
High (7–8 events)	42%	71%
Medium (5–6 events)	46	22
Low (Less than 5 events)	12	7

Source: Author's survey of Herri Batasuna activists.
Chi^2: $p = .04$; Cramer's V: .32

all cases where the ratio of ETA victims per thousand members of a municipality exceeds 0.20 percent, the proportion of Basque speakers within the community exceeds 0.25 percent, and those in which the proportion of ETA members per thousand of population are greatest also have the highest percentage of Basque speakers. These patterns of association strongly support the arguments presented previously regarding the relationship between militant Basque nationalism, primordial sentiments, and the experience of cultural or physical repression by institutions of the state. Data from the Herri Batasuna survey enables us to see if a similar relationship exists between familiarity with the Basque language and attitudes toward the use of violence to secure political objectives.

Table 6.10, which illustrates the relationship between Herri Batasuna activists' attitudes toward political violence and their familiarity with the Basque language reveals that, as hypothesized, support for political violence in the Basque Country is significantly related to ethnicity, as indicated by the ability to speak Basque. Indeed, activists who report that they speak and use Euskara daily and those who are fluent in Basque are twice as likely to perceive acts of political violence as effective as those who do not. The following comment by José Luíz Alvarez Enparanza, "Txillardegi," who has remained a leading intellectual figure within the MLVN, provides some insights into this relationship: "If I were far from being a Basque patriot, I would smile. But because I am one, I feel shame and disgust. This incessant abandonment of a marvelous national language, and its subordination, now happily accepted, to the language of our eternal oppressors, is intolerably painful for true patriots."[19] For these activists, it is not merely the political identity of the Basque provinces that is at stake; rather, the importance of this conflict lies beyond politics. It is, in essence, a struggle for the survival of a culture whose most distinguishing feature, its language, has been threatened with extinction for both economic-demographic and political reasons. Any political compromise with Spain that fails to guarantee the primacy of

Table 6.10. Herri Batasuna Activists' Perception of the Efficacy of Armed Struggle by Fluency in Euskara

Level of Ability	Percent Finding Armed Struggle Effective
Fluent or Semifluent	68%
Limited or None	32%

Source: Author's interviews/survey of Herri Batasuna activists (N=154)
Chi^2: p = .04; Cramer's V: .29

Euskara in the Basque provinces is therefore unacceptable. For these activists, the unwillingness of Madrid thus far to allow the Basque government to introduce obligatory education in Basque continues to justify the armed struggle of ETA.

Given that Euskara continues to flourish in the small villages and towns of Gipuzkoa and Bizkaia, it is not surprising that, with the exceptions of the provincial capitals, Donostia, Bilbao, Gasteiz, and Iruñea, the majority of ETA members have been recruited from these towns. Clark (1984, 211), for example, recounts that San Gregorio, a small village (population 500–600) in Gipuzkoa, often had as many as eleven *etarras* in exile at one time. Also, given the importance of security to clandestine organization, the recruitment process is less risky for both recruiters and recruits when they know each other well, as in small towns, villages, and distinct neighborhoods in large cities. In such cases, established social networks clearly help to ensure a general base of loyalty and reduce the risk that a clandestine organization takes in contacting a potential militant.

Social Background, Political Experiences, and Environment

Using data from the Herri Batasuna survey, I can now provide a more sophisticated reconstruction of the activists' social and political backgrounds and experiences. Given our definitions of ideologues, radicals, and politicos, we would expect that ideologues would be the most familiar with the Basque language and would come predominantly from the provinces of Gipuzkoa and Bizkaia, where support for radical nationalism, as indicated by support for Herri Batasuna, is highest, and that these activists would have been recruited during periods of low regime responsiveness (periods 2 and 3 in Table 6.6). Finally, we might expect these activists to be least concerned with specifically economic issues. Politicos should represent almost a mirror image of ideologues. We might expect radicals to be somewhat less fluent than ideologues, and to come from areas characterized by a high level of social mobilization, regardless of province, and to be concerned with economic issues.[20] Table 6.11, which presents the regression equations,[21] provides strong support for the proposed model of movement activism. For each type of activist, the expected patterns are present and significant.

Summary

"Parties," as Kitschelt (1990, 20) has stated, "do not develop in a social vacuum but emerge from patterns of socioeconomic stratification, structures of political domination, and cultural identities that shape the demands and visions of their constituencies." This chapter has shown that support for mili-

Table 6.11. Determinants of Movement Activism by Type of Activist

	Ideologues	Radicals	Politicos
Language/Ethnicity 0 = Fluent	−.16***	.07*	.08*
Organizational Support Gipuzkoa/Bizkaia = 0	−.16**	.19**	.06*
Regime Responsiveness Periods 1 and 4 = 0	.13***	.08*	−.07*
Economic Interests	−.05	.21***	.17**
Adjusted R^2 (N=114)	.18***	.15***	.12***

Source: Author's survey of Herri Batasuna activists.
*p = .05; **p = .01; ***p = .001.

tant Irish and Basque nationalism is highest in areas where "primordial" elements of Irish and Basque ethnicity, particularly language, remain strongest. An analysis of the social backgrounds of Sinn Fein and Herri Batasuna activists revealed that ideologues, in general, were recruited from the most parochial areas of Ireland and the Basque Country, while radicals and politicos came from more urban areas. As hypothesized, the internal composition of Sinn Fein and Herri Batasuna—the relative strength of ideologues, radicals, and politicos, and their ability to form coalitions with each other—has been influenced by shifts in the level of regime repression in those areas most affected by the coercive actions of state security forces. Finally, the operational capacity of ETA was shown to be greatest in these areas of tightly knit communities. This finding provides strong support for the relationship between the indigenous organizational strength of a revolutionary nationalist movement and its engagement in armed struggle.

7

People, Places, and Political Violence: Some Concluding Comparisons

In an analysis of recruitment into clandestine political organizations in Italy, della Porta (1988, 163) found that these organizations also recruited their militants from "tight-knit networks of social relations in which political ties were strengthened by primary solidarity based on friendship and kinship relations." Doug McAdam (1988) in his insightful study of the participants in the Freedom Summer of the American civil rights movement reveals similar findings. These findings, together with those from the Northern Ireland and Basque cases, offer strong support for the argument that individuals who are well-integrated in their communities and belong to tight-knit political networks have the greatest propensity to join social movement organizations and to participate in acts of violent political protest. Also consistent with the arguments presented in this study was della Porta's finding regarding the importance attributed by Red Brigade recruits to their prior experience of violence. Although della Porta focuses on the recruits' previous experience of violence in terms of their participation in violent activities, her observation that the recruits frequently cited the use of violence by right-wing activists and the police as justification for their involvement in illegal and violent activities supports the interaction between the experience of violence and the willingness to engage in acts of violence evident among Irish and Basque activists. Her analysis of the activists' political biographies leads della Porta to the following conclusion:

> My analysis suggests that participation in violent practices produces a
> kind of militant for whom political commitment is identified with

physical violence rather than with negotiation. The lack of possibilities for concrete gains through bargaining activities increases the need for symbolic substitutes, which are often found in radical ideologies that maintain that social changes can be obtained only through a long war against the enemy. (1988, 167)

The emergence of such militants and the spread of organizations that adopted violence as a tactic in Italy, she maintains, was closely related to the long cycle of political protest that continued throughout the late 1960s and early 1970s.[1] Harsh social conflicts, combined with the state's failure to provide timely policy responses and the relatively high level of police intervention, favored a gradual deterioration of the repertoires of protest. Once the protest cycle was over, networks of militants more accustomed to physical violence than mediation constituted a potential base for violent political groups.[2] The presence of violent repertoires and a generation of militants socialized to violence, she suggests, created the conditions that led political entrepreneurs to orient their efforts to a specific constituency of those who use radical forms of action and, consequently, to continue to operate after the protest cycle had ended. Clearly, the relationships between exposure to violence and the propensity to engage in acts of violence, between inadequate or coercive responses by the state to challengers' demands and the spread of violent patterns of political behavior, and between recruitment and social integration that this study has demonstrated mirror quite closely those described by della Porta.

Clearly, much more cross-national and longitudinal research is needed to assess the explanatory potential of the proposed model. In particular, its applicability to class-based as well as ethnically based organizations should be explored. Should the model prove robust, however, it suggests that both militant movements and those governments confronted with violent political opposition might be better served by allowing, rather than excluding, electoral competition as a strategy for securing political goals. For insurgent movements, electoral competition increases the opportunities for participation by supporters who are unwilling or unable to participate in violent actions, potentially granting the organization a sufficient power in numbers to secure its political goals. For incumbent regimes, allowing insurgents to contest elections and offering them the opportunity to participate in the negotiation and decision-making process may result in a permanent cessation of violence, as in Columbia and South Africa, and a willingness to compromise on issues once regarded as absolutes.

Most of the coercive and legal responses described in the Basque and

Irish cases and alluded to in others have a long history. In internal wars, as in any war, winning is usually more important to governments than adhering to the laws of insurrection or warfare. The problem, however, in Northern Ireland and the Basque Country is that both the state and the paramilitary actors are seeking to secure the consent of a substantial minority to a particular constitutional regime. In such cases, the advantage for government actors is likely to lie with a strategy of adhering as closely as possible to ordinary standards of policing and justice while maintaining reasonable security and order and taking practical political measures aimed at removing the underlying causes of the political violence. For the paramilitaries, the best strategy may be to allow their political voices the opportunity to negotiate in a climate of security for all parties to the conflict.

Internal wars, especially of the ethnic variety, are inevitably, to paraphrase Hobbes, mean, nasty, brutish, and very dirty wars. Forcing Protestant civilians to drive bombs into barracks, the literal butchering of Catholic civilians, the use of gangs and death squads, the kidnapping of businessmen, the execution of Spanish politicians, the deliberate dispersion of IRA and ETA prisoners far from their families, and the use of shoot-to-kill tactics against unarmed IRA volunteers and *etarras* are equal in their abuse of human rights. No party, therefore, to the conflicts in either Northern Ireland or the Basque Country can claim clean hands, but neither can any party claim a monopoly on suffering.

History has repeatedly shown that security measures alone are incapable of resolving the Northern Ireland conflict or ending the violence in the Basque Country. Of course, without these policies, the conflicts might have been much worse. However, to the extent that IRA and ETA military operations increased with the introduction and lifting of extremely repressive measures, it appears that unless governments are prepared and able to abrogate civil and constitutional rights for extended periods of time, extreme measures do little to diminish the appeal of armed struggle as a strategy for militant nationalists.

Given that the principal justification claimed by the IRA and ETA for their strategy of struggle is their inability to secure their political objectives through existing political institutions, a more promising path to resolution, and one supported by the findings of this study, appears to be the provision of incentives for the inclusion, rather than the exclusion, of the political representatives of the IRA and ETA in the political decision-making process. The historical analysis of Sinn Fein and Herri Batasuna has illustrated that as the parties have gained influence within the political process, they have become increasingly committed to that process.

The relegation of antisystem parties to the sidelines of the political arena, Sani (1976, 3) suggests, leads to the reinforcement "of whatever antisystem feelings they might actually have had within them: if not antisystem, they certainly become antiestablishment." Under these circumstances, the gulf between government and opposition widens, and the result is reciprocal distrust. Such strategies, while likely to bring about the consolidation of a fragmented party system, also tend to result in a consolidation of government coalitions characterized by the lack of rotation of political forces and political impasse. The immobility of the Northern Irish party system and the local Basque government provides ample evidence for this argument.

The significance and the costs of prior strategies of delegitimation to all parties that have benefitted from such strategies become clear when, as a result of some modification in the strength of the contending parties or other pressures, the coalition formula that has prevailed becomes politically unviable. When the removal of the antisystem stigma becomes necessary or desirable, parties discover that relegitimation turns out to be extremely difficult and can succeed only slowly, being vulnerable to reversals influenced by domestic or international events. Similarly, I would argue that organizations that have committed acts of violence in the pursuit of political goals will find it difficult to convince their former targets that they would respect their right to express their political opinions freely.

The difficulty for each actor in these situations lies in the need to alter the image of the "other" to make it compatible with the requirements of the new alignment. Sani's description of the effect that the partial delegitimation of the Italian Communist Party (Partito Comunista Italiano, PCI) and the Italian Social Movement (Movimiento Sociale Italiano, MSI) has had on government in Italy provides important insights into the current political impasses in Northern Ireland and the Basque Country, as well as those now confronting Bosnia, Israel, the Autonomous Palestinian Authority, and many other severely divided societies where party elites are discovering that transforming a prior enemy into a prospective partner at the mass level is far more difficult than the creation of an enemy. "[When] the logic of the decisions inspired by historically determined ends is, perhaps, no longer appropriate to the designs of the political elites; the mass level consequences of those decisions are still very much in evidence and far more difficult to change" (Sani 1976, 32). My findings suggest that violence inflicted to exclude groups from power begets violence in order to seize power and leads to the creation of a cycle that can continue for generations, contributing to a further polarization of the parties in conflict. Power has, and will, come from the gun barrel, but only at the cost of civil and constitutional rights, which is often a price willingly paid by those who lack the political will to devolve power or by those who lack the political opportunity to exercise influence in the decision-making process.

On a more optimistic note, this study does support a more positive conclusion regarding the conflicts in Northern Ireland and the Basque Country, and in other severely divided societies in which militant social movement organizations are active. In both cases, participation by these organizations in the political process has resulted in an increasing commitment to the parliamentary process by all parties to the conflict, and when access to the decision-making process has appeared to provide the parties with a *real*, not merely symbolic, chance to influence the resolution of the existing conflicts, violence has been placed "on hold." Decisions by all the parties involved to discuss the demands of each party may offer an alternative solution to armed struggle. In South Africa, the inclusion of the African National Congress (ANC) in the political process resulted in its decision to abandon support of armed struggle as a strategy of political change. The Autonomous Palestine Authority was secured without a "decommissioning" of arms. Similarly, the Dayton talks facilitated an end to ethnic cleansing in the former Yugoslavia and have fostered a fragile peace.

Many would argue that those who engage in violence against the state should not be allowed to participate in the institutions of the state. If that is the argument, then political parties representing those organizations should be banned. To encourage the participation of these parties in the electoral process, while at the same time refusing to treat their representatives like any other legitimately elected representatives, is to impose a double standard on the democratic process. The policy of excluding legally elected representatives from access to government resources, as well as the refusal of political representatives of the government parties to meet with representatives of Sinn Fein and Herri Batasuna, has contributed most to the profound distrust between the parties to the conflicts, rendering any negotiation process more difficult. The imposition of this double standard of "representative democracy," of legalizing, yet concomitantly delegitimating these parties, serves only to give credence to those who portray the liberal democratic process as its opposite: illiberal and undemocratic.

I agree that it is extremely awkward, if not impossible, for governments to negotiate "political issues" with "terrorists." It is possible, however, for governments to negotiate such issues with the legally elected representatives of the political parties that represent the interests of the "terrorist" organizations. From this perspective, Sinn Fein and Herri Batasuna represent not only the appropriate parties with whom their respective governments could negotiate political issues but also, and more importantly, the only agents whose decisions would be accepted as legitimate by those who support the armed struggle of the IRA and ETA. In both Ireland and the Basque Country, the governments' insistence on the decommissioning of weapons has, I would argue, inhibited the ability of Sinn Fein and Herri Batasuna to shift the nationalist struggle from the military to the purely political arena. Indeed, as numerous IRA and ETA strategists have noted, the most significant thing they have to offer in the prenegotiation stage is their ability to end the violence. To play that card before negotiations have begun, they point out, is to risk losing the game before it starts.

While some within the Republican Movement and the MLVN, and within the parties and governments opposed to them, may have vested interests in perpetuating their respective conflicts because it enables them to pursue other objectives they regard as important, the *overwhelming* majority seek a resolution to, not a continuation of, the conflicts. Only a dialogue among all parties to the conflict that allows common interests to arise, or at least allows cooperation to avoid a common bad, can offer hope of reaching the necessary political solution to these most political of conflicts. If the IRA and ETA are to disengage permanently, the forces of the British and Spanish states must likewise disengage and entrust the politics to politicians. This is the republican and *abertzale* challenge to the British and Spanish governments. Those in Westminster and the Cortes should acknowledge that this challenge is also their opportunity, and peace the more likely prize.

Appendix 1

Methodology and Data

On theoretical grounds, Sinn Fein and Herri Batasuna were selected for study on the basis of three essential considerations. First, they offer the possibility of comparing variations in the key relationships under investigation across both space and time. Second, their historical development provides the possibility for both intraunit and interunit comparison, thus reducing somewhat the problem of "small *N*, many variables." Their history also made possible an examination of decisions to reject and to adopt electoral politics, as each organization, prior to its present commitment to engage in institutional politics, had previously rejected entering the electoral process. Finally, the extensive involvement of these organizations in electoral campaigns in the past twenty years makes it possible to study the effects of their participation in institutional politics on their choices of political strategies and organizational structures.

In regard to more practical concerns, I chose these cases because the leadership of each organization granted me the necessary permission to carry out the proposed study and offered to cooperate in the research programs. That few empirical investigations of the internal dynamics of parties linked to paramilitary organizations have been undertaken is understandable, given the security concerns of these organizations and the ambiguous position that these parties, and those who investigate them, often inhabit in relation to the law. That Sinn Fein and Herri Batasuna were willing to permit a limited exploration of their internal organizational structures is, I believe, indicative of the changes in ideology, strategy, and organization that they were experiencing as they were changing from conspiratorial support groups for their comrades in arms to distinct, legal, public, and participatory political parties.

The most important sources of the study are one hundred interviews with the members and former members of the leadership, elected representatives, and grassroots activists in Sinn Fein and Herri Batasuna. It should be noted that unless otherwise indicated, all translations of interviews with Herri Batasuna activists, as well as those of other excerpts from Spanish or French language sources are my own. As a secondary source, I rely on a survey questionnaire distributed to Herri Batasuna activists, which, to the best of my knowledge, is the only existing survey of its militants.

The interviews were conducted throughout Ireland and the southern Basque provinces. Each lasted between forty minutes and four hours. The selection of interviewees was designed to ensure as diverse a range, both geographically and professionally, of activist experience as possible. Years of paramilitary or party activism, residence in urban and rural areas and areas of strong or weak support, and positions of leadership or office-holding within the organization or, externally, in local councils or national parliaments helped to determine the final selections of the interviewees. Using an open and semistructured format, the interviews were designed to cover the social and political backgrounds of the activists, their pathways to activism, their participation in the organizations, and most specifically, the internal debates and discussion regarding the creation of political strategy. A content analysis (Krippendorf 1980) of responses to all the topics covered in the interviews was prepared. This analysis was used to identify general patterns and variations in the pattern of responses.

Additional interviews were carried out in 1995 with ten of the original republican interviewees in order to address issues related to the IRA cease-fire of 31 August 1994. During the period April–August 1997, I carried out a further set of interviews with seven of the original Sinn Fein activists and with five additional members of the republican movement to assess the implications of the collapse of the IRA cease-fire in February 1996 and its subsequent reinstatement in July 1997. During this same period, I was able to interview five Herri Batasuna activists in Ireland, three of whom, by chance, had responded to my questionnaire. These interviews provided information regarding key issues currently being debated within Herri Batasuna.

The survey questionnaire, which was distributed to Herri Batasuna activists in 1989, was designed to focus as closely as possible on the same issues covered in the interviews. The data collection followed common survey methodology. A sample questionnaire was submitted to the Herri Batasuna leadership for examination. Objections were raised to a few questions, but acceptable substitutes were easily negotiated. The questionnaire was pretested by a small group of party activists and then revised to eliminate as many ambiguities of interpretation as possible. To ensure as wide a geographic distribution as possible, the questionnaire was distributed between mid-October and mid-December 1989 at local party meetings held in Araba, Gipuzkoa, Bizkaia, and Nafarroa. The activists completed the questionnaires without interviewer assistance. Of the 125 prepared for distribution, 108 were returned, yielding an excellent return rate of 82 percent. I also distributed the questionnaire to an additional set of twelve activists, four from each of the provinces in the Spanish state who were elected representatives. Although respondents do not represent a true random sample of Herri Batasuna activists, the sampling bias is limited, partly because the distribution of the survey was specifically designed to include as diverse a range as possible of party activism, both vertically and horizontally, and because attendance at party meetings normally exceeds 60 percent—a fact that also partially explains the high number of completed questionnaires returned. The sample clearly reaches beyond a restricted group of national or local party activists and a narrow geographic base. The results of the survey are used primarily for subnational comparisons of party activists and organizational structures.

A similar questionnaire was approved by the leadership of Sinn Fein. However, due to security concerns voiced by the membership, the leadership found it necessary to withdraw the offer. The unwillingness of the Sinn Fein activists to participate in the survey illustrates the conspiratorial background of the party as well as the high levels of repression that have characterized their political environment. For the purpose of public accessibility, the Sinn Fein questionnaire is included, rather than the Herri Batasuna questionnaire, which was prepared in Euskara and Spanish.

Appendix 2

Survey for Sinn Fein Activists

1. Year of birth _____

2. Sex

       1. Female ( )

       2. Male   ( )

3. Place of birth

       1. Ireland ( )

       2. Other   ( )

    a. If born in Ireland, please list county of birth. _____

4.   a. Place of mother's birth

       1. Ireland

       1a. County _____

       2. Other

    b. Place of father's birth

       1. Ireland

       1a. County _____

       2. Other

5. How many persons live in the town in which you reside?

       1. Under 500   ( )

       2. 500–1,000   ( )

3. 1,000–5,000   ( )

4. 5,000–15,000   ( )

5. 15,000–50,000   ( )

6. 50,000–100,000   ( )

7. 100,000–500,000   ( )

8. Over 500,000   ( )

6. If presently living in the six counties, have you ever lived elsewhere?

1. Yes   ( )

2. No   ( )

a. If yes, please indicate where. _____

7. Are you

1. Married   ( )

2. Single   ( )

3. Widow/Widower   ( )

4. Separated/Divorced   ( )

5. Living with male/female friend   ( )

8. Do you have children?

1. Yes   ( )

2. No   ( )

a. If yes, how many children do you have? _____

9. What is the highest level of education you have completed?

1. Primary   ( )

2. Secondary—Leaving Certificate   ( )

3. O-Levels   ( )

4. A-Levels   ( )

5. University   ( )

6. Professional or technical degree   ( )

10. What is the highest level of formal education that one of your parents achieved?

1. Primary   ( )

2. Secondary—Leaving Certificate   ( )

3. O-Levels   ( )

4. A-Levels   ( )
5. University   ( )
6. Professional or technical degree   ( )

11. What is your present occupation? It would be helpful if you could be
as specific as possible. If you are a student, unemployed, pensioner, etc.,
please indicate so.

_____

    a. If not presently working, what was your last occupation?

_____

    b. If a farmer, what is the size of your farm? _____ acres

12. If presently working, are you working
        1. Full time?   ( )
        2. Part time?   ( )
  a. Is this a
        1. Temporary job?   ( )
        2. Permanent job?   ( )
        3. Don't know   ( )

13. If employed, are your employer and fellow employees aware that you are
a member of Sinn Fein?
        1. Yes   ( )
        2. No   ( )

14. Have you ever experienced any disadvantages at work because of being
a member of SF?
        1. Yes   ( )
        2. No   ( )
  a. If yes, please describe. _____
  b. Have you been harassed by members of the Garda or British
    security forces?   Yes ( )   No ( )   If so, please describe.

_____

15. Based on your personal monthly income, would you consider yourself
        1. Very well off?   ( )
        2. Well off?   ( )
        3. Not good, not bad?   ( )

    4. Bad?   ( )
    5. Very bad?   ( )

16. Are you familiar with the Irish language?

    1. Yes   ( )
    2. No   ( )

  a. If yes, do you read and write Irish

    1. Fluently?   ( )
    2. Well?   ( )
    3. Some?   ( )
    4. Not at all?   ( )

  b. speak and understand Irish

    1. Fluently?   ( )
    2. Well?   ( )
    3. Some?   ( )
    4. Not at all?   ( )

17. If you speak Irish, how often do you speak Irish?

    1. All or almost all the time   ( )
    2. Several times a day   ( )
    3. Several times a week   ( )
    4. Seldom   ( )
    5. Never   ( )

  a. With whom and where do you tend to speak Irish?

  _____

18. When you were growing up, how interested was your family in politics?

  1. Very interested—parents, brothers or sisters were active in political
     work and the like.

  2. Interested—There was a lot of conversation about politics, although
     no one in the family was politically active.

  3. Average—Politics was discussed once in a while.

  4. Not very interested—Politics was rarely discussed.

  5. Not interested—Politics was never discussed.

  6. Can't remember.

19. Have you ever been

    a. arrested?   Yes ( ) No ( )

    b. imprisoned? Yes ( ) No ( ) If yes, how long _____

Have any members of your family been arrested?   Yes ( ) No ( )

    a. Have any family members been imprisoned?   Yes ( ) No ( )

    b. Have any family members been killed either
       by the Garda or British security forces?   Yes ( ) No ( )

20. Did your parents belong to a political party when you were growing up?

      ( ) 1. Yes

      ( ) 2. No

      ( ) 3. Don't know

    a. If yes, to which ones?

      1. Mother _____

      2. Father _____

    b. If no, which party, if any, did they generally support?

      1. Mother_____

      2. Father _____

21. In what year did you join Sinn Fein? _____

22. Below are listed several reasons persons have given for becoming involved in politics. How important are each of the following reasons to your participation in SF? Please circle the appropriate number.

	Extremely Important	Very Important	Not Very Important	Not Important
1. Personal friends or members of my family are active in the party as workers, candidates, etc.	1	2	3	4
2. I want to see particular candidates elected.	1	2	3	4
3. I enjoy the friendships and social contacts I have with other people in politics.	1	2	3	4

4. I want to get the party
and its candidates to
support the policies
I believe in.   1   2   3   4

5. I believe the party I
support is the only one
that really cares about
people like myself.   1   2   3   4

6. My party is the only
party that can achieve
the unification of
Ireland and end the
present conflict.   1   2   3   4

7. I feel I, personally, have
many good ideas to
contribute to the party   1   2   3   4

23. If asked why you decided to become active in Sinn Fein, what would you give as the single most important reason for your decision?

_____

24. Since joining Sinn Fein, how, if at all, have your attitudes changed in regards to the importance of electoral politics for Irish independence?

_____

25. Before joining SF, which, if any, party did you generally vote for?
( ) 1. NILP
( ) 2. SDLP
( ) 3. Peoples' Democracy
( ) 4. Republican Clubs
( ) 5. Fianna Fail
( ) 6. Fine Gael
( ) 7. Workers' Party
( ) 8. Labour
( ) 9. Other _____
( ) 10. None

26. Are you a member of a trades union organization?

( ) 1. Yes

( ) 2. No

a. If yes, please specify

Name _____

27. If a member of a trades union, what do you perceive to be the most important roles of trades unions in Ireland?

_____

28. Are you active in any groups, committees, or organizations outside of SF?

( ) 1. Yes

( ) 2. No

29. If yes, please give the name of group(s), where possible, and whether you were already a member before joining SF.

1. Environmental groups

Name		Active Before	
a._____	Yes ( )	No ( )	
b._____	Yes ( )	No ( )	

2. International support groups
(For example, Antiapartheid)

a._____   Yes ( )   No ( )

b._____   Yes ( )   No ( )

3. Feminist groups

a._____   Yes ( )   No ( )

b._____   Yes ( )   No ( )

4. Sports associations

a._____   Yes ( )   No ( )

b._____   Yes ( )   No ( )

5. Cultural/language groups

a._____   Yes ( )   No ( )

b._____   Yes ( )   No ( )

6. Religious/charitable groups

a._____   Yes ( )   No ( )

b._____   Yes ( )   No ( )

7. Other

    a._____ Yes ( ) No ( )

    b._____ Yes ( ) No ( )

30. Have you participated in any of the following political demonstrations?

    a. 1968 Civil Rights marches   1. Yes ( )   2. No ( )

    b. Anti-Internment marches   1. Yes ( )   2. No ( )

    c. Rent and rates strikes   1. Yes ( )   2. No ( )

    d. Bloody Sunday, 1972/Dublin Protest March   1. Yes ( )   2. No ( )

    e. H-Block/Armagh Committee demonstrations   1. Yes ( )   2. No ( )

    f. 1981 Hunger Strike demonstrations   1. Yes ( )   2. No ( )

    g. Strip-Search demonstrations   1. Yes ( )   2. No ( )

    h. International Women's Day demonstrations   1. Yes ( )   2. No ( )

    I. Plastic Bullets/Diplock/Supergrass demonstrations
      1. Yes ( )   2. No ( )

    j. Anti-Extradition demonstrations   1. Yes ( )   2. No ( )

    k. Anti-Sellafield/Environmental Marches   1. Yes ( )   2. No ( )

    l. Abortion/Divorce Referendum Demonstrations
      1. Yes ( )   2. No ( )

31. I would be most grateful if you could give the following details on your cumann.

    a. Name of comhairle ceantair to which cumann belongs _____

    b. Name of comhairle limisteir to which cumann belongs _____

    c. Number of members _____

    d. Number of women members _____

32. How has the membership of your cumann developed over the last 5 years?

    ( ) 1. Decreased

    ( ) 2. Remained the same

    ( ) 3. Increased

    ( ) 4. Greatly increased

    a. How many members who are presently active would you say were active 5 years ago?

( ) 1. Almost all
( ) 2. About half
( ) 3. Few
( ) 4. Very few
( ) 5. None

33. How often would you say you attend cumann meetings?

    ( ) 1. Always
    ( ) 2. Often
    ( ) 3. Occasionally

34. When you attend meetings, which of the following most closely describes your part in the meeting?

    ( ) 1. I listen only.
    ( ) 2. I participate sometimes.
    ( ) 3. I often participate.
    ( ) 4. I always participate.

35. How often are the following topics discussed at the cumann meetings? Please circle the number corresponding to the appropriate category.

	Always	Often	Rarely	Never
1. Local politics	1	2	3	4
2. Six-county politics	1	2	3	4
3. Twenty-six-county politics	1	2	3	4
4. European (EC) politics	1	2	3	4
5. International politics	1	2	3	4
6. Internal SF party issues (for example, finance, paper sales, head-office directives)	1	2	3	4

36. Regardless of how often topics are actually discussed, how interested are you personally in

	Very Interested	Quite Interested	Moderately Interested	Not Interested
1. Local politics?	1	2	3	4
2. Six-county politics?	1	2	3	4

3. Twenty-six-county
   politics?   1   2   3   4

4. European (EC)
   politics?   1   2   3   4

5. International politics?   1   2   3   4

6. Internal SF party
   issues?   1   2   3   4

37. If you think of the last party meeting you attended, were there any differences of opinion among participants concerning decisions to be made?

( ) 1. Yes

( ) 2. No

a. If yes, how are decisions generally reached?

( ) 1. There was discussion until unanimity was reached.

( ) 2. After discussion, they were reached by majority vote.

( ) 3. Decision was put off or referred to party officials.

( ) 4. Other; please specify. _____

38. Have you ever stood as a SF candidate for an elected political office?

( ) 1. Yes

( ) 2. No

a. If yes, do you presently hold an elected position?

( ) 1. Yes

( ) 2. No

39. Have you ever held a local, regional, or national party office?

( ) 1. Yes

( ) 2. No

a. If yes, please indicate at which level you held office and whether you are presently in office.

Level of Office

1. Local   Yes ( )   No ( )

2. District   Yes ( )   No ( )

3. Regional   Yes ( )   No ( )

4. National   Yes ( )   No ( )

40. How often would you say you participate in meetings of the following?

	Always	Often	Seldom	Never
1. National Party Conferences	1	2	3	4
2. National Party Executives	1	2	3	4
3. Comhairle Limisteir Conferences	1	2	3	4
4. Comhairle Ceantair Conferences	1	2	3	4
5. Local Party Conferences	1	2	3	4

41. How active would you consider yourself in SF at the following levels?

	Very Active	Active	Not Very Active	Not at All Active
1. At the local level	1	2	3	4
2. At the district level	1	2	3	4
3. At the regional level	1	2	3	4
4. At the national level	1	2	3	4

42. How would you describe the discussion of the political report for this year's Ard Fheis in your cumman meetings?

( ) 1. There were widely differing opinions.

( ) 2. There was little difference of opinion.

( ) 3. There was no difference of opinion.

( ) 4. There was no discussion.

43. Did you attend this year's party conference?

( ) 1. Yes—Voting delegate

( ) 2. Yes—Non-voting delegate

( ) 3. No

44. From a general point of view, how important, in your opinion, are the following functions of the Ard Fheis?

	Very Important	Important	Not So Important	Not Important
1. The sharing and conveyance of the opinion of the rank-and-file membership to the party leadership	1	2	3	4

2. The laying down of political and organizational guidelines	1	2	3	4
3. The election of the Ard Comhairle	1	2	3	4
4. The presentation of the party to the public	1	2	3	4
5. The preparation of electoral campaigns	1	2	3	4
6. The resolution of internal SF differences	1	2	3	4
7. The careful discussion in detail of the motions and changes in SF policy	1	2	3	4
8. The promotion of contacts between party workers and the leadership	1	2	3	4
9. The promotion of contacts between delegates from different parts of the country	1	2	3	4

10. Others; please specify. _____

45. To what extent, in your opinion, can an individual delegate who possesses specialized knowledge in certain areas influence decisions of the Ard Fheis in those areas? Please check the appropriate box.

	Pre-Conference Stage	At the Ard Fheis
1. Extensively	( )	( )
2. Rather extensively	( )	( )
3. Somewhat	( )	( )
4. Not very much	( )	( )
5. Not at all	( )	( )

46. I would like to ask you to think of your various party-related activities. Which of the following activities occupy you the most?

	Most Frequently	Frequently	Occasionally	Never
1. Recruiting new members	1	2	3	4
2. Organizing SF-sponsored social activities	1	2	3	4
3. Electoral campaigning, for example, canvassing	1	2	3	4
4. Participating in local council meetings	1	2	3	4
5. Participating in voluntary associations, for example, Green Cross, Community Advice Centres	1	2	3	4
6. Preparing party press statements	1	2	3	4
7. Speaking up for the party among friends and co-workers	1	2	3	4
8. Selling *AP/RN*, SF ballots, fundraising	1	2	3	4
9. Participating in developing and elaborating party policy documents	1	2	3	4
10. Maintaining party contacts with other parties and organizations in the country	1	2	3	4
11. Maintaining party contacts with other parties and organizations abroad	1	2	3	4
12. Party-administrative functions	1	2	3	4

13. Others; please specify. _____

47. How much time do you devote to party activities each week?

    ( ) 1. Up to 5 hours

    ( ) 2. 5–10 hours

( ) 3. 15–25 hours

( ) 4. 25–50 hours

( ) 5. 60–80 hours

( ) 6. more than 80 hours

48. Below are four statements about the party's place in political life. Please check your response to each statement.

	Strongly Agree	Agree	Disagree	Strongly Disagree
1. SF should always stand fast to its goals and principles of support for the armed struggle and democratic socialism, even if this should lead to a loss of votes.	1	2	3	4
2. SF should attempt to win the votes of as many voter groups as possible and to represent their interests in any political office.	1	2	3	4
3. Politics is more a matter of getting the best possible out of a given situation than strictly sticking to principles.	1	2	3	4
4. SF needs a firm ideological basis for its goals and policies.	1	2	3	4

49. In politics, the experiences of other countries are often raised as examples when discussing the planning of future policies and strategies. What other countries do you think can represent a useful comparison for Ireland? Please check the three you feel are most useful, placing a "1" next to the most useful, and so on.

( )   1. None

( )   2. Cuba

( )   3. Basque Country

( )   4. Denmark

( )   5. USA

( )   6. The Baltic States, Lithuania, Estonia, Latvia

( )   7. Algeria

( )   8. Nicaragua

( )   9. South Africa

( ) 10. Palestine

( ) 11. Other; please specify. _____

50. In regard to other Irish political parties, particularly at the grassroots level, would you say that your attitudes toward them are

	Somewhat Sympathetic?	Neutral?	Unfavorable?	Very Unfavorable?
1. Fianna Fail	1	2	3	4
2. Fine Gael	1	2	3	4
3. Labour	1	2	3	4
4. Progressive Democrats	1	2	3	4
5. SDLP	1	2	3	4
6. Workers' Party	1	2	3	4
7. Communist Party of Ireland	1	2	3	4
8. Other _____				

51. Please note what you think of the following statements:

	Agree Strongly	Agree	Neutral	Disagree	Disagree Strongly
a. Any SF member could represent the party in political office if given the opportunity to do so.	1	2	3	4	5
b. The influence that individuals hold in SF is less the result of the duties they exercise officially than the result of their presence and contributions in important meetings.	1	2	3	4	5

52. Suppose that in the next few years several members of Sinn Fein were elected to Dail Eireann. Would or wouldn't you approve of Sinn Fein's participating in a coalition government?

      ( ) 1. Approve strongly

      ( ) 2. Approve, but with some hesitation

      ( ) 3. Oppose

      ( ) 4. Strongly oppose

53. How effective, in your opinion, are the following forms of political activity in furthering the objectives of SF?

	Very Effective	Effective	Not Very Effective	Not Effective
1. Signing a petition or referendum	1	2	3	4
2. Participating in a political demonstration	1	2	3	4
3. Self-reduction of rent, rates	1	2	3	4
4. Armed struggle	1	2	3	4
5. Participating in trades union actions	1	2	3	4
6. Operating Citizens' Advice Centres	1	2	3	4
7. Participating in Local Councils	1	2	3	4
8. Participating with other anti-imperialist groups in political campaigns (i.e, anti-extradition, anti-EEC, SOSP-Lifers)	1	2	3	4

54. If a new six-county assembly is formed, would you

      ( ) 1. Very much support a decision by SF to stand candidates?

      ( ) 2. Support such a decision but with some reservations?

      ( ) 3. Not support such a decision?

      ( ) 4. Very much oppose such a decision?

55. Would you

very much support	( )
support with reservation	( )
not support	( )
very much oppose	( )

any SF candidates elected to a six-county assembly participating in that assembly?

56. In political matters people often speak of "the Left" and "the Right." How would you place yourself on this scale? Please circle the corresponding number.

Extreme   Extreme
  Left   Right
    10   9   8   7   6   5   4   3   2   1

57. According to you, what is the real influence, with respect to the
    (1) general policy program, (2) selection of candidates for elections,
    (3) party strategy of the following groups within SF?

	Very Important	Important	Neutral	Not Very Important	Not Important
A. General Political Policy					
1. The Ard Comhairle	1	2	3	4	5
2. Elected SF public officials	1	2	3	4	5
3. Other party officials	1	2	3	4	5
4. Grassroots activists	1	2	3	4	5
5. Ard Fheis	1	2	3	4	5
B. Selection of Candidates for Elections					
1. The Ard Comhairle	1	2	3	4	5
2. Elected SF public officials	1	2	3	4	5
3. Other party officials	1	2	3	4	5
4. Grassroots activists	1	2	3	4	5
5. Ard Fheis	1	2	3	4	5

C. Party Strategy

	Way Too Much	Too Much	About Right	Too Little	Way Too Little
1. The Ard Comhairle	1	2	3	4	5
2. Elected SF public officials	1	2	3	4	5
3. Other party officials	1	2	3	4	5
4. Grassroots activists	1	2	3	4	5
5. Ard Fheis	1	2	3	4	5

58. Now please indicate for each group whether, in your opinion, the group has too much or too little influence on the party's politics.

	Way Too Much	Too Much	About Right	Too Little	Way Too Little
A. General Political Program					
1. The Ard Comhairle	1	2	3	4	5
2. Elected SF public officials	1	2	3	4	5
3. Other party officials	1	2	3	4	5
4. Grassroots activists	1	2	3	4	5
5. Ard Fheis	1	2	3	4	5
B. Choosing Candidates for Elections					
1. The Ard Comhairle	1	2	3	4	5
2. Elected SF public officials	1	2	3	4	5
3. Other party officials	1	2	3	4	5
4. Grassroots activists	1	2	3	4	5
5. Ard Fheis	1	2	3	4	5
C. Party Strategy					
1. The Ard Comhairle	1	2	3	4	5
2. Elected SF public officials	1	2	3	4	5
3. Other party officials	1	2	3	4	5
4. Grassroots activists	1	2	3	4	5
5. Ard Fheis	1	2	3	4	5

59. Realizing that party democracy is not always easy to achieve, I have listed several explanations below. Please indicate for each one whether you agree or disagree.

	Agree Strongly	Agree	Disagree	Disagree Strongly
1. Like every party, SF must occasionally make decisions very rapidly. Therefore, there is not always enough time to consult with its members.	1	2	3	4
2. The party leadership does not make enough efforts to include the membership in making decisions.	1	2	3	4
3. Political problems on the national level are often very complicated. The grassroots members do not know enough about such problems. Therefore, discussion of the problems is difficult.	1	2	3	4
4. Grassroots members are not very interested in political problems at the national level.	1	2	3	4

60. Below you will find a list of important political issues. Please indicate your personal opinion on each issue.

	Agree Completely	Agree	Disagree	Disagree Completely
1. There should be far more active control over activities of multinational corporations operating in Ireland.	1	2	3	4
2. Greater effort should be made to protect the environment.	1	2	3	4
3. Women should be allowed to decide matters concerning abortion.	1	2	3	4
4. Differences in wealth between people should be evened out.	1	2	3	4

5. Privatization of major national
industries should be resisted.   1   2   3   4

6. Environmental regulations
should not be so strict that
industries currently in Ireland
would likely have to withdraw.   1   2   3   4

7. The principle of equal
opportunity for women and
men should be implemented
in all aspects of life.   1   2   3   4

8. The guarantee and extension
of individual liberties is a more
important goal for government
than the fostering of close com-
munity ties and associations.   1   2   3   4

9. Government should guarantee
that everyone who wants a
job can have one.   1   2   3   4

10. Policies should be developed
to reduce regional economic
differences within Ireland.   1   2   3   4

11. Government should fight
against inflation.   1   2   3   4

12. The number of hours in the
work week must be reduced,
even if this means a decrease
in salary.   1   2   3   4

61. Given that it is the stated policy of Sinn Fein to promote the participation of women in the party, I would now like to ask you to indicate
your opinion on the following statements about women in politics.
Please indicate how much you agree or disagree with each of the following statements:

	Strongly Agree	Agree	Uncertain	Disagree	Strongly Disagree
a. Family responsibilities have kept women from participating in politics.	1	2	3	4	5

b. Women don't support
other women who stand
for political office.   1   2   3   4   5

c. Women are taught not
to want political careers.   1   2   3   4   5

d. Men tend to prevent
women from seeking
political careers, either
directly or indirectly,
by not assuming equal
shares of family
responsibilities.   1   2   3   4   5

e. There will be many
more women standing
for political office in
the next few years.   1   2   3   4   5

f. There will be many
more women elected to
political office in the
next few years.   1   2   3   4   5

g. SF provides adequate
resources (childcare, for
example) to those
women who wish to
participate actively in
party activities.   1   2   3   4   5

h. Women who actively
participate in SF are
generally given positions
of major importance.   1   2   3   4   5

62. Lastly, below you will find a list of possible political goals for an Irish
government in the coming years. Please indicate in descending order
(1 = most important; 10 = least important) the importance that you
attribute to them.

( ) Give people more say in the decisions of government.

( ) Maintain a high rate of economic growth.

( ) Protect civil liberties.

( ) Fight against crime.

( ) Give people more say in how things are decided at work and in the community.

( ) Fight rising prices.

( ) Move toward a friendlier, less impersonal society.

( ) Maintain a stable economy.

( ) Move toward a society where ideas are more important than money.

( ) Promote equality to its maximum.

Thank you very much for your cooperation and patience in completing this questionnaire!

Notes

1. Unconstitutional Means to Constitutional Change

1. Gerry Doherty, quoted in *An Phoblacht/Republican News*, 23 May 1985, 9.

2. This prohibition first split the IRA in 1922 as a result of the ratification of the Anglo-Irish Treaty by the pro-treaty members of the Dail by a margin of seven votes (64–57). In April 1926, Eamon De Valera, unable to secure grassroots support within Sinn Fein for participation in Dail Eireann, left Sinn Fein and established the political party Fianna Fail. De Valera had argued that a move to take the party's seats in the Dail should be regarded as a question of tactics, not as a point of principle and that Sinn Fein would be foolish to squander the influence its representatives could wield by taking their seats if the required oath to the British monarch were dropped. The more militant faction within Sinn Fein argued that the basic question was not one of the oath, per se, but of the nature of the Irish "Free State" and its Parliament. This faction argued that true republicans, no matter how many seats they could win, should never lend legitimacy to a "puppet parliament whose strings were pulled from England" (internal SF document, 1928, in author's possession). For these activists, the Second Dail Eireann, which had been elected in 1921 prior to the treaty, remained the only legitimate assembly of the Irish people. Purged of the more moderate elements in both the political and military wings, the Republican Movement was now firmly committed to securing Ireland's independence through physical force.

3. *Etarra* is the word used by Basques to refer to members of ETA.

4. The Basque Parliament is located in Gasteiz (Vitoria) in the province of Araba (Alava).

5. Interview with author, Bilbao, 2 October 1989.

6. By armed struggle, I mean a strategy of political violence related to but distinct from its more advanced "cousins," guerrilla warfare and mass insurgency. Unlike those forms of struggle, in which military force is used to defeat the incumbent regime, a

strategy of armed struggle employs force as a means of inflicting largely symbolic defeats on the incumbent regime. Armed struggle is directed primarily toward securing the political rather than the military overthrow of the state. As Pedro Ibarra Guëll (1989: 28–29) notes, a strategy of armed struggle may be viewed from two distinct perspectives. From one perspective, armed struggle represents the first phase in a strategy of political violence that advances first from armed struggle to guerilla warfare and then from peoples' war to general insurrection and the overthrow of the existing regime. From the other, armed struggle represents an autonomous strategy, sufficient in itself, to achieve its desired goals. This study adopts the latter perspective.

7. See, for example, Marighella (1978).

8. I define as revolutionary any social movement with the goal of a radical change in the existing structures of a state or the dissolution of existing state borders and the establishment of a new state.

9. Paddy Bolger, interview in *IRIS,* 7 (November 1983): 7.

10. Sinn Fein, internal discussion document, July 1983, in author's possession.

11. ETA (Commandos Autonomous), internal discussion document (1979, 275).

12. Until amended in 1986, Sinn Fein's constitution stated that "[n]o person who is a member of any political party, organization or who approves of or supports the candidature of persons who, if elected, intend taking part in the proceedings of either the British or Partition Governments by which Ireland is ruled, or who approves of or supports the candidature of persons who sign any form or give any kind of written or verbal undertaking to take their seats in these institutions, shall be admitted to membership, or allowed to retain membership."

13. John Hannigan (1985, 39), for example, in a prescient analysis of Sinn Fein strategy, remarks, "[W]e need to know more about how military action and political outreach are reconciled and coordinated; . . . future research of this type should be of a more comparative nature, focusing on both variations in RMO structure and on different environments."

14. For more recent analyses of these questions, see Guelke (1993, 1995); della Porta (1992, 1995); Weinberg (1992, 1993, 1995); Wieviorka (1993); and Wickham-Crowley (1992).

15. Important exceptions include the work of Conversi (1993, 1996) on Basque and Catalan nationalism; White (1989, 1993) on Irish republicans; and McGarry and O'Leary (1990, 1995) on the Northern Ireland conflict.

16. Many of the best analyses to date have come from scholar/practitioners of conflict resolution. See, for example, Sisk (1996); Lund (1996); de Silva and Samarasinghe (1993).

17. Among the most insightful studies to date that address this issue is DeNardo (1985). Since the IRA cease-fire in 1994, a wave of books by journalists have chronicled the events leading to the cease-fire. See, for example, the works of McKittrick (1994, 1996); Mallie and McKittrick (1996); O'Brien (1995); and Coogan (1994).

18. As the work of Bowyer Bell (1979, 1988, 1990), which has inspired and guided most of those who followed his footsteps into the field in Northern Ireland, has illustrat-

ed, such research relies more on common sense, an open mind, and personal integrity, rather than some secret or dangerous entry into such groups.

19. These mass behavior theorists, in the tradition of Durkheim, viewed mass protests as symptoms of social anomie and societal disintegration, and perceived those who participated in collective behavior as fundamentally irrational and their actions as expressive rather than purposive.

20. See, for example, Freedman and Alexander (1983); Laqueur (1977, 1979, 1987); Parry (1976); Wilkinson (1986); and Wolfenstein (1971).

21. Attempts to verify empirically the relationship between deprivation, frustration, and aggression as proposed by Gurr (1970) and Davies (1962) have likewise proved futile. See Muller (1980). In recent works examining ethnic conflicts in general, Connor (1994, 153) suggests that while "the emphasis . . . is placed upon economic deprivation (real or imaginary) in ethnonational propaganda, economic arguments can act as a catalyst or exacerbator of national tensions; . . . this is something quite different from acknowledging economic deprivation as a necessary precondition of ethnonational conflict."

22. See, for example, Gamson (1988, 1990); Jenkins (1983, 1985); Jenkins and Klandermans (1995); Kitschelt (1986); Kreisi (1989); Klandermans (1988, 1989, 1995); McAdam (1985, 1988); Tarrow (1989, 1994); and Tilly (1978, 1993).

23. Iñaki Esnaola, quoted in *Tiempo de hoy* no. 252, 9–15 March 1987, 16.

24. HB activist and former *etarra*. Interview with author, 4 October 1989, Donostia.

25. Interview with author, 17 February 1989, Derry.

26. In the case of highly institutionalized radical parties such as Sinn Fein and Herri Batasuna, the same dynamic is used to explain the formation of party strategy and organization, only the direction of radicalism is reversed. In these cases, the more classical formulation of Michels's (1962) "iron law of oligarchy" applies; that is, a more moderate and compromising leadership betrays the radical masses.

27. Within organizations identified with a particular charismatic leader, for example, Sendero Luminoso (Shining Path) and Abimael Guzmán, the authority and control of the leader's grassroots activists are usually explained in terms of some variant of the charismatic leader-follower relationship. This type of relationship, according to McCormick (1988, 110) is based on four properties: (1) the group leader is believed to possess a unique vision and superhuman qualities; (2) followers unquestioningly accept the leader's views, statements, and judgments; (3) they comply with the leader's orders and directives without condition; and (4) they give the leader unqualified support and devotion. Many current analysts would argue that Gerry Adams, president of Sinn Fein, controls the party in a similar fashion. In contrast, I argue that Gerry Adams, though certainly a charismatic leader, is neither sufficiently powerful nor free to impose his strategic preferences on the organization.

28. As Klandermans and Johnston state in the introduction to *Social Movements and Culture* (1995, 3), "[T]he pendulum of Kuhn's normal science now seems to swing toward culture." This volume contains research by scholars at the forefront of cultural analyses of social movements.

29. Among the most compelling analyses of the use of ritual in situations of violent ethnic conflict are those of Feldman (1991) and Aretxaga (1988, 1997).

2. Splits in the Ranks

1. ETA, *Documentos* 10: 199–218.

2. ETA, *Zutik-Berri* no. 50, p. 3; quoted in Bruni (1987, 80).

3. Ibid., 81.

4. ETA, *Documentos* 18: 97.

5. Sinn Fein, *Carrigart,* 1987 (videocassette: 4 hr).

6. Martin McGuinness, quoted in *The Politics of Revolution: The Main Speeches and Debates from the 1986 Sinn Fein Ard Fheis* (Dublin: Sinn Fein, 1986), 26–27.

7. Sinn Fein, "Where Sinn Fein Stands," *An Phoblacht/Republican News,* February 1970, 2.

8. ETA, quoted in Bruni (1977, 106).

9. By terrorism, I refer explicitly to the threat or actual use of coercive force against civilians in order to effect political change. Throughout this work, terrorism is referred to only as a strategy. I disagree strongly with the characterization of movement organizations as "terrorist" organizations. State actors as well as insurgent actors at times employ terrorism as a strategy while maintaining a distinct organizational identity.

10. Daíthí O'Conaill, quoted in O'Malley (1983, 275).

11. As Connor (1994, xi) has noted, there is no difference between ethnonationalism and nationalism if the term *nationalism* is used in its purest form. When I use the terms *ethnonationalism/ethnonationalist movement,* I do so to emphasize the participants' identification with a distinct group of people seeking to establish a sovereign state for their nation. Throughout this work, however, ethnonationalism and nationalism may be regarded as synonyms.

12. Doug Bond, (1992, 3) defines "parapolitical" actions as those forms of nonviolent direct action that are nonconsensual and unilaterally initiated. Examples of parapolitical actions would include participation in illegal demonstrations, boycotts, reclaiming and resettling confiscated land, removing physical barriers placed by security forces to impede border crossings, and so on.

13. Herri Batasuna activist, interview with author, 19 October 1989, Bilbao.

14. Sinn Fein supporter, interview with author, 10 November 1988, Belfast.

15. See, for example, Bandura (1973); Stagner (1965); and Berkowitz (1962).

16. Members of the Royal Ulster Constabulary are colloquially referred to as "Peelers" in Northern Ireland after British Prime Minister Sir Robert Peel.

17. Sinn Fein supporter, interview with author, 3 March 1989, Belfast.

18. Joseba Artexe, Herri Batasuna activist, interview with author, 8 October 1989, Gasteiz.

19. See Lipúzcoa (1973, 59).

20. See de Olabuenaga (1985, 60). In his analysis of 1,500 responses of Basques over the age of 18 (500 in each of the four Basque provinces in the Spanish state), the au-

thor found that 16 percent of respondents had been ill treated by either the Guardia Civil or the National Police. If this figure is transposed to the entire Basque population, it indicates that over a quarter of a million Basques have personally experienced state violence.

21. McGarry and O'Leary (1995, 25) also note that the instrumental model of violence is "not without flaws. In particular it too easily assumes that there are shared interests and goals between activists and their constituencies . . . and that all political violence is strategically aimed at the state and its agencies, rather than being local opportunist or particularistic in its focus."

22. Given the role of IRA violence in precipitating the collapse of the Northern Ireland Parliament, it is not unreasonable to view the IRA campaign as having successfully secured tactical goals.

23. Threat of exit, I believe, has too often been overlooked as a means by which rank-and-file activists can control the leadership.

24. See Gamson (1975, 1990).

3. Resurgent Nationalism in Ireland and the Basque Country

1. See Rowthorn and Wayne (1988).

2. Sinn Fein's tally of 150,000 votes represented 56 percent of the Catholic electorate. Two Sinn Fein candidates were elected: Tom Mitchell for the Mid-Ulster constituency and Phil Clarke for Fermanagh/South Tyrone. At the time of election, both were serving prison sentences. The British government reacted to the results by taking away Mitchell's seat on the grounds that he was a convicted felon. Sinn Fein renominated Mitchell to stand in the Mid-Ulster by-election in August 1955, and he won again. The British again disqualified Mitchell, and another by-election was scheduled for May 1956. This time, the Nationalist Party decided to stand a candidate. Consequently, the Catholic vote was split, and a unionist finally won the seat.

3. The IRA, cited in Kevin Kelley (1982, 74).

4. Cronin (1980, 155).

5. Ibid., 156.

6. Coogan (1987, 385).

7. Bell (1979, 334).

8. Ibid., 337.

9. Peader O'Donnell, leader of the Republican Congress in the 1930s, quoted in Kelley (1982, 85).

10. Joe Austin, interview with author, 4 October 1988, Belfast.

11. Sinn Fein, untitled discussion document (1962), Political Collection, Linen Hall Library, Belfast.

12. The Civil Authorities (Special Powers) Act was introduced in 1922 and renewed annually until 1928, when it was extended for five years. At the end of 1933 it was made permanent. The Special Powers Act gave wide powers of arrest, questioning, search, detention, and internment to the police and other agents of the Northern Ireland Ministry of Home Affairs. See Hogan and Walker (1989, chapter 1).

13. In October 1920, the British government established the Ulster Special Constabulary (USC). It was based on the Ulster Volunteer Force, a totally Protestant paramilitary force that had been reorganized a few months earlier. Hence, the USC was from the outset exclusively Protestant. It was divided into three classes. Class A was for those willing to do full-time duty and be posted anywhere within Northern Ireland; Class B was for those willing to do part-time duty in their own locality; and Class C was for those willing to go on reserve and who could be called in an emergency. According to Hillyard (1983, 33), by August 1922 there were 7,000 A-Specials, 20,000 B-Specials, and 17,000 members in Class C. There were also 1,200 full-time members of the Royal Ulster Constabulary, which had replaced the Royal Irish Constabulary in the same year. The Specials, however, played the central role in establishing the authority of the new government in Northern Ireland.

14. T. Moore, interview with author, 17 February 1989, Derry.

15. Ibid.

16. Official Sinn Fein, *United Irishmen,* October 1968.

17. The "Bogside" refers to the predominantly Catholic area of Derry City. It has traditionally suffered from high rates of unemployment and inadequate housing. It remains one of the most militantly nationalist areas of Northern Ireland.

18. Coogan (1987, 425).

19. Amendments to the Sinn Fein constitution must be passed by two-thirds of the delegates present at the annual party conference.

20. By some accounts, five persons were killed. Approximately sixty civilians and fifteen soldiers were treated for injuries. Except for a restricted period allowed for shopping, residents were not allowed to leave their homes. Widespread accounts of soldiers ripping up floorboards, smashing crucifixes, and throwing holy pictures in toilets during house-to-house searches were reported. The curfew was broken by one thousand women from surrounding areas marching in with supplies of milk and bread; see Hall (1988) and Kelley (1982).

21. SDLP, "SDLP Statement," in *The Sinn Fein and SDLP Talks* (Dublin: Sinn Fein, 1989), 3.

22. See, for example, Irvin and Moxon-Browne (1989, 7–8); and O'Leary (1990, 12–15).

23. Unless otherwise specified, the term *IRA* will refer to those who joined the Provisional IRA and Sinn Fein following the 1970 Sinn Fein *ard fheis.*

24. The information used by the RUC to identify suspected republicans was quite dated, as an attempt to arrest a man who had been dead four years made quite evident. There was also a clear bias in the targets of arrest. Despite the activities of loyalist paramilitaries, only two of the 342 people arrested on August 9 were Protestant (see Farrell 1980, 276–86).

25. Sinn Fein activist, interview with author, 8 November 1988, Belfast.

26. It is widely believed among republicans that the actions of the British Army that day were designed to act as a shock treatment to the nationalist community and to halt the momentum of the Civil Rights Movement. Scholars familiar with the situation, such as Bell (1993) and Coogan (1994), concur with the republican analysis.

27. Sean McManus, Sinn Fein national organizer, interview with author, 8 April 1989, Sligo, Ireland. Similar comments regarding the impact of Bloody Sunday on their activism were made by many of the other activists I interviewed.

28. Many within the official organizations were discontent with the leadership's decision, and in December 1974 this group would split from the organizations to form the Irish Republican Socialist Party and the Irish National Liberation Army, who would offer yet another challenge to the Provisional leadership of the Republican Movement.

29. The death toll for the year included 103 British soldiers, 41 members of the RUC or UDR, and 323 civilians, of whom, according to Hall (1988, 42), 122 were classified as assassinations: 81 Catholics and 41 Protestants. It was the worst death toll to date in the conflict.

30. Pat McGeown, "British Counter-Insurgency Strategy," in *The Starry Plough* no. 1, n. d. (approximately 1992).

31. Brigadier Frank Kitson, Britain's principal counterinsurgency strategist, acknowledged as much in his classic text, *Low-Intensity Operations* (1971), stating, "It is in men's minds that wars of subversion have to be fought and decided."

32. Sinn Fein, *An Phoblacht/Republican News,* 18 February 1973, 2.

33. On 20 June, Daíthí O'Conaill and Gerry Adams met with Whitelaw's representatives, Philip Woodfield and Frank Steele. At this meeting the two delegations agreed to a bilateral truce. For the IRA this formal IRA-British agreement represented a significant political advance and justification for the campaign of the Provisionals, who could reasonably argue they had accomplished more than any other Irish party or politician since the treaty negotiations.

34. The Republican delegation consisted of Sean MacStiofain, Daíthí O'Conaill, Seamus Twomey, Ivor Bell, Martin McGuinness, and Gerry Adams. Dublin lawyer Myles Shevlin served as secretary for the republicans.

35. Note, however, that during this period, the British government had negotiated with the leadership of the IRA under the guise of community leadership regarding such issues as where and when barricades could be placed and taken down and other law-and-order problems, hooliganism being helpful to neither side.

36. The IRA delegation had made two proposals that it regarded as crucial to any future negotiation process. The first asked that the British government publicly declare that it was for the whole people of Ireland, acting and voting as a single unit, to decide the future of Ireland. This demand has remained crucial to republican participation in any peace process. The second proposal demanded that the British government announce its intent to withdraw all troops from Northern Ireland prior to 1 January 1975.

37. In Sinn Fein's record of the most recent set of negotiations with the British government, *Setting the Record Straight,* (1992, 28), a British official who participated in both sets of negotiations quotes Merlyn Rees as having stated, "We set out to con them and we did."

38. Operation Motorman, as Bell (1993, 340) noted, "would be the largest British military effort since the invasion of Suez, involving some twenty-six thousand troops,

armor, Centurion tanks with steel plows instead of guns, air surveillance, a naval expedition, and a propaganda effort."

39. See McGeown, "British Counter-Insurgency Strategy," 5.

40. Ruairí ÓBrádaigh, quoted in Bishop and Mallie (1987, 208).

41. The SDLP won nineteen of the seventy-eight seats. The Republican Clubs failed to elect a single candidate.

42. See Bell (1979, 416).

43. See Liam Clarke (1987, 24–25).

44. The IRA, "People's Assembly," internal strategy document (1975), Political Collection, Linen Hall Library, Belfast.

45. Sinn Fein, "Why Sinn Fein Asks You to Boycott the Convention Elections," Election pamphlet, Political Collection, Linen Hall Library, Belfast.

46. IRA volunteer, quoted in Kelley (1982, 241).

47. Martin McGuinness, quoted in Mallie (1989, 218). McGuinness also noted that as the level of operations dropped, so did morale and numbers, leaving him with "inferior" material to restructure—the reason the IRA had given for agreeing to the ceasefire in the first place.

48. Joe Austin, interview with author, 8 October 1988, Belfast.

49. Republican activist, interview with author, 15 March 1989, Omagh.

50. The term *H-Blocks* refers to the wings of the Maze prison in Northern Ireland. The Maze prison is referred to as Long Kesh by republicans.

51. Principal founding figures of ETA were José Manuel Aguirre, José María Benito de Valle, Julen Madariaga, and José Luis Alvarez Enparanza ("Txillardegi").

52. See, especially Daniele Conversi's (1996) analysis of Basque and Catalan nationalism. Conversi provides an outstanding interpretation of the internal divisions within ETA, focusing especially on the ways in which different conceptions of Basque identity have influenced the evolution of the Basque nationalist movement.

53. During the period 1901–1980, the total net migrations for the Basque provinces were, respectively, Araba (+57,195); Bizkaia (+312,557); Gipuzkoa (+157,575); Nafarroa (–81,058). For more information, see *EGIN,* 1977–1982.

54. The leading intellectual influence within the *tercermundista* faction was Frederico Krutwig Sagredo, whose work, *Vasconia,* written under the pseudonym F. Sarrailh de Ihartza, articulated the action-repression-action theory that guided ETA strategy during this period.

55. Etxebarrieta's writings focused on how the politico-military strategies of Mao Tse-Tung could be adopted to the Basque struggle.

56. ETA, *Documentos,* vol. 18, p. 56.

57. See Ortzi [Francisco Letamendia] (1978, 51).

58. Since this group, led by José María Ezkubi, used the magazine *Saioak* to express their views, they also became known as the *Saioak* group.

59. Clark (1984, 67).

60. See Portell (1974, 172–173).

61. See Onaindia (1980, 109).

4. Sinn Fein and Herri Batasuna

1. The orations given annually in June at the grave of Wolfe Tone, the leader of the 1798 United Irishmen rebellion, have historically been used by republicans to announce the direction the movement would be taking in the coming year.

2. Jimmy Drumm, Sinn Fein activist, quoted in Kelley (1982, 265).

3. Joe Austin, interview with author, 8 October 1988, Belfast.

4. The prisoners' five demands were for the rights (1) to wear their own clothes; (2) to refrain from prison work; (3) to associate freely with one another; (4) to organize recreational facilities and to have one letter, visit, and parcel a week; and (5) to have lost remission time fully restored.

5. Tom Hartley, Sinn Fein general secretary, interview with author, 5 March 1989, Belfast.

6. Jim McAllister, Sinn Fein activist, interview with author, 18 March 1989, Crossmaglen, Northern Ireland.

7. Mitchell McLaughlin, interview with author, 19 March 1989, Derry.

8. Anonymous, quoted in author's interview with Ivan Barr, Sinn Fein councillor, in Strabane, Co. Fermanagh, 6 November 1988.

9. Teresa Moore, interview with author, 3 April 1989, Derry.

10. John Hume, leader of SDLP, quoted in O'Malley (1983, 124).

11. Interview with Jim Gibney, Sinn Fein activist, 8 April 1989, Belfast.

12. See Browne (1981, 6).

13. The "Sands Bill," which barred convicted felons from contesting elections, had been implemented in June 1981. Carron, who had been Bobby Sands's election agent, was nominated as a proxy candidate for the prisoners. Needless to say, the IRA made much of the legislative changes, claiming that the British had changed the rules of their own parliamentary game because they no longer liked the way it was being played by Irish republicans.

14. IRA, quoted in *IRIS* 1 (November 1981), 3.

15. Bobby Lavery, Sinn Fein activist and elected representative, interview with author, 10 November 1988, Belfast.

16. John Doyle, quoted in *An Phoblacht/Republican News,* 5 August 1982, 4 (hereafter cited as *AP/RN*).

17. The "Sticks," or "Stickies," is the name given by IRA and Sinn Fein supporters to those who remained in the Official IRA and Sinn Fein after the 1970 split. Their name derives from the fact that the traditional Easter Lily emblem sold by Sinn Fein to commemorate the Easter 1916 Uprising is attached to the lapel with a pin, while that sold by the Officials is attached with a sticky glue backing.

18. P. Short, quoted in *AP/RN,* 9 September 1982, 8.

19. IRA, quoted in *AP/RN,* 2 September 1981, 1.

20. IRA, quoted in *AP/RN,* 18 September 1982, 2.

21. Sinn Fein, editorial in *AP/RN,* 5 September 1981, 3.

22. IRA, quoted in *AP/RN,* 7 October 1982, 1.

23. Sinn Fein, internal discussion paper, in author's possession, 1982, 2.

24. Ibid., 4.

25. Bobby Lavery, Sinn Fein Belfast City Councillor, interview with author, 14 March 1989, Belfast.

26. IRA, quoted in *AP/RN,* 16 September 1982, 6.

27. Gerry Adams, interview with author, 7 December 1989, Belfast.

28. Gerry Adams, cited in Michael Farrell, "The Armalite and the Ballot Box," *Magill* (July 1983), 13.

29. For detailed analyses of the assembly election and its functioning, see O'Leary, Elliot, and Wilford (1988), and Elliot and Wilford, *The 1982 Northern Ireland Assembly Election* (Glasgow: Centre for the Study of Public Policy, University of Strathclyde, 1983).

30. The Northern Ireland Forum elections of May 1996 witnessed the consolidation of three additional Unionist bloc parties: the Progressive Unionist Party and the Unionist Democratic Party, both of which are linked to Protestant paramilitary groups, and the UK Unionist Party, represented by Robert McCartney and Conor Cruise O'Brien. The election of candidates representing the Women's Coalition would strengthen the political "center."

31. See Ulster Marketing Survey (1989, 3).

32. See Elliott and Smith (1985, 36).

33. Data from a 1989 survey (Ulster Marketing Survey, 1989: Table 1.1) of the Northern Irish electorate underlines the difference in the age profile more starkly: whereas the 18–24 age group is the only group in which Sinn Fein is overrepresented in relation to its overall support, the same age group is the only one in which the SDLP is underrepresented. It appears that the electoral battle between the two parties will continue to be fought among the youngest Catholic voters.

34. See MORI survey (1984).

35. The level of ETA-related deaths was considerably higher. Clark (1984, 126–28) has calculated that approximately 700 people were injured as a result of ETA operations. Among the most significant of the ETA attacks were (1) the 17 March 1978 bombing of the Leméniz nuclear plant, which resulted in two deaths and the injuring of fourteen construction workers; (2) the 21 March 1978 bombing of the motor vehicle pool of the Spanish government ministries in Madrid, which injured 14; the 20 November 1978 machine-gun attack on national police playing a soccer match, which killed two and wounded eleven; (4) the 29 July 1979 simultaneous bombings of the airport and two railroad stations in Madrid, which left six dead and approximately one hundred wounded; and (5) the 22 July 1980 bombing of a Guardia Civil convoy in Logroño, which killed one and injured thirty-four.

36. Iruñea (Pamplona), the provincial capital of Nafarroa (Navarra), is widely regarded as the historic center of Euskadi. Nafarroa also represents over 60 percent of the Basque territory and is the most agriculturally productive area of the ethnonation. The exclusion of Nafarroa from the autonomous Basque community was viewed both as a symbolic assault on the Basque ethnonation and an attempt by Madrid to reduce the viability of an independent Basque state.

37. Although the vote had been divided fairly evenly among the Basque and Spanish parties prior to the Second Republic, the Spanish Right made considerable gains in Nafarroa in 1936, becoming the dominant party.

38. Miguel de Castells Arteche, "Amnistía y Elecciones," *Punto y Hora,* 14–20 April 1977, 19.

39. Zabaleta was one of the founding members of EHAS, the party formed from the merger of HAS and EAS.

40. Patxi Zabaleta, "Elecciones en Euskadi: Tocan a Fuego," *Punto y Hora,* 14–20 April 1977, 8.

41. HASI, "Ponencia KAS," *Second Congress,* September 1983, 17. Internal document in author's possession.

42. Herri Batasuna, "Ponencia sobre participación en las instituciones," April 1983, 19. Internal document in author's possession.

43. This platform, which remains the platform of ETA(m) today, was derived from the ETA(pm) manifesto issued for Aberri Eguna (Homeland Day) in 1975.

44. Eduardo Moreno ("Pertur") was one of the ETA leaders who was most in favor of a turn to electoral politics. He disappeared under suspicious circumstances after meeting with his more pro–armed struggle rival for the leadership of ETA(pm), Miguel Angel Apalategui Ayerbe ("Apala").

45. Parties such as HASI, which explicitly advocated separation from Spain, were not legalized and could not participate in the elections.

46. ETA, cited in Bruni (1987, 266–67).

47. HASI, *First Congress Report,* May 1978, 4. Internal party document in author's possession.

48. "Acuerdo inicial de partidos de la izquierda abertzale entre las municipales," editorial in *Egin,* 25 October 1977, 5.

49. Herri Batasuna, "Carta abierta de la Mesa Nacional de HB al EBB del PNV," cited in *Egin,* 6 February 1982, 1–2.

50. Gilen Azoaga, "Los Abertzales Ante el Referendum Constitucional," *Punto y Hora,* 29 June–5 July 1978, 34–35.

51. See *EGIN, 1977–1982,* 182–86.

52. ETA, cited in Ibarra Güell (1989: 117).

53. Pablo Gorostiaga, Herri Batasuna activist and elected representative, interview with author, 6 November 1989, Laudio.

54. ETA, "ETA frente a las elecciones generales," quoted in Bruni (1987, 278).

55. Election results appear in *EGIN,1994,* 151.

56. Herri Batasuna, quoted in *Punto y Hora,* 12–19 March 1979, 3.

57. Herri Batasuna, quoted in *Egin,* 14 March 1979, 8.

58. See *EGIN,1994,* 151.

59. By 5 July, more than a dozen bombings had rocked many of Spain's most luxurious resorts; see Clark (1984, 113).

60. ETA(m), "Communication to Euskadi Press," August 1979, quoted in Bruni (1987, 284).

61. ETA(pm), interview given to an *El País* journalist in November 1979, quoted in Bruni (1987, 284).

62. The combined abstention rate for the three provinces of Araba, Gipuzkoa, and Bizkaia was 40.2 percent. Of the 59.8 percent who voted, over 80 percent voted for the statute.

63. See FOESSA (1981) for the year 1979 and *EGIN, 1977–1982,* 194.

64. On a scale from 1 (extreme left) to 10 (extreme right), the positions of the party were HB, 2.29; EE, 2.68; and the PNV, 4.67. See FOESSA (1981) and Gunther, Sani, and Shabad (1988, 373–75).

65. See *EGIN, 1994,* 151.

66. According to Clark (1984, 118) eighty-nine people were killed by ETA in 1980.

5. Republicans and Abertzales

1. Brigadier James Glover, a former General Commanding Officer of British Forces in Northern Ireland, drew up a secret report for the Army entitled "Northern Ireland: Future Terrorist Trends," which detailed the army's assessment of the IRA. The report, quoted in full in Cronin (1980, 339–57), concluded that "[o]ur evidence of the caliber of the rank-and-file terrorists does not support the view that they are merely mindless hooligans drawn from the unemployed and unemployable. . . . PIRA is essentially a working-class organization based in the ghetto areas of the cities and in the poor rural areas. The Provisionals' campaign of violence is likely to continue while the British remain in Northern Ireland. . . . We see little prospect of political development of a kind which would seriously undermine the Provisionals' position. PIRA . . . will still be able to attract enough people with the leadership talent, good education, and manual skills to continue to enhance their all-around professionalism."

2. Ricardo Garcia Damborenea, PSOE party leader, quoted in *Epoca,* 25 May 1987, 53.

3. Mr. W. A. F. Agnew, OUP elected representative for Newtownabbey, quoted in *Northern Ireland Assembly Official Report: Government Attitudes to Sinn Fein,* 1984, vol. 12, 246.

4. Conor Cruise O'Brien, in the *London Observer,* 3 October 1982, 5. As Fine Gael minister of posts and telegraphs in 1973, O'Brien was responsible for the introduction of Section 31 of the Irish Broadcasting Act, which, until 1994, prohibited interviews with representatives of Sinn Fein on radio or television.

5. Mr. David Wells, Official Unionist Party member of the Northern Ireland Assembly, quoted in *Northern Ireland Assembly Official Report: Government Attitudes to Sinn Fein,* 1984, vol. 12, 267–68.

6. Javier Pradera, editor of *El País,* quoted in *Egin,* 6 March 1979, 8.

7. Joseba Elósegui, PNV elected representative, quoted in *Egin,* 26 October 1982, 4.

8. José María Benegas, PSOE elected representative, quoted in *Egin,* 19 June 1986, 7.

9. Manuel Fraga Iribarne, AP elected representative, quoted in *Egin,* 6 June 1986, 7.

10. Inazio Oliveri, PNV elected representative, quoted in *Egin,* 24 June 1986, 14.

11. Juan María Bandrés, president of EE, quoted in *Egin,* 14 June 1987, 7.

12. Xavier Arzallus, PNV leader, quoted in *Punto y Hora,* 22–29 October 1987, 18.

13. Inazio Oliveri, EA elected representative, quoted in *Egin,* 11 June 1987, 11.

14. During the period 1978–1988, unemployment in Euskadi Sur exceeded the unemployment rate for the rest of Spain. See *EGIN, 1989,* 198.

15. In Sinn Fein, full-time activists generally have received approximately the same amount as they would receive in unemployment benefits. Herri Batasuna full-time activists similarly receive a minimum wage.

16. HB activist, interview with author, 8 December 1989, Tolosa.

17. See, for example, Policy Studies Institute (1987a, 1987b).

18. SF activist, interview with author, 5 March 1989, Belfast.

19. HB activist and former *etarra,* interview with author, 2 October 1989, Bilbao.

20. HB activist, interview with author, 5 December 1989, Donostia.

21. De Olabuenaga (1985, 74–75) found that while 58 percent of HB respondents expressed a fear of unjust arrest, only 17 percent of PNV voters expressed such fears.

22. HB activist, interview with author, 5 October 1989, Galdakao.

23. SF activist, interview with author, 15 October 1988, Portadown.

24. *Iris Bheag* first appeared in August 1987, less than a year after the Ó Brádaigh faction had walked out as a result of the party's decision to take any seats won in the Irish Parliament. Many of the items contributed by the leadership to the magazine appear to represent an attempt to gauge the membership's attitudes on those issues.

25. Tippex (pseudonym), *Iris Bheag* 1 (1987), 2.

26. Penfold (pseudonym), quoted in *Iris Bheag* 2 (1987), 3.

27. Ibid., 5.

28. Owen (pseudonym), *Iris Bheag* 8 (1988), 5.

29. See Clark (1984, 94–96).

30. ETA, *Hautsi* 2 (January 1973), quoted in Bruni (1987), 151.

31. SF, "Six-County Strategy Paper" (1984), 2, in author's possession.

32. Ibid., 3.

33. Ed Cairns, quoted in Horowitz (1985, 134).

34. Sixty-seven percent of the Sinn Fein activists declaring independence as their primary goal were fluent Gaelic speakers. All of the Herri Batasuna activists in this category were fluent in Euskara, three being native speakers, one having learned the language as a teenager.

35. See, for example, Paul R. Brass, "Ethnicity and Nationality Formation," *Ethnicity* 3 (September 1976) and Robert Melson and Howard Wolpe, "Modernization and the Politics of Communalism: Theoretical Perspective," *American Political Science Review* 64 (December 1970). For an excellent critique of the tendency of American scholars, in particular, to exaggerate the influence of economic factors on the mobilization of ethnonational movements, see Walker Connor's chapter, "American Scholarship in the Post-World War II Era," in Connor (1994, 28–66).

36. SF activist, interview with author, 20 April 1998, Co. Roscommon.

37. SF activist, interview with author, 3 November 1989, Co. Fermanagh.

38. *Ikastola* is the term for schools in which Euskara is the primary language of instruction.

39. Pero (pseudonym), "Nationalism and Socialism," *Iris Bheag* 9 (1988), 13.

40. HB activist, interview with author, 18 October 1989, Gazteiz.

41. Sinn Fein, "The Effects on Developing Such Strategy on Sinn Fein's Attitudes, for example, towards Armed Struggle, Abstentionism, Social Policy, etc." (internal discussion paper), 1983, in author's possession.

42. Gorka Martinez Bilbao, HB activist, interview with author, 17 November 1989, Bilbao.

43. SF activist, interview with author, 3 October 1988, Derry.

44. HB member of executive committee, interview with author, 17 November 1989, Bilbao.

45. SF activist, interview with author, 3 October 1988, Derry.

46. HB member of executive committee, interview with author, 17 November 1989, Bilbao.

47. Armstrong (pseudonym), "Broad Front Bullshit," *Iris Bheag* 18 (1989), 8.

48. HB activist, interview with author, 4 October 1989, Bilbao.

49. The indices used to distinguish the three types in the survey sample included the respondent's perception of the effectiveness of armed struggle (very effective—not effective), and his or her position (agree strongly—disagree strongly) on participation in electoral politics and political institutions. In the HB survey sample, 70 percent of respondents viewed attacks on security forces as effective and 53 percent viewed attacks on security forces in which civilians were killed as effective. Sixty-five percent were opposed to routine political participation in government institutions.

50. Among the survey respondents, 48 percent reported having participated in 7–8 key protests, and 29 percent reported participating in 5–6 events.

51. Pablo Gorostiaga, HB elected representative, interview with author 21 November 1989, Laudio.

52. SF activist, interview with author, 20 April 1989, Dublin.

53. In the SF sample, 65 percent identified themselves as opportunists, 35 percent as pragmatists. In the HB interview sample, 45 percent identified as opportunists and 55 percent as pragmatists. In the HB survey sample, 47 percent identified as opportunists, 53 percent as pragmatists.

54. Sinn Fein internal strategy document, 1984, in author's possession.

55. HB activist, interview with author, 7 November 1989, Galdakao.

56. Gerry Adams (1982, 157–58).

57. Iñaki Piñedo, interview with author, 23 November 1989, Gazteiz.

58. Pat Doherty, SF party organizer, 5 May 1989, Dublin.

59. Tasio Erkizia, quoted in *Askatzen* (HB Foreign Affairs bulletin) 5 (April 1988), 3.

60. HB activist, interview with author, 20 November 1989, Bilbao.

61. Sinn Fein, "Needs of the Struggle in the 26 Counties" (internal discussion document), 1987, in author's possession.

62. SF activist, interview with author, 20 April 1989, Dublin.

63. Groupy (pseudonym), "The Single European Act," *Iris Bheag* 1 (1987), 7.

64. Results from the analysis of the Herri Batasuna survey indicated that the distribution of types among those activists was quite similar to that of the interview sample. The indices used to determine the distribution of activists in the survey included their view of the efficacy of armed struggle, the relative value of adherence to organizational principles or political gains, and their degree of support for the party's participation in political institutions. See questions 48, 52, and 54 in the questionnaire in appendix 2.

6. Regime Responsiveness, Recruitment, and Movement Strategies

1. HMSO. *Report of the Commission to Consider Legal Procedures to Deal with Terrorist Activities in Northern Ireland.* Cmd 5185. 1972.

2. See Irish Information Partnership, *Agenda,* 1989.

3. The term *supergrass* has its origins in the colloquial use of the phrase "to grass," or to inform on someone. *Supergrass,* which derives from a pop song verse that refers to the "whispering grass," was used to refer explicitly to informers recruited by the British security forces to infiltrate the IRA and testify against large numbers of IRA volunteers. Perhaps the most notorious of the "supergrasses" was Christopher Black, whose testimony resulted in thirty-five convictions with sentences totaling 4022 years.

4. In 1973 the ratio of charges to yearly shootings and explosions was 24 percent. By 1985, the ratio had risen to 152 percent. See Rowthorn and Wayne (1988), appendix 4.

5. Brendan O'Brien (1995, 129).

6. According to Tom Hartley, one of the party theorists involved with drafting the *Scenario for Peace* document, the plan had emerged from the ongoing debate within the Republican Movement, which while publicly committed to a long-war strategy, was nonetheless cognizant of that strategy's limitations and was searching for a strategy that would enable Sinn Fein to overcome its political isolation and carry the struggle forward in the political arena. Perhaps one of the most telling indicators of the context of the internal debate was the recognition, albeit limited, of the need for Protestant participation in any political settlement (interview with author, 3 April 1996, Lexington, Ky.).

7. In the aftermath of the Garvaghy Road march, serious rioting broke out in Belfast and Derry, and divisions between the communities were further intensified. In July 1997, the British government again decided that forcing the Orange March down the Garvaghy Road, despite the intense opposition of the nationalist residents of the community through which the Orangemen marched, was the "least worst option." Following the march, rioting again erupted throughout the six Northern counties, and the INLA declared that it would shoot any Orangeman attempting to march through the nationalist Ormeau community in Belfast on 12 July. Failing to receive assurances from the RUC of its ability to protect the marchers, the Orange Order canceled or rerouted its most contentious 12 July marches, signaling a significant change in the internal balance of political power in Northern Ireland.

8. In their analysis of all deaths related to the Northern Irish conflict, researchers

with the Northern Ireland *Cost of the Troubles Study* (University of Ulster–INCORE) research group have determined that Belfast suffered, both absolutely and proportionately, the greatest number of conflict-related fatalities.

9. Portell (1974, 156–57).

10. Amnesty International, *Report of an Amnesty International Mission to Spain 3–28 October 1979* (London: Amnesty International, 1980); see also Amnesty International, *Spain: The Question of Torture* (London: Amnesty International, 1985).

11. See Clark (1990, 246).

12. In my conversations with MLVN activists, the bombing was more generally regarded as an attempt by ETA to strengthen its negotiating hand by illustrating both its popular political support and its military capabilities. In particular, the choice of Barcelona as the site for the bombing was perceived as a demonstration of ETA's capacity to disrupt the 1992 Olympics.

13. The Madrid anti-terrorist pact was signed by representatives of all the parties elected to the Cortes, with the exception of EA and HB, on 5 November 1987. The Basque anti-ETA pact, known as the Ajuria Enea Pact, was signed by all parties participating in the Basque Parliament on 12 January 1988; the EA representative signed "with reservations."

14. The Basque anti-ETA pact takes its name from the official residence of the president of the Basque Parliament in Gasteiz.

15. Herri Batasuna's vote fell from 251,849 in the 1987 European Union elections to 215, 878 in the June 1989 European Union elections.

16. In 1983, the distribution of persons arrested under antiterrorist legislation in Euskadi Sur was, respectively, Araba, 10 percent; Nafarroa, 12 percent; Gipuzkoa, 38 percent; Bizkaia, 40 percent. In 1988, the distribution was Araba, 11 percent; Nafarroa, 12 percent; Gipuzkoa, 38 percent; Bizkaia, 34 percent.

17. The ratio of victims to the population of each province, per 1,000, was 0.14 for Araba; 0.05 for Nafarroa; 0.13 for Bizkaia, and 0.34 for Gipuzkoa.

18. The distribution of the 504 *etarras* imprisoned in 1986–87 by province was Araba, 5 percent; Nafarroa, 10 percent; Gipuzkoa, 38 percent; Bizkaia, 40 percent; other, 7 percent.

19. Txillardegi, "Testimonios personales de la crisis teoríco política que motive mi salida de ETA," *Cuaderno de Formación de IPES* 1 (1980), 37.

20. As an indicator of concern with economic issues, I created a variable by combining scores on membership in a trade union (1 if a member, 0 otherwise), attitudes toward economic well-being (1 if not well off, 0 if well off), and ranking of issues regarding economic issues (1 if two or more issues ranked important, 0 if not).

21. I have used both ordinary least squares and logistic regression techniques as the dependent variables; types of activists are dummy variables. Since both sets of equations were statistically significant, I have chosen to present the results of the OLS estimation, as the results are more readily interpretable.

7. People, Places, and Political Violence

1. These findings are mirrored quite closely in the works of Perez-Agote (1984), White (1993), and Zulaika (1988).

2. Wieviorka (1993), in his study of members of the Red Brigades, Prima Linea, and members of the radical Basque nationalist movement, expands the analysis regarding the relationship between state and antistate violence by arguing that the emergence of antistate terrorist violence is a response to the collapse of mass-based social movements. In the Basque case, however, Wieviorka concludes that ETA continues to exist because it has succeeded in retaining its links to the broader Basque public through its political wing, Herri Batasuna, and the other constituent organizations that comprise the Basque Movement for National Liberation (MLVN).

References

Books and Articles

Adams, Gerry. 1986. *The Politics of Irish Freedom*. Kerry: Brandon Publishers.

Ahmad, Eqbal. 1971. "Revolutionary Warfare and Counterinsurgency." In *National Liberation and Revolution in the Third World*, ed. Norman Miller and Roderick Aya. New York: Free Press.

Akenson, Donald. 1992.*God's Peoples: Covenant and Land in South Africa, Israel, and Ulster*. Ithaca, N.Y.: Cornell University Press.

Alexander, Yonah, and Alan O'Day, eds. 1986. *Ireland's Terrorist Dilemma*. Dordrecht: Martinus Nijhoff.

Alinsky, Saul. 1972. *Rules for Radicals: A Pragmatic Primer for Realistic Radicals*. New York: Vintage Books.

Amnesty International. 1980. *Report of an Amnesty International Mission to Spain*. 28 October 1979. London: Amnesty International.

———. 1985. *Spain: The Question of Torture*. London: Amnesty International.

Apalategi, Jokin, and Paulo Iztueta. 1977. *El Marxismo y la cuestión nacional Vasca*. Zarauz: Itxaropena.

Arregi, Natxo. 1981. *Memorias del KAS, 1975–1978*. San Sebastián: Hordago.

Arteaga, Federico de. 1971. *ETA y el proceso de Burgos*. Madrid: Aguado.

Arthur, Paul. 1984. *The Government and Politics of Northern Ireland*. London: Longman.

———. 1990. "Republican Violence in Northern Ireland: The Rationale." In *Political Violence: Ireland in a Comparative Perspective*, ed. John Darby, N. Hodge, and A. C. Hepburn. Belfast: Appletree Press.

Aretxaga, Begoña. 1988. *Los funerales en el nacionalismo Vasco*. San Sebastián: Baroja 1997.

———. 1993. "Striking with Hunger: Cultural Meanings of Political Violence in

Northern Ireland." In *The Violence Within: Cultural and Political Opposition in Divided Nations,* ed. Kay B. Warren. Oxford: Westview Press.

———. 1997. *Shattering Silence: Women, Nationalism and Political Subjectivity in Northern Ireland.* Princeton: Princeton University Press.

Bandura, Albert. 1973. *Aggression: A Social Learning Experience.* Englewood Cliffs, N.J.: Prentice-Hall.

Barnes, Samuel H. 1976. *Party Democracy: Politics in a Socialist Federation.* New Haven, Conn.: Yale University Press.

Barnes, Samuel, and Max Kasse, eds. 1979. *Political Action: Mass Participation in Five Western Democracies.* Beverly Hills, Calif.: Sage.

Barry, Brian. 1978. *Sociologists, Economists, and Democracy.* Chicago: University of Chicago Press.

Beach, Stephen W. 1977. "Social Movement Radicalization: The Case of the People's Democracy in Northern Ireland." *Sociological Quarterly* 18: 305–18.

Bell, J. Bowyer. 1979. *The Secret Army: A History of the IRA, 1916–1979.* Dublin: Academy Press.

———. 1988. *The Gun in Politics: An Analysis of Irish Political Conflict, 1916–1986.* New Brunswick, N.J.: Transaction Books.

———.1990. *IRA Tactics and Targets: An Analysis of Tactical Aspects of the Armed Struggle 1969–1989.* Swords, County Dublin: Poolbeg Press.

———. 1993. *The Irish Troubles: A Generation of Violence, 1967–1992.* Dublin: Gill and Macmillan.

Berkowitz, Leonard. 1962. *Aggression: A Social Psychological Analysis.* New York: McGraw-Hill.

Berman, Paul. 1974. *Revolutionary Organization.* Lexington, Mass.: D. C. Heath.

Birrell, Derek. 1972. "Relative Deprivation as a Factor in the Conflict in Northern Ireland." *Sociological Review* 20 (3): 317–44.

Bishop, Patrick, and Eamonn Mallie. 1987. *The Provisional IRA.* London: Hutchinson.

Bond, Douglas. 1992. "Nonviolent Direct Action and the Diffusion of Power." In *Justice Without Violence,* ed. Paul Wehr, Heidi Burgess, and Guy Burgess. Boulder, Colo.: University of Colorado Conflict Resolution Consortium.

Bowles, Samuel, and Herbert Gintis. 1986. *Democracy and Capitalism: Property, Community and the Contradiction of Modern Social Thought.* New York: Basic Books.

Brass, Paul R. 1976. "Ethnicity and Nationality Formation." *Ethnicity* 3 (September 1976).

Brawngart, Richard G., and Margaret M. Brawngart, 1987. "Generational Politics." In *Annual Review of Political Science* 2: 34–83.

Breuilly, John. 1985. *Nationalism and the State.* Chicago: University of Chicago Press.

Browne, Vincent. 1981. "H-Block Crisis: Courage, Lies, and Confusion." *Magill* 6 (August): 5–8.

Bruce, Steve. 1992. *The Red Hand: Protestant Paramilitaries in Northern Ireland.* Oxford: Oxford University Press.

————. 1994. *The Edge of the Union: The Ulster Loyalist Political Vision.* Oxford: Oxford University Press.

Bruni, Luigi. 1987. *E.T.A.: Historia politica de una lucha armada.* Bilbao: Txalaparta.

Budge, Ian, Ivor Crewe, and Dennis Farlie, eds. 1976. *Party Identification and Beyond.* London: John Wiley.

Burton, Frank. 1978. *The Politics of Legitimacy.* London: Routledge and Kegan Paul.

Cameron, David R. 1974. "Toward a Theory of Political Mobilization." *Journal of Politics* 36: 133–71.

Castells, Miguel. 1977. "Amnistia y elecciones." *Punto y Hora,* 14–20 April, 19.

————. 1982. *Radiografia de un modelo represivo.* San Sebastián: Ediciones Vascas.

Clark, Peter B., and James Q. Wilson. 1961. "Incentive Systems: A Theory of Organization." *Administrative Science Quarterly* 6: 129–66.

Clark, Robert P. 1980. *The Basques: The Franco Years and Beyond.* Reno: University of Nevada Press.

————. 1981. "Language and Politics in Spain's Basque Provinces." *West European Politics* 4: 85–103.

————. 1984. *The Basque Insurgents: ETA, 1952–1980.* Madison: University of Wisconsin Press.

————. 1990. *Negotiating with ETA: Obstacles to Peace in the Basque Country, 1975–1988.* Reno: University of Nevada Press.

Clarke, Liam. 1987. *Broadening the Battlefield: The H-Blocks and the Rise of Sinn Fein.* Dublin: Gill and Macmillan.

Connor, Walker. 1972. "Nation-Building or Nation-Destroying?" *World Politics* 24: 319–55.

————. 1973. "The Politics of Ethnonationalism." *Journal of International Affairs* 27: 1–21.

————. 1994. *Ethnonationalism: The Quest for Understanding.* Princeton: Princeton University Press.

Conversi, Daniele. 1990. "Language or Race? The Choice of Core Values in the Development of Catalan and Basque Nationalisms." *Ethnic and Racial Studies* 13 (1): 189–200.

————. 1993. "Domino Effects or Internal Developments? The Influences of International Events and Political Ideologies on Catalan and Basque Nationalism." *West European Politics* 16 (3): 245–70.

————. 1994. "Reassessing Current Theories of Nationalism: Nationalism as Boundary Maintenance and Creation." *Nationalism and Ethnic Politics* 1 (1): 73–85.

————. 1996. *The Basques, the Catalans, and Spain: Alternative Routes to Nationalist Mobilization.* Reno: University of Nevada Press.

Coogan, Tim Pat. 1987. *The IRA.* 2d ed. London: The Pall Mall Press.

————. 1994. *The IRA: A History.* Niwot, Colo.: Roberts Rinehart Publishers.

Cormack, R. J., and R. D. Osborne, eds. 1983. *Religion, Education, and Employment in Northern Ireland.* Belfast: Appletree Press.

Cormack, R. J., R. D. Osborne, and W. T. Thompson. 1980. *Into Work: Young School*

Leavers and the Structure of Opportunity in Belfast. 5th Report. Belfast: Fair Employment Agency.

Crelinsten, Ronald D. 1988. "The Internal Dynamics of the FLQ During the October Crisis of 1970." In *Inside Terrorist Organizations,* ed. David Rapoport. New York: Columbia University Press.

Crenshaw, Martha.1985. "An Organizational Approach to the Analysis of Political Terrorism." *Orbis* 29: 465–88.

———. 1988. "Theories of Terrorism: Instrumental and Organizational Approaches." In *Inside Terrorist Organizations,* ed. David C. Rapoport. New York: Columbia University Press.

———. 1990. "The Logic of Terrorism: Terrorist Behavior as a Product of Strategic Choice." In *Origins of Terrorism: Psychologies, Ideologies, Theologies, States of Mind,* ed. Walter Reich. Cambridge: Cambridge University Press.

Cronin, Sean. 1980. *Irish Nationalism.* Dublin: Academy Press.

Curtis, Liz. 1984. *Ireland: The Propaganda War.* London: Pluto Press.

Darby, John. 1983. *Northern Ireland: The Background to the Conflict.* Belfast: Appletree Press.

———. 1990. "Northern Ireland: The Persistence and Limitations of Violence." In *Conflict and Peacemaking in Multiethnic Societies,* ed. Joseph V. Montville. Lexington, Mass.: D. C. Heath.

Davies, James C. 1962. "Toward a Theory of Revolution." *American Sociological Review* 27: 5–19.

———. 1969. "The J-Curve of Rising and Declining Satisfactions as Cause of Some Great Revolutions and a Contained Rebellion." In *Violence in America: Historical and Comparative Perspectives,* ed. Hugh Davis Graham and Ted Robert Gurr. Washington, D.C.: U.S. Government Printing Office.

de Ihartza, Fernando Sarrailh [Federico Krutwig]. 1963. *Vasconia.* Buenos Aires: Ediciones Norbait.

de la Cueva, Justo. 1988. *La Escisión del PNV.* Bilbao: Txalaparta.

della Porta, Donatella. 1988. "Recruitment Processes in Clandestine Political Organizations: Italian Left-Wing Terrorism." In *From Structure to Action: Comparing Social Movement Research across Cultures,* ed. Bert Klandermans, Hanspeter Kriesi, and Sidney Tarrow. London: JAI Press.

———. 1992. "Life Histories in the Analysis of Social Movement Activists." In *Studying Collective Action,* ed. Mario Diani and Ron Eyerman. London: Sage.

———. 1995. *Social Movements, Political Violence, and the State: A Comparative Analysis of Italy and Germany.* Cambridge and New York: Cambridge University Press.

della Porta, Donatella, and Sidney Tarrow. 1986. "Unwanted Children: Political Violence and the Cycle of Protest in Italy, 1966–1973." *European Journal of Political Research* 14: 607–32.

DeNardo, James. 1985. *Power in Numbers.* Princeton: Princeton University Press.

de Olabuenaga, José I. Ruiz.1985. *Violencia y ansiedad en el País Vasco.* Bilbao: Ediciones Tarttalo.

De Silva, K. M. and S.W. R. Samarasinghe. 1993. *Peace Accords and Ethnic Conflict.* New York: St. Martin's Press.

Douglass, William A., ed. 1985. *Basque Politics: A Case Study in Ethnic Nationalism.* Reno, Nev.: University of Nevada Press.

Douglass, William, and Joseba Zulaika. 1990. "On the Interpretation of Terrorist Violence: ETA and the Basque Political Process." *Comparative Studies in Society and History* 32 (2): 238–57.

Downs, Anthony. 1967. *An Economic Theory of Democracy.* New York: Harper and Row.

Dunn, John. 1989. *Modern Revolutions.* Cambridge: Cambridge University Press.

Duverger, Maurice. 1954. *Political Parties: Their Organization and Activity in the Modern State.* Trans. Thomas Ebermann and Ranier Trampert. London: Methuen.

Eckstein, Harry. 1970. "On the Etiology of Internal Wars." In *Struggles in the State,* ed. George A. Kelly and Clifford W. Brown. London: John Wiley and Sons.

———. 1975. "Case Study and Theory in Political Science." In *Handbook of Political Science,* ed. F. I. Greenstein and N. W. Polsby. Reading, Mass.: Addison-Wesley.

Eckstein, Susan, ed. 1989. *Power and Popular Protest: Latin American Social Movements.* Berkeley: University of California Press.

Edelman, Murray. 1971. *Politics as Symbolic Action.* Chicago: Markham.

Eldersveld, Samuel J. 1964. *Political Parties: A Behavioral Analysis.* Chicago: Rand McNally.

Elliott, Sydney, and F. J. Smith. 1985. *Northern Ireland: The District Council Elections of 1985.* Belfast: Queen's University Belfast.

Elliott, Sydney, and R. A. Wilford. 1982. *The 1982 Northern Ireland Assembly Election.* Glasgow: Centre for the Study of Public Policy, Strathclyde.

Enloe, Cynthia H. 1973. *Ethnic Conflict and Political Development.* Boston: Little, Brown.

Esman, Milton, ed. 1977. *Ethnic Conflict in the Western World.* Ithaca, N.Y.: Cornell University Press.

———. 1990. "Political and Psychological Factors in Ethnic Conflict." In *Conflict and Peacemaking in Multiethnic Societies,* ed. Joseph V. Montville. Lexington, Mass.: D.C. Heath.

———. 1994. *Ethnic Politics.* Ithaca, N.Y.: Cornell University Press.

Etzioni, Amatai. 1975. *A Comparative Analysis of Complex Organizations.* New York: Free Press.

Farrell, Michael. 1980. *Northern Ireland: The Orange State.* 2d ed. London: Pluto Press.

Feierabend, Ivo K., Rosalind L. Feierabend, and Ted R. Gurr, eds. 1972. *Anger, Violence, and Politics: Theories and Approaches.* Englewood Cliffs, N.J.: Prentice-Hall.

Feldman, Allen. 1991. *Formations of Violence: The Narrative of the Body and Political Terror in Northern Ireland.* Chicago: University of Chicago Press.

Freedman, Lawrence Z., and Yonah Alexander, eds. 1983. *Perspectives on Terrorism.* Wilmington, Del.: Scholarly Resources.

Gamson, William A. 1975. *The Strategy of Social Protest.* Homewood, Ill.: The Dorsey Press.

————. 1988. "Political Discourse and Collective Action." In *From Structure to Action: Comparing Social Movement Research across Cultures.* Vol.1, ed. Bert Klandermans, Hanspeter Kriesi, and Sidney Tarrow. Greenwich, Conn: JAI Press.

————. 1990. *The Strategy of Social Protest.* 2d. ed., rev. Belmont, Calif.: Wadsworth.

Garmendia, José A. 1979. *Historia de ETA.* 2 vols. San Sebastián: L. Haranburu.

Gay, Peter. 1962. *The Dilemma of Democratic Socialism.* New York: Collier Books.

George, Alexander L. 1979. "Case Studies and Theory Development: The Method of Structured, Focused Comparison." In *Diplomacy: New Approaches in History, Theory, and Policy,* ed. Paul Gordon Lauren. New York: Free Press.

Goodspeed, Donald James. 1962. *The Conspirators: A Study of the Coup d'État.* New York: Viking Press.

Gordon, Charles C., and Nicholas Babchuk. 1959. "A Typology of Voluntary Organizations." *American Sociological Review* 24: 22–29.

Guelke, Adrian. 1983. "The 'Ballot Bomb': The Northern Ireland Assembly Election and the Provisional IRA." Paper prepared for the European Consortium for Political Research, Freiburg, West Germany, 20–25 March, 3.

————. 1988. *Northern Ireland: The International Perspective.* Dublin: Gill and Macmillan.

————. 1993. *Interdependence and Transition: The Cases of South Africa and Northern Ireland.* South Africa: South African Institute of International Affairs.

————. 1995. *The Age of Terrorism and the International Political System.* London: I. B. Tauris Publishers.

Gunther, Richard, Giacamo Sani, and Goldie Shabad. 1988. *Spain After Franco: The Making of a Competitive Party System.* Berkeley: University of California Press.

Gurr, Ted Robert. 1970. *Why Men Rebel.* Princeton: Princeton University Press.

————. 1993. *Minorities at Risk: A Global View of Ethnopolitical Conflicts.* Washington, DC: United States Institute of Peace Press.

Hadden, Tom, Kevin Boyle, and Colm Campbell. 1987. "Emergency Law in Northern Ireland: The Context." In *Justice Under Fire: The Abuse of Civil Liberties in Northern Ireland,* ed. Anthony Jennings. London: Pluto Press.

Hall, Michael. 1988. *Twenty Years: A Concise Chronology of Events in Northern Ireland, 1968–1988.* Newtownabbey, N. Ireland: Island Publications.

Hannigan, John A. 1985. "The Armalite and the Ballot Box: Dilemmas of Strategy and Ideology in the Provisional IRA." *Social Problems* 33: 31–40.

Hargrove, Erwin C. 1970. "Nationality, Values, and Change." In *Comparative Politics* 2, 3: 473–500.

Hechter, Michael. 1973. *Internal Colonialism: The Celtic Fringe in British National Development, 1536–1966.* Berkeley: University of California Press.

Herman, Edward S., and Frank Brodhead. 1984. *Demonstration Elections: U.S. Staged Elections in the Dominican Republic, Vietnam, and El Salvador.* Boston: South End Press.

Hewitt, Christopher. 1981. "Catholic Grievances, Catholic Nationalism, and Violence in Northern Ireland During the Civil Rights Period: A Reconsideration." *British Journal of Sociology* 32: 362–80.

————. 1983. "Discrimination in Northern Ireland: A Rejoinder." *British Journal of Sociology* 34: 446–51.

————. 1984. *The Effectiveness of Anti-Terrorist Policies.* New York: University Press of America.

————. 1987. "Explaining Violence in Northern Ireland." *British Journal of Sociology* 38: 88–93.

Hibbs, Douglas A. 1973. *Mass Political Violence: A Cross-National Causal Analysis.* New York: John Wiley.

Hillyard, Paddy. 1983. "Law and Order." In *Northern Ireland: The Background to the Conflict,* ed. John Darby. Belfast: Appletree Press.

Hirschman, Albert O. 1970. *Exit, Voice, and Loyalty.* Cambridge, Mass.: Harvard University Press.

————. 1982. *Shifting Involvement: Private Interest and Public Action.* Princeton: Princeton University Press.

Hoffer, Eric. 1951. *The True Believer: Thoughts on the Nature of Mass Movements.* New York: Mentor Books.

Hogan, Gerard, and Clive Walker. 1989. *Political Violence and the Law in Ireland.* Manchester: Manchester University Press.

Horowitz, Donald L. 1985. *Ethnic Groups in Conflict.* Berkeley: University of California Press.

————. 1990. "Making Moderation Pay." In *Conflict and Peacemaking in Multiethnic Societies,* ed. Joseph V. Montville. Lexington, Mass.: D. C. Heath.

————. 1993. "Democracy in Divided Societies." *Journal of Democracy* 4 (4): 18–38.

Hutchinson, John. 1987. *The Dynamics of Cultural Nationalism: The Gaelic Revival and the Creation of the Irish Nation State.* London: Allen and Unwin.

Ibarra Güell, Pedro. 1989. *La Evolución Estratégica de ETA.* Donostia: Kriselu.

Irvin, Cynthia L. 1992. "Terrorists' Perspectives: Interviews." In *Terrorism and the Media,* ed. David L. Paletz and Alex P. Schmid. London: Sage.

Irvin, Cynthia L., Francisco S. Llera, and José M. Mata. 1993. "ETA: From Secret Army to Social Movement: The Post-Franco Schism of the Basque Nationalist Movement." *Terrorism and Political Violence* 5 (3): 106–34.

Irvin, Cynthia L., and Edward Moxon-Browne. 1989. "Not Many Floating Voters Here." *Fortnight* no. 270 (May): 6–8.

Janda, Kenneth. 1980. *Political Parties: A Cross-National Survey.* New York: Free Press.

Jauregui Bereciartu, Gurutz. 1981. *Ideología y estrategia política de ETA: Análisis de su evolución entre 1959 y 1968.* Madrid: Siglo XXI.

————. 1994. *The Decline of the Nation State.* Reno, Nev.: University of Nevada Press.

Jaureguiberry, Francis. 1983. *Question nationale et mouvements sociaux au Pays Basque Sud.* Ph.D. diss., Ecole des Hautes Etudes en Sciences Sociaux, Paris.

Jenkins, J. Craig. 1983. "Resource Mobilization Theory and the Study of Social Movements." *American Review of Sociology* 9: 527–53.

————. 1985. *The Politics of Insurgency: The Farmworkers' Movement in the 1960s.* New York: Columbia University Press.

Jenkins, J. Craig, and Bert Klandermans, eds. 1995. *The Politics of Social Protest: Comparative Perspectives on States and Social Movements.* Minneapolis: University of Minnesota Press.

Jennings, Anthony, ed. 1987. *Justice Under Fire: The Abuse of Civil Liberties in Northern Ireland.* London: Pluto Press.

Johnson, Chalmers. 1966. *Revolutionary Change.* Boston: Little, Brown.

Kelley, Kevin. 1982. *The Longest War: Northern Ireland and the IRA.* London: Zed Press.

Keniston, Kenneth. 1970. *The Uncommitted: Alienated Youth in American Society.* New York: Dell Publishing Company.

Kimmel, Michael S. 1990. *Revolution: A Sociological Interpretation.* Philadelphia: Temple University Press.

Kitschelt, Herbert. 1986. "Political Opportunity Structures and Political Protest: Anti-Nuclear Movements in Four Countries." *British Journal of Political Science* 16: 57–85.

———. 1988. "Organization and Strategy in Belgian and West German Ecology Parties: A New Dynamic of Party Politics in Western Europe?" *Comparative Politics* 20: 127–54.

———. 1989. *Logics of Party Formation: Structure and Strategy in the Belgian and West German Ecology Parties.* Ithaca, N.Y.: Cornell University Press.

———. 1990. *Beyond the European Left: Ideology and Political Action in the Belgian Ecology Parties.* Durham, N.C.: Duke University Press.

Kitson, Frank. 1971. *Low Intensity Operations: Subversion, Insurgency, Peace-Keeping.* London: Faber.

Klandermans, Bert. 1984. "Mobilization and Participation: Social Psychological Expansions of Resource Mobilization Theory." *American Sociological Review* 49: 583–600.

———. 1988. "The Formation and Mobilization of Consensus." In *International Social Movement Research,* vol. 1, ed. Bert Klandermans, Hanspeter Kriesi, and Sidney Tarrow. Greenwich, Conn.: JAI Press.

Klandermans, Bert, and Hank Johnston, eds. 1995. *Social Movements and Culture.* Minneapolis: University of Minnesota Press.

Klare, Michael T., and Peter Kornbluh, eds. 1988. *Low-Intensity Warfare: Counterinsurgency, Proinsurgency, and Antiterrorism in the Eighties.* New York: Pantheon Books.

Knoke, David. "Incentives in Collective Action Organizations." *American Sociological Review* 53, 3: 311–29.

Knoke, David, and Christine Wright-Isak. 1982. "Individual Motives and Organizational Incentive Systems." *Research in the Sociology of Organizations* 1: 209–54.

Kreisi, Hanspeter. 1988. "The Interdependence of Structure and Action: Some Reflections on the State of the Art." In *From Structure to Action: Social Movement Participation across Cultures,* International Social Movement Research, vol. 1, ed. Bert Klandermass, Hanspeter Kriesi, and Sidney Tarrow. Greenwood, Conn.: JAI Press.

Kreisi, Hanspeter, Rudd Koopmans, Jan Willem Dyvendak, and Marco G. Giugni, eds. 1995. *New Social Movements in Western Europe.* Minneapolis: University of Minnesota Press.

Krippendorf, Klaus. 1980. *Content Analysis: An Introduction to Its Methodology.* Beverly Hills, Calif.: Sage.

Lange, Peter. 1975. "The PCI at the Local Level: A Study of Strategic Performance." In *Communism in Italy and France,* ed. Donald Blackmer and Sidney Tarrow. Princeton: Princeton University Press.

Laqueur, Walter. 1979. *Terrorism.* Boston: Little, Brown.

———. 1987. *The Age of Terrorism.* Boston: Little, Brown.

Laswell, H. D. 1960. *Psychopathology and Politics.* New York: Viking Press.

———. 1962. *Power and Personality.* New York: Viking Press.

Le Bon, Gustav. 1960. *The Crowd: A Study of the Popular Mind.* New York: Viking Press.

Lee, J. J. 1985. *Ireland: Politics and Society, 1912–1985.* Cambridge: Cambridge University Press.

Leiden, Carl, and Karl M. Schmitt. 1968. *The Politics of Violence: Revolution in the Modern World.* Englewood Cliffs, N.J.: Prentice-Hall.

Levi, Margaret, and Michael Hechter. 1985. "A Rational Choice Approach to the Rise and Decline of Ethnoregional Parties." In *New Nationalisms of the Developed West,* ed. Edward A. Tiryakian and Ronald Rogowski. Boston: Allen and Unwin.

Lijphart, Arend. 1971. "Comparative Politics and the Comparative Method." *American Political Science Review* 65: 682–93.

———. 1975. "The Comparable-Case Strategy in Comparative Research." *Comparative Political Studies* 8: 158–77.

———. 1977. *Democracy in Plural Societies.* New Haven, Conn.: Yale University Press.

———. 1990. "The Political Consequences of Electoral Laws, 1945–85." *American Political Science Review* 84: 481–96.

Linz, Juan J. 1973. "Early State-Building and Late Peripheral Nationalisms against the State: The Case of Spain." In *Building States and Nations,* ed. S. N. Eisenstadt and Stein Rokkan. Beverly Hills: Sage.

———. 1980. "The Basques in Spain: Nationalism and Political Conflict in a New Democracy." In *Resolving Nationality Conflicts: The Role of Public Opinon,* ed. W. Phillips Davison and Leon Gordenker. New York: Praeger.

———. 1985. "From Primordialism to Nationalism." In *New Nationalisms of the Developed West,* ed. Edward A. Tiryakian and Ronald Rogowski. Boston: Allen and Unwin.

Linz, Juan J., Manuel Gómez Reino, Francisco A. Orizo, and Darío Vila. 1986. *Conflicto en Euskadi.* Madrid: Espasa-Calpe.

Lipset, Seymour M., and Stein Rokkan, eds. 1967. *Party Systems and Voter Alignments: Cross-National Perspectives.* New York: Free Press.

Lipúzcoa, Manu Elu. 1973. *La iglesia como problema en el País Vasco.* Buenos Aires: Editorial Vasca Ekin.

Llera, Francisco J. 1984. "El sistema de partidos Vasco: Distancia ideológica y legitimación política." *Revista Española de Investigaciones Sociológicas* 28: 171–206.

———. 1985. *Postfranquismo y fuerzas políticas en Euskadi: Sociología electoral del País Vasco.* Bilbao: Universidad del País Vasco.

Lund, Michael S. 1996. *Preventing Violent Conflicts: A Strategy for Preventive Diplomacy.* Washington, D.C.: United States Institute of Peace Press.

Lustick, Ian. 1985. *State-Building Failure in British Ireland and French Algeria.* Berkeley: Institute of International Studies, University of California.

———. 1993. *Unsettled States, Disputed Lands: Britain and Ireland, France and Algeria, and the West-Bank-Gaza.* New York: Cornell University Press.

Mair, Peter. 1979. "The Autonomy of the Political: The Development of the Irish Party System." *Comparative Politics* 11: 445–65.

Mallie, Eamonn, and Patrick Bishop. 1987. *The Provisional IRA.* London: Heinemann.

Mallie, Eamonn, and David McKittrick. 1996. *The Fight for Peace: The Secret Story behind the Irish Peace Process.* London: Heinemann.

March, James G., and Johan P. Olsen. 1976. *Ambiguity and Choice in Organizations.* Bergen, Norway: Universitetsforlaget.

Marighella, Carlos. 1978. *The Minimanual of the Urban Guerrilla.* San Francisco: Patrick Arguello Press.

Mayo, Patricia. 1974. *The Roots of Identity: Three National Movements in Contemporary European Politics. Wales, Euzkadi, and Brittany.* London: Allen Lane.

McAdam, Doug. 1985. *Political Process and the Development of Black Insurgency, 1930–1970.* Chicago: The University of Chicago Press.

———. 1988. "Micromobilization Contexts and Recruitment to Activism." In *From Structure to Action,* ed. Bert Klandermans, Hanspeter Kriesi, and Sidney Tarrow. Greenwich, Conn.: JAI Press.

———. 1990. *Freedom Summer.* New York: Oxford University Press.

McAllister, Ian, and Sarah Nelson. 1979. "Modern Developments in the Northern Irish Party System." *Parliamentary Affairs* 32: 279–316.

McCann, Eamonn. 1980. *War in an Irish Town.* London: Pluto Press.

McCormick, Gordon H. 1988. "The Shining Path and Peruvian Terrorism." In *Inside Terrorist Organizations,* ed. David C. Rapoport. New York: Columbia University Press.

McGarry, John, and Brendan O'Leary, eds. 1990. *The Future of Northern Ireland.* Oxford: Oxford University Press.

———. 1995. *Explaining Northern Ireland: Broken Images.* Oxford: Blackwell Publishers.

McKittrick, David. 1994. *Endgame: The Search for Peace in Northern Ireland.* Belfast: Blackstaff Press.

———. 1996. *The Nervous Peace.* Belfast: Blackstaff Press.

Melson, Robert, and Howard Wolpe. 1970. "Modernization and the Politics of Communalism: Theoretical Perspective." *American Political Science Review* 64 (December 1970).

Merkl, Peter H., ed. 1980. *Western European Party Systems: Trends and Prospects.* New York: Free Press.

———. 1986. *Political Violence and Terror: Motifs and Motivations.* Berkeley: University of California Press.

Meyer, Joan W., and Brian Rowan. 1987. "Institutionalized Organizations: Formal Structure as Myth and Ceremony." *American Journal of Sociology* 83: 340–63.

Michels, Robert. [1911] 1962. *Political Parties.* English edition. New York: Free Press.

Moxon-Browne, Edward. 1983. *Nation, Class, and Creed in Northern Ireland.* Aldershot, England: Gower.

Muller, Edward N. 1980. "The Psychology of Political Protest and Violence." In *Handbook of Political Conflict: Theory and Research,* ed. Ted Gurr. New York: Free Press.

Muller, Edward N., and Karl-Dieter Opp. 1986. "Rational Choice and Rebellious Collective Action." *American Political Science Review* 80: 472–87.

Muller, Edward N., and Mitchell A. Seligson. 1987. "Inequality and Insurgency." *American Political Science Review* 81: 425–51.

Murray, Dominic, and John Darby. 1978. *The Vocational Aspirations and Expectations of School Leavers in Londonderry and Strabane.* 6th Report. Belfast: Fair Employment Agency.

Nairn, Tom. 1977. *The Breakup of Britain.* London: New Left Books.

Nuñez-Astrain, Luis C. 1977. *Clases Sociales en Euskadi.* San Sebastián: Editorial Txertoa.

———. 1980. *Euskadi Sur Electoral.* San Sebastián: Ediciones Vascas.

Oberschall, Anthony. 1973. *Social Conflict and Social Movements.* Englewood Cliffs, N.J.: Prentice-Hall.

O'Brien, Brendan. 1995. *The Long War: The IRA and Sinn Fein.* Dublin: The O'Brien Press.

O'Hegarty, P. S. 1919. *Sinn Fein: An Illumination.* Dublin: Maunsel.

O'Leary, Brendan. 1990. "More Green, Fewer Orange." *Fortnight* no. 281 (February): 12–15.

O'Leary, Brendan, and John McGarry. 1993. *The Politics of Antagonism: Understanding Northern Ireland.* London and Atlantic Heights, N.J.: Athlone

O'Leary, Brendan, Tom Lyne, Jim Marshall, and Bob Rowthorn. 1993. *Northern Ireland: Sharing Authority.* London: Institute of Public Research.

O'Leary, Cornelius, Sydney Elliot, and R. A. Wolford. 1988. *The Northern Ireland Assembly, 1982–1986: A Constitutional Experiment.* London: C. Hurst and Company.

Olson, Mancur. 1965. *The Logic of Collective Action: Public Goods and the Theory of Groups.* Cambridge: Harvard University Press.

O'Malley, Padraig. 1983. *The Uncivil Wars: Ireland Today.* Belfast: Blackstaff Press.

———. 1990a. *Northern Ireland: Questions of Nuance.* Belfast: Blackstaff Press.

———. 1990b. *Biting at the Grave: The Irish Hunger Strikes and the Politics of Despair.* Belfast: Appletree Press.

Onaindia, Mario. 1979. *Euskadiko Ezkerra ante el Estatuto.* Bilbao: Euskadiko Ezkerra.

———. 1980. *La lucha de clases en Euskadi, 1939–80.* San Sebastián: Hórdago.

Oots, Kent Layne. 1986. *A Political Organization Approach to Transnational Terrorism.* Westport, Conn.: Greenwood Press.

Ortzi [Francisco Letamendia]. 1975. *Historia de Euskadi: El nacionalismo Vasco y ETA.* Barcelona: Ruedo Ibérico.

———. 1976. *Los Vascos ayer, hoy, y mañana.* San Sebastián: Editorial Txertoa.

———. 1978. *Los Vascos: Sintesis de su historia.* San Sebastián: Hórdago.

———. 1979. *El no Vasco a la reforma.* 2 vols. San Sebastián: Editorial Txertoa.

Osborne, Robert, and Robert J. Cormack. 1983. *Religion, Education, and Employment: Aspects of Equal Opportunity in Northern Ireland.* Belfast: Appletree Press.

Panebianco, Angelo. 1988. *Political Parties: Organization and Power.* Cambridge: Cambridge University Press.

Parry, Albert. 1976. *Terrorism: From Robespierre to Arafat.* New York: Vanguard Press.

Payne, Stanley. 1975. *Basque Nationalism.* Reno: University of Nevada Press.

Pérez-Agote, Alfonso. 1984. *La reproducción del nacionalismo: El caso vasco.* Madrid: Centro de Investigaciones Sociológicos.

Perrow, Charles. 1986. *Complex Organizations: A Critical Essay.* 3d ed. Glencoe, Ill: Scott, Foresman.

Pfeffer, Jeffrey, and Gerald Salancik. 1978. *The External Control of Organizations.* New York: Harper and Row.

Pierson, Christopher. 1986. *Marxist Theory and Democratic Politics.* Berkeley: University of California Press.

Pinard, Maurice. 1971. *The Rise of a Third Party.* Englewood Cliffs: N.J.: Prentice-Hall.

Piven, Frances Fox, and Richard A. Cloward. 1979. *Poor People's Movements.* New York: Vintage Books.

Poole, Michael. 1990. "The Geographical Location of Political Violence." In *Political Violence: Ireland in Comparative Perspective,* ed. John Darby, N. Hodge, and A. C. Hepburn. Belfast: Appletree Press.

Portell, José María. 1974. *Los hombres de ETA.* Barcelona: DOPESA.

Preston, Paul. 1986. *The Triumph of Democracy in Spain.* London: Methuen.

Probert, Belinda. 1978. *Beyond Orange and Green: The Political Economy of the Northern Ireland Crisis.* London: Verso.

Przeworski, Adam, and John Sprague. 1986. *Paper Stones: A History of Electoral Socialism.* Chicago: University of Chicago Press.

Ragin, Charles. 1979. "Ethnic Political Mobilization: The Welsh Case." *American Sociological Review* 44: 619–35.

Rapoport, David C., ed. 1988. *Inside Terrorist Organizations.* New York: Columbia University Press.

Rawkins, Phillip. 1985. "Living in the House of Power: Welsh Nationalism and the Dilemma of Antisystem Politics." In *New Nationalisms of the Developed West,* ed. Edward A. Tiryakian and R. Rogowski. Boston: Allen and Unwin.

Reinares, Fernando, ed. 1982. *Terrorismo y sociedad democrática.* Madrid: Akal.

———. 1984. *Violencia y política en Euskadi.* Bilbao: Desclée de Brouwer.

Rejai, Mostafa, and Kay Phillips. 1979. *Leaders of Revolution.* Beverly Hills: Sage.

Richardson, John M., Jr., and Jianxin Wang. 1993. "Peace Accords: Seeking Conflict-Resolution in Deeply Divided Societies." In *Peace Accords and Ethnic Conflicts,* ed. K. M. de Silva and S. W. R. de A. Samarasinghe. London: Frances Pinter.

Rincón, Luciano. 1985. *ETA (1974–1984).* Barcelona: Plaza y Janés.

Robertson, David. 1976. *A Theory of Party Competition.* London: John Wiley.

Rogowski, Ronald. 1973. *Rational Legitimacy.* Princeton: Princeton University Press.

Rose, Richard. 1971. *Governing without Consensus.* London: Faber.

Rowthorn, Bob, and Naomi Wayne. 1988. *Northern Ireland: The Political Economy of Conflict.* Cambridge: Polity Press.

Samarasinghe, S. W. R. de A., and Reed Coughlan. 1991. *Economic Dimensions of Ethnic Conflict.* New York: St. Martin's Press.

Sani, Giacomo. 1976. "Mass Constraints on Political Realignments: Perceptions of Anti-System Parties in Italy." *British Journal of Political Science* 6: 1–31.

Sartori, Giovanni. 1966. "European Political Parties: The Case of Polarized Pluralism." In *Political Parties and Political Development,* ed. J. Palombara and M. Weiner. Princeton: Princeton University Press.

———. 1976. *Parties and Party Systems: A Framework for Analysis.* New York: Cambridge University Press.

Sartori, Giovanni, and Giacomo Sani. 1983. "Polarization, Fragmentation, and Competition in Western Democracies." In *Western European Party Systems: Continuity and Change,* ed. Hans Daalder and Peter Mair. Beverly Hills, Calif.: Sage.

Schlesinger, Joseph A. 1984. "On the Theory of Party Organization." *The Journal of Politics* 46: 369–98.

Schorske, Carl. 1970. *German Social Democracy, 1905–1917.* New York: Russell and Russell.

Scott, W. Richard. 1987. *Organizations: Rational, Natural, and Open Systems.* 2d ed. Englewood Cliffs, N.J.: Prentice-Hall.

Silver, Morris. 1974. "Political Revolution and Repression: An Economic Approach." *Public Choice* 17: 63–71.

Silverman, David. 1970. *The Theory of Organizations.* London: Heinemann.

Sinn Fein. [1985]. "Fighting Elections." Internal discussion document in author's possession.

———. 1986. *The Politics of Revolution: The Main Speeches and Debates from the 1986 Sinn Fein Ard Fheis.* Dublin: Sinn Fein.

———. 1989. *The Sinn Fein and SDLP Talks.* Dublin: Sinn Fein.

———. 1992. *Setting the Record Straight.* Dublin: Sinn Fein.

Sisk, Timothy D. 1996. *Power Sharing and International Mediation in Ethnic Conflicts.* Washington, D.C.: United States Institute of Peace.

Skocpol, Theda. 1979. *States and Social Revolutions.* New York: Cambridge University Press.

Sluka, Jeffrey. 1989. *Hearts and Minds, Water and Fish: Support for the IRA and INLA in a Northern Irish Ghetto.* Greenwich, Conn.: JAI Press.

Smelser, Neil. 1963. *Theory of Collective Action.* New York: The Free Press.

Smith, Anthony D. 1971. *Theories of Nationalism.* London: Duckworth.

———. 1981. *The Ethnic Revival.* New York: Cambridge University Press.

———. 1984. "Ethnic Myths and Ethnic Revivals," *European Journal of Sociology* 25: 283–305.

Smith, M. L. R. 1991. *The Role of the Military Instrument in Irish Republican Thinking: An Evolutionary Analysis.* Ph.D. thesis, King's College, University of London.

Stagner, Ross. 1965. "The Psychology of Human Conflict." In *The Nature of Human Conflict,* ed. Elton B. McNeil. Englewood Cliffs, N.J.: Prentice-Hall.

Sullivan, John. 1988. *ETA and Basque Nationalism.* London: Routledge.

Sutton, Michael. 1994. *An Index of Deaths from the Conflict in Ireland, 1969–1993.* Belfast: Beyond the Pale Publications.

Taber, Robert. 1970. *The War of the Flea: A Study of Guerrilla Warfare Theory and Practice.* New York: Citadel Press.

Tarrow, Sidney. 1983. *Struggling to Reform: Social Movements, Resource Mobilization, and Policy Change During Cycles of Protest.* Ithaca, N.Y.: Cornell University Center for International Studies.

———. 1989. *Struggle, Politics, and Reform: Collective Action, Social Movements, and Cycles of Protest.* Ithaca, N.Y.: Cornell University, Western Societies Program Occasional Paper 21.

———. 1994. *Power in Movement: Social Movements, Collective Action, and Mass Politics.* New York and London: Cambridge University Press.

Taylor, Stan. 1984. *Social Science and Revolutions.* New York: St. Martin's Press.

Teague, Paul, ed. 1987. *Beyond the Rhetoric: Politics, the Economy, and Social Policy in Northern Ireland.* London: Lawrence and Wishart.

Tejerina, Benjamin. 1992. *Nacionalismo y lengua.* Madrid: Centro de Investigaciones Sociológicos.

Tilly, Charles. 1978. *From Mobilization to Revolution.* Reading, Mass.: Addison-Wesley.

———. 1985. *Big Structures, Large Processes, Huge Comparisons.* New York: Russell Sage Foundation.

———. 1993. *European Revolutions, 1492–1992.* Oxford, UK: Blackwell.

Tinker, Jerry M. 1969. *Strategies of Revolutionary Warfare.* New Delhi: Chand.

Tiryakian, Edward A., and Ronald Rogowski, eds. 1985. *New Nationalisms of the Developed West.* Boston: Allen and Unwin.

Tullock, Gordon. 1971. "The Paradox of Revolution." *Public Choice* 17: 63–71.

Unzueta, Patxo. 1988. *Los nietos de la IRA: Nacionalismo y violencia en el País Vasco.* Madrid: El País and Aguilar.

Urry, John. 1973. *Reference Groups and the Theory of Revolution.* London: Unwin Hyman.

Urwin, Derek. 1970. "Social Cleavages and Political Parties in Belgium: Problems of Institutionalization." *Political Studies* 18: 320–40.

Weber, Max. [1920] 1978. *Economy and Society.* Berkeley: University of California Press.

Weinberg, Leonard. 1992. *Political Parties and Terrorist Groups.* London: Frank Cass.

———. 1993. *Encounters with the Contemporary Radical Right.* Boulder, Colo.: Westview Press.

———. 1995. *The Transformation of Italian Communism.* New Brunswick, N.J.: Transaction Publishers.

Wellhofer, E. Spenser. 1974. "Political Parties as Communities of Fate: Tests with Argentine Political Party Elites." *American Journal of Political Science,* 2: 347–63.

White, Robert W. 1988. "Commitment, Efficacy and Personal Sacrifice among Irish Republicans." *Journal of Political and Military Sociology* 16: 77–90.

———. 1989. "From Peaceful Protest to Guerrilla War: Micromobilization of the Provisional Irish Republican Army. *American Journal of Sociology* 94: 1277–1302.

———. 1993. *Provisional Irish Republicans: An Oral and Interpretive History.* Westport, Conn.: Greenwood Press.

Whyte, John. 1990. *Interpreting Northern Ireland.* Oxford: Clarendon Press.

Wickham-Crowley, Timothy. 1992. *Guerrillas and Revolution in Latin America: A Comparative Study of Insurgents and Regimes Since 1956.* Princeton, N.J.: Princeton University Press.

Wieviorka, Michel. 1993. *The Making of Terrorism.* Trans. David Gordon White. Chicago: University of Chicago Press.

Wilkinson, Paul. 1986. *Terrorism and the Liberal State.* New York: New York University Press.

Wilson, James Q. 1962. *The Amateur Democrat: Club Politics in Three Cities.* Chicago: University of Chicago Press.

———. 1973. *Political Organizations.* New York: Basic Books.

Wolfenstein, E. V. 1971. *Revolutionary Personality: Lenin, Trotsky, Ghandi.* Princeton: Princeton University Press.

Wright, Frank. 1987. *Northern Ireland: A Comparative Analysis.* Dublin: Gill and Macmillan.

Wright, William E., ed. 1971. *A Comparative Study of Party Organization.* Columbus, Ohio: Charles E. Merrill.

Young, Crawford. 1976. *The Politics of Cultural Pluralism.* Madison, Wis.: University of Wisconsin Press.

Zald, Mayer N., and Roberta Ash. 1970. "Social Movement Organizations: Growth, Decay, and Change." In *Protest, Reform, and Revolt,* ed. Joseph R. Gusfield. New York: John Wiley.

Zald, Mayer N., and J. D. McCarthy. 1970. *The Dynamics of Social Movements: Resource Mobilization, Social Control, and Tactics.* Boston: Little, Brown.

Zariski, Raphael. 1989. "Ethnic Extremism among Ethnoterritorial Minorities in Western Europe." *Comparative Politics* 22, 2: 253–72.

Zirakzadeh, Cyrus Ernesto. 1991. *A Rebellious People: Basques, Protest, and Politics.* Reno: University of Nevada Press.

Zulaika, Joseba. 1988. *Basque Violence: Metaphor and Sacrament.* Reno: University of Nevada Press.

Zulaika, Joseba, and William Douglass. 1996. *Terror and Taboo: The Follies, Fables, and Faces of Terrorism.* New York: Routledge.

Newspapers

An Phoblacht/Republican News (AP/RN), Dublin and Belfast, weekly
Belfast Telegraph, Belfast, daily
Deia, Bilbao, daily

El diario Vasco, San Sebastián, daily
Egin, San Sebastián, daily
El País, Madrid, daily
Guardian, London, daily
Irish News, Belfast, daily
Irish Times, Dublin, daily
Le Monde, Paris, daily
Liberation, Paris, daily
Observer, London, weekly
Times, London, daily
United Irishmen, Dublin, monthly

Magazines

Askatzen, Herri Batasuna, monthly
Batasuna, ETA, 1967–80
Cambio 16, 1973–89, Madrid, weekly
EGIN (1977–1982, 1 vol); annual 1983–present
Fortnight, 1976–90, Belfast, monthly
Hautsi, 1974–77
Herria 2000 Eliza, 1981, Bilbao
IPES, 1980–89, Bilbao
IRIS, 1981–90, Dublin and Belfast
Magill, Dublin, monthly
Punto y Hora, 1976–90, San Sebastián, weekly
Starry Plough, Dublin, occasional publication
Zutik, ETA, 1960–70
Zutik, ETA-Berri, 1967–69
Zutik, ETA-V, 1971–84
Zutik, ETA-Militar, 1974–77

Government and Other Documents

Documentos. 1979–1981. San Sebastián: Hordago.
FOESSA. 1981. *Informe sociológico sobre el cambio político en España, 1975–1981.*
    Madrid: Fundación FOESSA.
Her Majesty's Stationary Office. 1969a. *Disturbances in Northern Ireland: Report of the*
    Commission Appointed by the Governor of Northern Ireland (Cameron Report). Cmd.
    532. Belfast: HMSO.
———. 1969b. *Report of the Advisory Committee on Police in Northern Ireland (Hunt*
    Report). Cmd. 535. Belfast: HMSO.
———. 1971. *Report of the Enquiry into Allegations against the Security Forces of Physical*
    Brutality in Northern Ireland Arising out of Events on 9 August 1971 (Compton
    Report). Cmd. 4823. Belfast: HMSO.

————. 1972a. *Violence and Civil Disturbances in Northern Ireland in 1969 (Scarman Report)*. Cmd. 566. Belfast: HMSO.

————. 1972b. *Report of the Committee of Privy Councillors Appointed to Consider Authorized Procedures for the Interrogation of Persons Suspected of Terrorism (Parker Report)*. Cmd. 4091. Belfast: HMSO.

————.1972c. *Report of the Tribunal Appointed to Inquire into the Events on Sunday 30 January 1972 Which Led to Loss of Life in Connection with the Procession in Londonderry on That Day (Widgery Report)*. H.C. 220. Belfast: HMSO.

————.1972d. *Report of the Commission to Consider Legal Procedures to Deal with Terrorist Activities in Northern Ireland (Diplock Report)*. Cmd. 5185. Belfast: HMSO.

INCORE and the Urban Institute. *Cost of the Troubles Study.* Marie-Smyth, Project Director. University of Ulster (ongoing).

Irish Information Partnership. *Agendas, 1984–1990.* London: Irish Information Partnership.

MORI (Market and Opinion Research International). Unpublished Northern Ireland Opinion Poll JN2428, 20–23 June 1984.

Northern Ireland Office. 1984. *Northern Ireland Assembly Official Report: Government Attitudes to Sinn Fein.* Vol. 12.

Policy Studies Institute. 1987a. *Equality and Inequality in Northern Ireland: Employment and Unemployment.* London: Policy Studies Institute.

————. 1987b. *Equality and Inequality in Northern Ireland: Perceptions and Views.* London: Policy Studies Institute.

Ulster Marketing Survey. "Inter-Party Talks: Northern Ireland Public Opinion Poll." Belfast: Ulster Marketing Survey, February 1989.

Index

strategy, 57, 102; role in peace process, 210–11; views of Sinn Fein, 105–6; voter profile, 103–5

Solidaridad de Trabajadores Vascos (STV, or Solidarity of Basque Workers), 76

South, Sean, 50

Spanish government: characterizations of Herri Batasuna voters, 131–34; counterinsurgency policy, 189–99; negotiations with ETA, 199

Spanish left, 123

Spanish Ministry of Interior, 113

special category status, 60, 66

Stalker, John, 186

strategic change, 12; behavioral approach, 15–17; choice of strategies, 25; discourses on, 25; effect of regime responsiveness, 30–36; instrumental approach, 12–15; opportunities and constraints, 25; rational-choice model, 15–17; subgroups and change, 29–30; synthetic model, 17–19, 46–47

Suárez, Adolfo, 123

Sunningdale Agreement, 63–64

supergrass, 185

Tarrow, Sidney, 5

Thatcher, Margaret, 1–2, 4, 130, 186

Tone, Wolfe, 52

Twomey, Seamus, 61

"Txiki" (Jon Paredes Manot), 114

"Txillardegi" (José Luis Alvarez Enparanza), 3

Ulster Defense Regiment (UDR), 27

Ulster Workers Council, 63

Umkonto we Sizwe, 6

White, Robert, 8

Whitelaw, William, 60

Wolfe Tone Society, 52–54

Workers Party. *See* Official Sinn Fein

Yoldi, Juan Carlos, 3

Zabala, Lorenzo, 76

CYNTHIA L. IRVIN is assistant professor of political science at the University of Kentucky and a former United States Institute of Peace Jennings-Randolph Peace Scholar. She is currently working on a book on the role of international economic assistance in the Northern Irish peace process.